CASS SERIES ON SOVIET (RUSSIAN) MI

RACE FOR THE REICHSTAG

CASS SERIES ON SOVIET (RUSSIAN) MILITARY EXPERIENCE
Series Editor: David M. Glantz
ISSN: 1462-0944

This series focuses on Soviet military experiences in specific campaigns or operations

1. David M. Glantz, *From the Don to the Dnepr, Soviet Offensive Operations, December 1942 to August 1943*. (ISBN 0 7146 3401 8 cloth, 0 7146 4064 6 paper)
2. David Glantz, *The Initial Period of War on the Eastern Front: 22 June–August 1941*. (ISBN 0 7146 3375 5 cloth, 0 7146 4298 3 paper)
3. Carl Van Dyke, *The Soviet Invasion of Finland, 1939–40*. (ISBN 0 7146 4653 5 cloth, 0 7146 4314 9 paper)
4. Leonid D. Grenkerich, *The Soviet Partisan Movement 1941–1944*, edited and with a Foreword by David M. Glantz. (ISBN 0 7146 4874 4 cloth, 0 7146 4428 5 paper)
5. Tony Le Tissier, *Race for the Reichstag: The 1945 Battle for Berlin*. (ISBN 0 7146 4929 5 cloth, 0 7146 4489 7 paper)
6. Robert Seely, *Russo-Chechen Conflict, 1800–2000: A Deadly Embrace*. (ISBN 0 7146 4992 9 cloth, 0 7146 8060 5 paper)

CASS SERIES ON THE SOVIET (RUSSIAN) STUDY OF WAR
Series Editor: David M. Glantz
ISSN: 1462-0960

This series examines what Soviet military theorists and commanders learned from the study of their own military operations.

1. Harold S. Orenstein, translator and editor, *Soviet Documents on the Use of War Experience*, Volume I, *The Initial Period of War 1941*, with an Introduction by David M. Glantz. (ISBN 0 7146 3392 5 cloth)
2. Harold S. Orenstein, translator and editor, *Soviet Documents on the Use of War Experience*, Volume II, *The Winter Campaign 1941–1942*, with an Introduction by David M. Glantz. (ISBN 0 7146 3393 3 cloth)
3. Joseph G. Welsh, translator, *Red Armor Combat Orders: Combat Regulations for Tank and Mechanized Forces 1944*, edited and with an Introduction by Richard N. Armstrong. (ISBN 0 7146 3401 8 cloth)
4. Harold S. Orenstein, translator and editor, *Soviet Documents on the Use of War Experience*, Volume III, *Military Operations 1941 and 1942*, with an Introduction by David M. Glantz. (ISBN 0 7146 3402 6 cloth)
5. William A. Burhans, translator, *The Nature of the Operations of Modern Armies* by V.K. Triandafillov, edited by Jacob W. Kipp, with an Introduction by James J. Schneider. (ISBN 0 7146 4501 X cloth, 0 7146 4118 9 paper)
6. Harold S. Orenstein, translator, *The Evolution of Soviet Operational Art, 1927–1991: The Documentary Basis*, Volume I, *Operational Art, 1927–1964*, with an Introduction by David M. Glantz. (ISBN 0 7146 4547 8 cloth, 0 7146 4228 2 paper)
7. Harold S. Orenstein, translator, *The Evolution of Soviet Operational Art, 1927–1991: The Documentary Basis*, Volume II, *Operational Art, 1965–1991*, with an Introduction by David M. Glantz. (ISBN 0 7146 4548 6 cloth, 0 7146 4229 0 paper)
8. Richard N. Armstrong and Joseph G. Welsh, *Winter Warfare: Red Army Orders and Experiences*. (ISBN 0 7146 4699 7 cloth, 0 7146 4237 1 paper)
9. Lester W. Grau, *The Bear Went Over the Mountain: Soviet Combat Tactics in Afghanistan*. (ISBN 0 7146 4874 4 cloth, 0 7146 4413 7 paper)
10. David M. Glantz and Harold S. Orenstein, *The Battle for Kursk 1943: The Soviet General Staff Study*. (ISBN 0 7146 4933 3 cloth, 0 7146 4493 5 paper)
11. Niklas Zetterling and Anders Frankson, *Kursk 1943: A Statistical Analysis*. (ISBN 0 7146 5052 8 cloth, 0 7146 8103 2 paper)
12. David M. Glantz and Harold S. Orenstein, *Belorussia 1944: The Soviet General Staff Study*. (ISBN 0 7146 5102 8)

RACE FOR THE REICHSTAG

THE 1945 BATTLE FOR BERLIN

Tony Le Tissier

FRANK CASS
LONDON • PORTLAND, OR

First published in 1999
First published in paperback in Great Britain by
FRANK CASS PUBLISHERS
Crown House, 47 Chase Side
Southgate, London N14 5BP

and in the United States of America by
FRANK CASS PUBLISHERS
c/o ISBS, 5824 N.E. Hassalo Street
Portland, Oregon 97213-3644

Website: www.frankcass.com

British Library Cataloguing in Publication Data:

Le Tissier, Tony, 1932–
  Race for the Reichstag: the 1945 battle for Berlin. –
(Cass series on Soviet (Russian) military experience; no. 5)
1. Berlin, Battle of, 1945 2. World War, 1939–1945 –
Campaigns – Germany – Berlin 3. Soviet Union – History,
Military
I. Title
940.5'421'3'155

ISBN 0-7146-4929-5 (cloth)
ISBN 0-7146-4489-7 (paper)
ISSN 1462-0944

Library of Congress Cataloging-in-Publication Data:

Le Tissier, Tony, 1932–
  Race for the Reichstag: the 1945 Battle for Berlin / Tony Le
Tissier.
    p.   cm. – (Cass series on Soviet (Russian) Military
experience, ISSN 1462-0944; 4)
  Includes bibliographical references and indexes.
  ISBN 0-7146-4929-5 (cloth). – ISBN 0-7146-4489-7 (paper).
  1. Berlin, Battle of, 1945. I. Title. II. Series.
D757.9.B4L44   1999
940.54'213155–dc21   99-13500
                                                          CIP

Typeset by Vitaset, Paddock Wood, Kent
Printed in Great Britain by
Bookcraft (Bath) Ltd, Midsomer Norton, Somerset

CONTENTS

MAPS

ILLUSTRATIONS

FOREWORD

For the Red Army, the Battle for Berlin was the final battle in a long and tortuous struggle for victory in mankind's most devastating war. For the German Wehrmacht, the Battle of Berlin represented the final desperate attempt to preserve the existence of Adolf Hitler's putative thousand-year Third Reich. Momentous as the battle was for both sides, the ferocity with which it was fought still defies the imagination, since its outcome and the outcome of the war as a whole was no longer in doubt. During over four years of war, the pendulum of success had swung wildly between Germany and the Soviet Union. In summer 1941, and again in summer 1942, German fortunes soared as its armies drove inexorably forward, first towards Leningrad and Moscow, and then to the banks of the distant Don and Volga Rivers. In turn, Soviet fortunes rose each winter as the Red Army won equally unprecedented victories at Moscow and Stalingrad. During the climactic Battle of Kursk in summer 1943, the tide finally turned decisively in the Soviets' favour. Thereafter, the Red Army embarked on a nearly continuous march to victory against an increasingly exhausted and threadbare Wehrmacht. By early April 1945 the scarred armies of the two antagonists faced one another along the banks of the Oder River, only 40 kilometres from Berlin. By then, Soviet victory was but one battle away and there was no doubt over which army would emerge supreme. Nonetheless, memories, reputations and simple pride on the one side, and a stoic determination to atone for 29 million casualties and years of immeasurable suffering on the other, made the ensuing Battle for Berlin one of the fiercest and most costly battles of the war.

In this, his third, book on the Battle for Berlin, Tony Le Tissier focuses on the final battle for the Reichstag, the seat and virtual symbol of German power. Exploiting a wide range of Soviet sources and unprecedented German archival and memoir materials, the author has created a detailed and touchingly human mosaic out of the immensely complex, agonizing and almost ceremonial struggle for the final hundreds of metres of soil under

Wehrmacht control. The result is a fitting memorial to the soldiers who were sacrificed in the name of victory or their Führer during the final battle of this most terrible war.

David M. Glantz
Carlisle, Pennsylvania
March, 1999

PREFACE

This account of the battle for Berlin was originally compiled some 20 years ago from the source material then available as an attempt to produce a definitive account of the battle for the city of Berlin. It took another ten years before an encounter with the author Len Deighton opened the way to publication. Subsequent historical events opening up access to places, people and information hitherto denied me, and this, together with feedback from the later German editions, have enabled an extensive revision of the original work, which I described as being 'rather like the reconstruction of an ancient vase from an incomplete set of fragments'.

I believe that my original edition was the first publication to draw attention to the extent and consequences of the bitter rivalry between Marshals Zhukov and Koniev that Stalin was so skilfully manipulating from Moscow. The veil is now lifted on further aspects of this battle hitherto masked by decades of Soviet propaganda.

To assist the reader through the complexities of this operation, I have endeavoured to illustrate the various parts and phases with a series of maps and drawings, incorporating as many of the place-names mentioned in the text as were feasible. Reference to the maps on which these names appear has been included in the index. I have also used breaks in the text to indicate switching between the narration of German and Soviet aspects and between those of the rival marshals.

ACKNOWLEDGEMENTS

The original work upon which this book is based would not have been possible without the active encouragement and assistance of many people, among them Tom Bonas, Michael Craster, Professor Christopher Donnelly, David Dunkelly, the late David Forrer, Dr Jürgen Freymuth, Professor Dr Werner Knopp of the Stiftung Preussischer Kulturbesitz in Berlin, Otto Spitz of the Berlin Verlag and Oberstleutnant Dr Rohde of the Militärgeschichtliches Forschungsamt in Freiburg.

I also wish to thank the many people who have helped me with my further research in producing this greatly revised text, including Horst Denkinger, Oberst a.D. Theodor von Dufving, Professor Dr Walter Kroemer, Lothar Loewe, the late Willi Rogmann, Oberst a.D. Skorning, Lennart Westberg of Sundsvall, Sweden, Horst Wilke and Oberst a.D. Horst Zobel.

I am especially grateful to Dorothée Freifrau von Hammerstein-Equord for all her invaluable assistance over the years.

For much of the material on which the maps are based I am indebted to the friendly co-operation of the staffs of the Institut für Geodäsie; Department V of the Senator für Bau- und Wohnungswesen; the Landesarchiv; the Landesbildstelle and Firma Röhll – all in Berlin – the Air Photo Library of the University of Keele; the Royal Air Force Museum, Hendon; and the former Soviet Army Museum, Karlshorst.

Thanks are also due to the staffs of the former 38 Regional Library, Royal Army Education Corps; the former US Army Nicholson Memorial (previously Crump Hall) Library; the Staatsbibliothek and Amerika-Gedenk-Bibliothek in Berlin; and the Imperial War Museum in London.

I am also grateful to Colonel (ER) Pierre Rocolle for his kind permission to allow me to include translations of French eyewitness statements taken from his *Götterdämmerung – La Prise de Berlin*; to Helmuth Altner for permission to quote the Oranienburg Hitlerjugend story from his *Totentanz Berlin*; to the Chief of the Military History Office, HQ USAREUR, for permission to include quotations from Wilhelm Willemer's *The German Defense of Berlin*; and to Friedhelm Schöneck for permission to include an extract from his *Die Zange*.

My recent association with Bengt and Irmgard von zur Mühlen of Chronos-Film GmbH, in connection with their film *Der Todeskampf der Reichshauptstadt – Ein General, der Führer und zwei Millionen Berliner*, the production of the English-language version *The Fate of Hitler's Capital* and assistance with the production of the book of the film, proved extremely fruitful and I would like to express my gratitude for their friendly co-operation and generosity with original material and photographs.

ABBREVIATIONS

A	Army
AA	Anti-Aircraft
AD	Army Detachment
AGp	Army Group
APC	Armoured Personnel Carrier
Armd	Armoured
Arty	Artillery
Aslt	Assault
A/Tk	Anti-Tank
AVM	Air Vice-Marshal
B/Bde	Brigade
BDM	Bund-Deutscher-Mädel (German Girls' League)
Bn	Battalion
Br	Bridge
BVG	Berlin Transport Authority
Bye Fr	Byelorussian Front
C	Corps
Cav	Cavalry
Civs	Civilians
Col.	Colonel
Coy	Company
CP	Command Post
D/Div	Division
Engr	Engineer
Fd	Field
GA	Guards Artillery
GC	Guards Rifle Corps
GCC	Guards Cavalry Corps
Gds	Guards

Gen.	General
GMB	Guards Mechanized Brigade
GMC	Guards Mechanized Corps
Grn	Garrison
GTA	Guards Tank Army
GTB	Guards Tank Brigade
GTC	Guards Tank Corps
How	Howitzer
Hy	Heavy
Ind	Independent
Inf	Infantry
Jagd Pz	Hunting Tank
'K'	'Kurmark'
LMG	Light Machine-gun
Lt	Light/Lieutenant
Lw	Luftwaffe
'M'	'Müncheberg'
Maj.	Major
MB	Mechanized Brigade
MC	Mechanized Corps
M/C	Motorcycle
Mech	Mechanized
Med	Medium
Mor	Mortar
Mot	Motorized
Mtn	Mountain
OKH	Oberkommande-der-Heeres
OKW	Oberkommande-der-Wehrmacht
Para	Parachute
Pol	Police/Polish
Pol A	Polish Army
Pz	Panzer
PzA	Panzer Army
PzC	Panzer Corps
PzGr	Panzergrenadier
R/Regt	Regiment
RAD	Reichsarbeitsdienst (State Labour Service)
Res	Reserve
RHSA	Reichshauptsicherheitsamt (State Main Security Office)
RL	Rocket Launcher

SA	Shock Army/Sturmabteilung (Storm Detachment)
SP	Self-propelled
SPG	Self-propelled gun
Stn	Station
Str	Strasse
Sy	Security
TB	Tank Brigade
TC	Tank Corps
Tk	Tank
Tps	Troops
Tpt	Transport
Trg	Training
Ukr Fr	Ukrainian Front
V	Volks (People's)
VGr	Volksgrenadier
VGr(D)	Volksgrenadier (Division)
Vol	Volunteer
VS	Volkssturm (Home Guard)

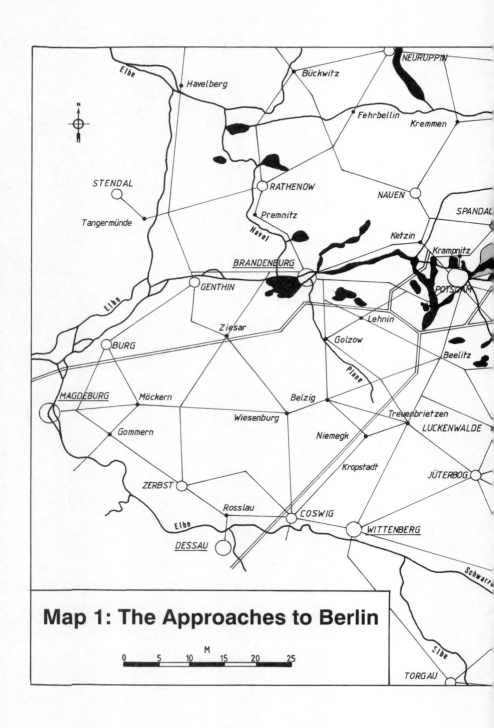

Map 1: The Approaches to Berlin

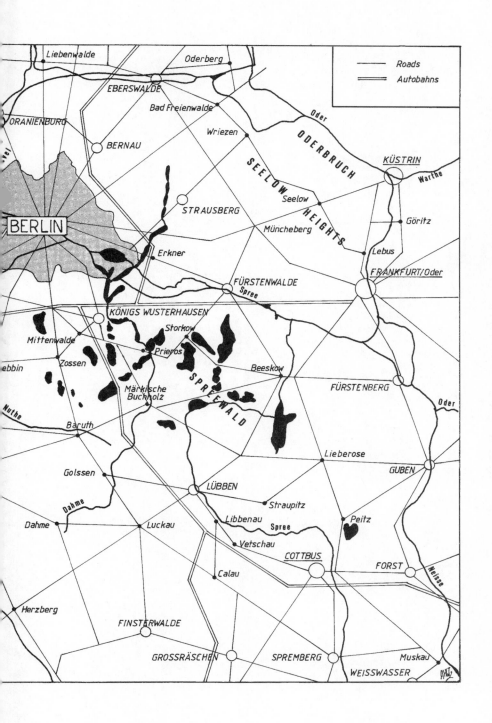

1

THE GOAL

At the time of writing the Reichstag building is nothing but an empty shell, gutted and roofless, encased in protective scaffolding while it undergoes transformation into the seat of the German Federal Parliament, the Bundestag, to the design of a team of British engineers, for by the turn of the century Berlin is due to regain its position as the capital of a reunited Germany. Just before this transformation began, the building underwent a short and unusual phase as an object of art when Christo and his team wrapped it in a glittering silver material, drawing hundreds of thousands of spectators to this extraordinary spectacle.

The last time the building had attracted visitors in such numbers was in 1945, when it was the goal of every Soviet soldier who could make it; the focus of attention of six converging Soviet armies. Workmen have erased the last of their cyrillic inscriptions from the interior but the other souvenirs of that time from bombing, siege artillery, field artillery, rockets, mortars, heavy machine-guns and small-arms will continue to mark the exterior, even if only discernible from the replacement stonework.

Why the Reichstag building should have been chosen by the Soviets as their goal in Berlin has puzzled many people, for by 1945 it had already been a burnt-out shell for 12 years and appeared to be of no significance to the Nazi regime. Indeed, despite its purpose and the inscription over the entrance *Dem deutschen Volke* ('To the German People'), the building had in fact been completed in 1894 to a design by Paul Wallot that could be interpreted as a symbol of the new German imperial state, the central dome representing the imperial crown and the four corner towers, the four kingdoms of Bavaria, Prussia, Saxony and Württenburg that the Second Reich incorporated among other territories. The Kaiser ruled through his own appointed ministers, who were not answerable to the parliament, whose authority was thus severely limited, despite genuine democratic aims on its part. The German defeat in 1918, the revolution and the Kaiser's abdication left a parliament so

1

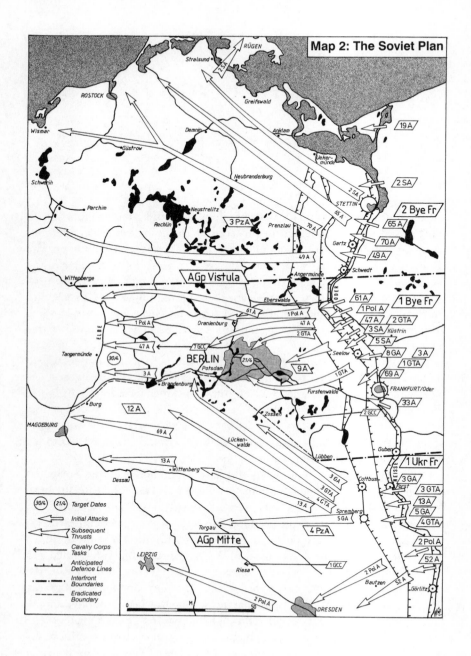

Map 2: The Soviet Plan

inexperienced in democracy that it could only squabble its way through the generally disastrous years of the Weimar Republic. Soon after Adolf Hitler came to power in 1933 the Reichstag building was gutted by a fire, which the Nazis blamed on their political enemies in the Communist Party, although it is most likely that they started it themselves. Hitler used this as an excuse to obtain sweeping powers from the ailing President Hindenburg, by which all political opponents were rounded up and incarcerated in improvised concentration camps. The windows and doorways of the burnt-out building were bricked up for security reasons and the parliament moved into the Kroll Opera House across Königsplatz (Platz der Republik) from the Reichstag building. That the Nazis intended to restore the building in due course is evident from the plans and models for the new Germania prepared by Albert Speer for Hitler's Third Reich capital, but in these the Reichstag building is completely dwarfed by the vast palaces and the Great Hall that were to flank Königsplatz. Work on this grandiose project had already begun, as we shall see later in this account.

Nevertheless, for the Soviets, the word 'Reichstag' came to acquire all the significance of the German Kremlin, embodying the nucleus of Nazi power, the lair of the fascist beast that they were out to destroy.

As a military goal, the Reichstag building was practical through its size and shape and particularly from its comparative isolation from other buildings, so that no matter how badly damaged nearby buildings might be, or how blocked with debris the streets, the Reichstag building itself remained clearly identifiable.

It has been said that the cry 'On to the Reichstag!' was first raised after the great tank battle of Kursk in 1943. By 1945 the Reichstag was the coveted victor's prize, the acquisition of which would spell the end of the Great Patriotic War that had devastated their country.

Generalissimo Joseph Stalin had promised his deputy supreme commander, Marshal Georgi Konstantinovich Zhukov, the taking of Berlin with his 1st Byelorussian Front (army group), and that was what Zhukov expected from the overall plans for 'Operation Berlin' discussed and approved in Moscow at the beginning of April that year. However, at the last minute Stalin had made an important alteration. The General Staff had drawn the operational boundary between Zhukov and Marshal Ivan S. Koniev's 1st Ukrainian Front from Guben on the Neisse via Michendorf to Schönebeck on the Elbe but, in response to Koniev's plea, with which the General Staff were in accord, Stalin had silently erased the boundary beyond Lübben, thereby implying that whatever happened beyond that point would be up to the commanders.

3

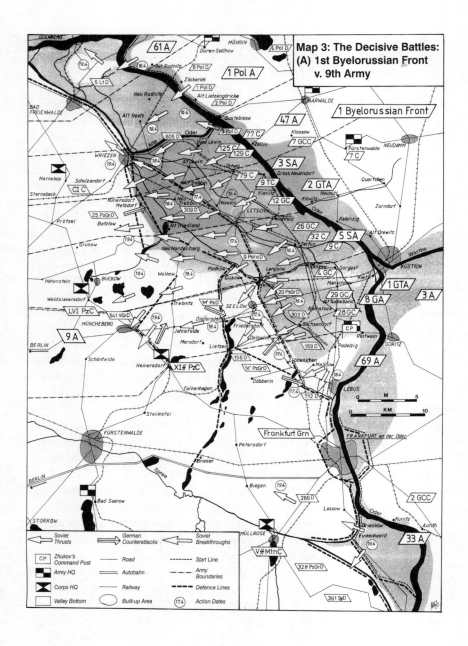

Map 3: The Decisive Battles:
(A) 1st Byelorussian Front
v. 9th Army

This was also an opportunity for Stalin to exploit the bitter rivalry that existed between the two marshals in order to ensure his own continuing supremacy in the Soviet Union as the unchallenged leader and bringer of victory. Both these marshals, Zhukov in particular, were too popular to suit his taste and needed humbling. With the outcome of the war virtually a foregone conclusion, Stalin could afford to play one against the other while he planned for a postwar world in which the Soviet Union would not only hold a dominant position in Europe but in the world at large. So he could allow 'Operation Berlin' to become a race for glory between the two rival marshals, but he would be holding the reins.[1]

As early as 1942 Stalin had sought some means of curbing Zhukov and had tasked Viktor S. Abakumov, Head of the Special Department (later to be known as SMERSH) with finding evidence that could be used against him. Although technically the Special Department belonged to Lavrenty Berya's Ministry of the Interior, Abakumov had direct access to Stalin, bypassing his chief. Abakumov began by arresting a previous Chief of Operations to Zhukov in the defence of Moscow, but could exact nothing incriminating from him. Nevertheless, Abakumov persisted in his task, a fact of which Zhukov was not unaware, and his virtual demotion to army group commander in 1944 after previous co-ordinating groups of fronts, coupled with Stalin's new coolness towards him, were alarming signals not to be ignored.[2]

Whatever the cause, Zhukov's handling of the assault on the Seelow Heights that opened the first phase of his part of 'Operation Berlin' on 16 April had been well below par. Instead of breaking though the German defences on the first day so as to be able to launch his two tank armies on Berlin in a classic pincer movement, his persistent head-on battering of General Theodor Busse's 9th Army's defences, goaded on by Stalin's reports of Koniev's success against General Fritz-Herbert Gräser's 4th Panzer Army to the south, had cost him enormous casualties in men and equipment, and absorbed the last of his reserves.

Stalin was so perturbed by Zhukov's lack of success on the direct route to Berlin that he ordered Marshal Konstanin K. Rokossovsky to begin his part of the operation immediately, two days ahead of schedule. Rokossovsky's 2nd Byelorussian Front was still regrouping from his successful mopping-up operations in Pomerania and East Prussia, and so on the morning of 18 April opened its offensive against General Hasso von Manteuffel's 3rd Panzer Army between Schwedt and Stettin virtually off the march. This was a particularly difficult operation, involving the crossing of both the east and west branches of the Oder, which were separated by a two-mile-wide strip of flooded marshland bordered by dykes.[3] Under these circumstances the effectiveness

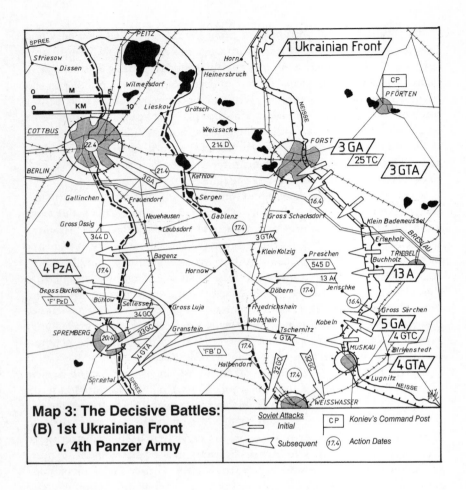

Map 3: The Decisive Battles:
(B) 1st Ukrainian Front
v. 4th Panzer Army

of the artillery support was severely reduced and it fell to the air forces to make up this deficiency.[4]

This initial phase of crossing the two branches of the Oder took two days to accomplish, so that it was not until 20 April that the Soviets were able to come to grips with the German defences, by which time Zhukov had broken through on the way to Berlin and intervention from the north was no longer necessary. Although Rokossovsky's operation played no direct part in the taking of Berlin, it successfully prevented the 3rd Panzer Army from intervening in the main operation and contributed significantly toward the final collapse of the German armed forces.

Meanwhile Koniev had had a successful two-day battle between the Neisse and Upper Spree Rivers, routing his opponents, who fell back on their third line of defence on the Upper Spree, where they concentrated on the towns of Cottbus and Spremberg, which had the only bridges capable of taking heavy armour. However, Koniev's troops found an unmarked ford by which his two tank armies were brought in readiness for a thrust northward still virtually intact.

While making his radio-telephone report to Stalin on the night of 17 April, Stalin made the impractical suggestion that Zhukov's armour might be brought south to exploit Koniev's breach. Koniev eagerly seized the opportunity to suggest that his own tank armies make for Berlin instead, and after a short deliberation Stalin agreed. The 1st Byelorussian Front was informed of this move next day, but Zhukov apparently still assumed that Koniev's troops would not approach closer than Potsdam, as had previously been agreed in Moscow.[5]

However, the orders that Koniev produced that night in confirmation of his verbal instructions included the following points, which confirmed his determination to beat Zhukov into Berlin:

> In keeping with the orders of the Supreme High Command, I order:
> 1. Commander 3rd Guards Tank Army: on the night of 17 Apr 45 the Army will force the Spree and advance rapidly in the general direction of Vetschau, Golssen, Baruth, Teltow and the southern outskirts of Berlin. The task of the Army is to break into Berlin from the south on the night of 20 Apr 45.
> 2. Commander 4th Guards Tank Army: on the night of 17 Apr 45 the Army will force the Spree north of Spremberg and advance rapidly in the general direction of Drebkau, Calau, Dahme and Luckenwalde. By the end of 20 Apr 45 the Army will capture the area of Beelitz, Treuenbrietzen and Luckenwalde, and, on the night of 20 Apr 45,

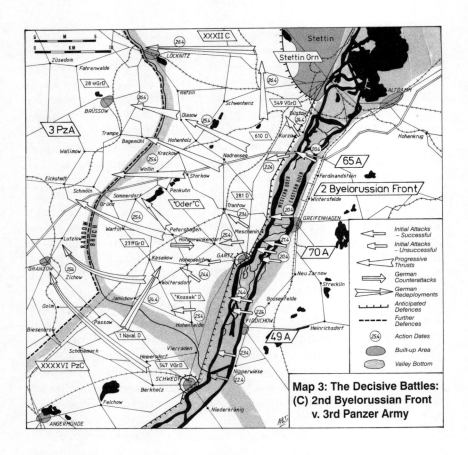

Map 3: The Decisive Battles:
(C) 2nd Byelorussian Front
v. 3rd Panzer Army

Potsdam and the southwestern part of Berlin. When turning toward Potsdam the Army will secure the Treuenbrietzen area with the 5th Guards Mechanised Corps. Reconnaissance will be made in the direction of Senftenburg, Finsterwalde and Herzberg.

3. The tanks will advance daringly and resolutely in the main direction. They will bypass towns and large communities and not engage in protracted frontal fighting. I demand a firm understanding that the success of the tank armies depends on the boldness of the manoeuvre and the swiftness of the operation.

4. Point 3 is to be impressed upon the minds of the corps and brigade commanders.[6]

That same day (19 April) Berlin saw its second influx of refugees in the year with sad columns streaming in from the south and east, this time from towns and villages abandoned nearby. Some of the city's inhabitants also started to depart discreetly to seek shelter elsewhere. The roads around the capital were filling with people on the move, their precious belongings loaded on farm-carts, bicycles, prams and pushcarts of all kinds, making it difficult for military and other official traffic to get through.[7]

This fateful day left a breach 19 miles wide in the German lines from Wriezen to Behlendorf and the remains of the 9th Army split into three main components. In the north General Friedrich Sixt's CI Corps, with their southern flank and rear suddenly exposed, were obliged to retire into a bridgehead around Eberswalde south of the Finow Canal, thus opening the way for Colonel General P.A. Belov's 61st Army and Lieutenant-General S.G. Poplowski's 1st Polish Army to break through to the west.[8] In the centre General Helmuth Weidling's LVI Panzer Corps withdrew toward Berlin and the only bridges that could enable it to reconnect with the main body to the south, while exacting a heavy toll on the way. General Busses' immediate command was now reduced to the remnants of SS General Mathias Kleinheisterkamp's XI SS Panzer Corps, Colonel Ernst Biehler's Frankfurt Garrison and SS General Friedrich Jackeln's V SS Mountain Corps, all of whom were still trying to hold on to their original positions. With Hitler's instructions to hold firm on the Oder, Busse was forced to adopt an all-round defensive position, initially extending his northern flank through Lietzen, Heinersdorf and Fürstenwalde, and moving his headquarters into the Spreewald, where thousands of refugees were already seeking refuge among his units in the woods and marshes. That night Lieutenant-General Wagner's V Corps, consisting of the 21st Panzer, 35th SS Police Grenadier, 36th SS

Grenadier, 275th and 342nd Infantry Divisions, was assigned to his command from the 4th Panzer Army in a logical regrouping.[9]

With Hitler's permission, the eastern suburbs of Frankfurt-an-der-Oder were abandoned to the Soviets so that Colonel Biehler's garrison could concentrate on defending their positions around the main part of the city on the west bank, where they continued to give a good account of themselves against the 69th Army.[10]

During the course of the day General Busse made an urgent appeal for the Berlin forward defence line to be manned with whatever forces were available as a fallback position for his collapsing front. Consequently General Reymann, commander of the Berlin Defence Area, was ordered to despatch ten Volkssturm battalions and a flak battery of the 'Grossdeutschland' Guard Regiment from his meagre resources forthwith.[11] These reinforcements were again rushed forward in commandeered buses and taxis in a manner reminiscent of the Battle of the Marne. Von Oven, an official in Goebbels' Propaganda Ministry, wrote in his diary for 20 April:

> The situation deteriorated during the night. The Minister was in lively, earnest telephone conversation with General Burgdorf, saying that reinforcement of the Oder Front with four battalions is simply not enough and that the Führer must now decide finally whether to despatch all the Berlin forces to the Oder Front. No doubt he also realizes that should the 9th Army's front be broken, quite clearly the 9th Army could no longer be counted upon defending Berlin.
>
> The Führer's reply arrives early in the morning. It is that Berlin is to be defended outside the city boundary. Immediately all the soldiers available in Berlin are to be sent to the Front in convoys of buses standing by. Our warmest wishes go with them.[12]

2

BERLIN

Greater Berlin, whose boundaries were established in 1920, is a city comparable in size with Greater London, encompassing some 341 square miles, measuring about 23 miles from north to south and 28 miles from east to west, with over half this area consisting of woods, parks, fields and lakes.

Berlin's blackened ruins still housed the organs of government of what remained of the Third Reich. Here too remained Adolf Hitler, whose haphazard, bankrupt dictatorship was clearly reflected in the state of his capital and its motley defenders preparing to meet the Soviet offensive. As the seat of government and a leading industrial city, Berlin had been a prime bombing target for much of the war, despite the fact that it lay at the extreme range of UK-based aircraft and was usually obscured by cloud so that only blind area-bombing was possible. Having endured a total of 450 raids, Berlin became the most heavily bombed city in Germany, the US Army Air Force and the Royal Air Force dropping in total some 45,517 tons of bombs and mines on it.

The frequency and size of the raids had gradually increased, and from mid-February 1945 onward Berlin suffered almost continual aerial bombardment for 30 days and nights. The damage was worst in the centre, where Mitte District sustained 78 per cent total destruction and Tiergarten District 48 per cent. Although three-quarters of this damage was attributable to fire, the broad streets characteristic of much of Berlin had prevented the larger conflagrations experienced in other German cities.

The prewar population of this spacious city of 4,321,000 inhabitants had been reduced by evacuation, wartime redeployment of labour and air raid casualties. Despite a large influx of refugees from the eastern provinces in early 1945, it was now down to somewhere between two and two and a half million. It is estimated that the bombing alone killed 50,000 Berliners, but it significantly failed to extinguish the spirit of the survivors. Indeed, the gradual build-up in the attacks seems to have conditioned the inhabitants to survival under the most appalling conditions, producing an indifference to their own suffering, and preparing them for the rigours of the forthcoming battle.[1]

This build-up had also enabled the city authorities and civil defence organizations to prepare for the worst of the ordeals. Following some heavy raids in August 1943, Joseph Goebbels, as Gauleiter of Berlin, had secured the evacuation of a million inhabitants and closed the schools, thereby reducing the burden of 'useless mouths'. For those that remained, air raid shelters were eventually produced with a total capacity of 300,000 persons. All suitable cellars were reinforced, their exits masked with brick walls and fitted with steel doors. Public shelters were also prepared under gasometers and other buildings with concrete foundations, and in the lateral galleries of some U-Bahn (underground railway) stations. Then numerous massive concrete shelters were built with roofs over three feet thick, each consisting of either 18 or 36 compartments, according to the model, and capable of accommodating several hundred people.[2]

All the principal ministries were provided with their own shelters, such as the one under Goebbels' Propaganda Ministry, which was just across Wilhelmstrasse from Hitler's Chancellery. The special Führerbunker lay under several layers of earth and concrete, beneath the Old Chancellery building, and was connected again by tunnels with other bunkers under and behind the New Chancellery building, sheltering the staff, bodyguards and a fleet of vehicles.

There was a large two-storey shelter below Alexanderplatz, accessible from the U-Bahn system, another large shelter beneath Saarlandstrasse (Stresemannstrasse) and a special shelter for diplomats and other customers of the Adlon Hotel under Pariser Platz.[3]

In addition to these shelters, three enormous towers were constructed in the parks at Friedrichshain, Humboldthain and at the Zoo for the dual purpose of sheltering the population and providing elevated platforms for the anti-aircraft artillery. These massive flak-towers were veritable fortresses, being both bomb-proof and shell-proof, with walls six feet thick and heavy steel doors over all the apertures. The largest was that at the Zoo, being 132 feet high with five storeys above ground. The top floor contained the barracks for the 100-strong garrison, the fourth a fully equipped and staffed hospital intended primarily for VIPs, the third served as a secure warehouse for some of Berlin's art and museum treasures, while the lower floors contained a specially reserved section for Deutschlandsender (the official broadcasting service), military kitchens, canteens and clothing stores, and could also provide shelter for 12,000 people.

The tower was completely self-contained with its own water and power supplies, and was well stocked with food and ammunition for sustaining a siege. However, it did have its drawbacks, for when the guns were in action and the rattling ammunition hoists were conveying shells up from the basement magazines, the noise within the building was almost unbearable. Also, the security it offered attracted far more people than it was designed for, so that it was permanently overcrowded.

Each of these three main flak-towers carried an eight-gun battery of 128mm calibre on twin mountings, for which the radar, range-finders and other electronic support was mounted on adjacent control towers of similar height but lesser size, and all the towers were ringed with platforms carrying 12 multi-barrelled 20mm or 37mm 'pom-poms'.

The control tower for the Zoo bunker, which was located opposite in the Tiergarten across the Landwehr Canal, contained the headquarters of the Luftwaffe's 1st 'Berlin' Flak Division, and was destined to serve as a communications centre for the defence.

There were a dozen other permanent flak positions situated at various points in the city, usually on the flat roofs of official buildings, and these were to prove useful in accommodating command posts and in acting as defensive positions in the coming land battle.

All the Luftwaffe anti-aircraft artillery stationed in the city belonged to the 1st 'Berlin' Flak Division and was independent of the normal military garrison. Originally the Berlin Flak, as it was called, numbered some 500 batteries, but the city's defences had been denuded to reinforce the Oder defences, and now all that remained were the batteries installed on the flak-towers and a few others at various vantage points around the capital. There was an important battery on the edge of the Tiergarten near the Shell Haus, another on Königsplatz (Platz der Republik) in front of the Reichstag, one on Königin-Luise-Platz outside the Botanical Gardens, one in the Grunewald, and a group outside Tempelhof Airport. These flak batteries could be expected to provide valuable support in the land battle, both against aircraft and in the anti-tank role. Unfortunately they were not all they appeared, for, since February 1943, 15–17-year-old secondary schoolboys of the Hitlerjugend had replaced all but a few key adult personnel on the home defence batteries, the younger boys assisting the Luftwaffehelferinnen (female auxiliaries) with the searchlights, radar and communications systems. Usually on reaching the age of 17 these boys would go on to Reichsarbeitsdienst and then Wehrmacht service, but since January 1945 many of the experienced older boys had been kept back in order to keep the three flak-towers fully operational.[4]

The Berlin Garrison Headquarters were traditionally located opposite the Zeughaus (Arsenal) on the Unter-den-Linden, and administered a motley collection of units: military police checking for stragglers and deserters, several battalions of sub-standard troops guarding installations, bridges and other vulnerable points, as well as the thousands of prisoners-of-war and slave-labourers employed in the city, some penal units, an engineer battalion, and two battalions of the 'Grossdeutschland' Guard Regiment retained for ceremonial duties. These garrison troops also assisted in clearing the streets of debris after air raids. The garrison formed part of Wehrkreis (Military Area) III, which was administered by Headquarters III Corps in peacetime, and by a Deputy Headquarters on the Hohenzollerndamm when the III Corps went off to war. Deputy Headquarters III Corps in turn came under the Reserve or Home Army, whose command had been given to Heinrich Himmler, Reichsführer-SS, after the abortive attempt on Hitler's life of 20 July 1944.[5]

At the beginning of February 1945, Hitler had declared Berlin a *Festung* (fortress), ordering the strengthening, supply and tactical deployment of the garrison in preparation for the defence of the city, but had not designated exactly what troops were to be used for this purpose. At the same time the Commander Deputy Headquarters III Corps had become Commander Berlin Defence Area, a logical step now that most of Wehrkreis III was either overrun or in the combat zone. However, for various reasons, including two rapid changes of commanders and the overriding commitment to reinforce the front, it was not until the day after Lieutenant-General Hellmuth Reymann, previously commanding the 11th Infantry Division, replaced his sick predecessor, Lieutenant-General Bruno Ritter von Hauenschild, on 8 March that a plan for the defence of the city as a separate entity was issued. At the time of his appointment Hitler told Reymann that, should the need arise, sufficient front-line troops would be made available to him to man the defences, and Reymann understood that they would come from Army Group 'Weichsel' (Vistula) on the Oder Front.[6] Hitler also told Reymann that he would be leaving Berlin and that Reymann could use the Führerbunker for his command post.[7]

General Reymann had found the double appointment unworkable and, at his request, another general had been appointed to the Wehrkreis Headquarters, which was eventually evacuated before the battle and took no part in it. In any case the entrenched personnel of the Wehrkreis Headquarters had failed to take the defensive planning seriously and continued to wage a paper war with the Defence Area Headquarters, whose unusual status directly under Hitler bypassed the normal chain of command and subsequent responsibility of superior military headquarters. The Defence Area Headquarters staff was skeletal when Colonel Hans Refior joined it as Chief-of-Staff on 20 March, the resources available to it consisted of:

14

The 1st 'Berlin' Flak Division, under Luftwaffe Major-General Sydow, which would only come under command once the land battle commenced,

The 'Grossdeutschland' Guard Regiment, consisting of two half-battalions with a total of nine companies,

A Territorial Battalion,

An SS Police Territorial Battalion,

A Panzer Company of immobile, dug-in tanks,

An Anti-Tank Company of Mark I tanks, each mounted with six Panzerfaust anti-tank weapons,

An Engineer Battalion of two companies, specialising in air raid damage work,

An *ad hoc* Engineer Battalion of two companies, formed from engineers cut off from their parent units.

Twenty Volkssturm Battalions of the first category that had already been mustered,

Twenty Volkssturm Battalions of the second category yet to be mustered, and

Several Batteries of captured Yugoslav and Belgian guns manned by Hitlerjugend crews at the Döberitz Training Area.[8]

The 35-page defence plan produced by Major Sprotte, the Operations Officer of his new staff, in a style totally uncharacteristic of General Reymann's own, nevertheless went out under the latter's signature in the haste of the moment. The basic concept of the plan was naturally conditioned by the nature of the terrain. The main threat was from Soviet armour, for which much of the ground was eminently suitable, with a good network of roads and open sandy ground, often screened by woodland, providing covered approaches. Although the irrigated fields in the northeast and the many ditches, canals and streams provided effective anti-tank obstacles, only the Havel Lakes in the west, the Spree River running through the city centre, and the Müggelsee and the Dahme River in the southeast could be relied upon as more positive barriers to movement. However, further out at an average distance of 25 miles from the city centre, there was a belt of woods and lakes running between the Alte Oder River near Bad Freienwalde to south of Königs Wusterhausen on the Dahme, offering a readily adaptable defensive position.

The system incorporated ideas put forward by Hitler and Goebbels, and consisted basically of the following:

1. A Forward Defence Line in the east, utilising the chain of natural obstacles between the Dahme and Alte Oder Rivers, and extending for about 50 miles.

2. An obstacle belt blocking major road junctions north and south of the city.
3. An Outer Defence Ring based roughly on the line of the city boundary, with alternative fallback positions wherever practicable.
4. An Inner Defence Ring based on the S-Bahn (suburban railway) circuit.
5. An innermost keep, named 'Zitadelle' (citadel), based on the island formed by the River Spree and the Landwehr Canal, with external bastions 'Ost' and 'West' around Alexanderplatz and the Knie (Ernst-Reuter-Platz) respectively, encompassing all the more important government buildings, including Hitler's Reichs Chancellery.[9]

The area between the Outer Defence Ring and 'Zitadelle' was divided clockwise into eight Defence Sectors labelled 'A' to 'H', and it was intended that the defence would be conducted in depth within these individual sectors. A commander with the powers of a Divisional Commander was nominated for each sector in the plan as follows:

'A' – Lieutenant-Colonel Bärenfänger
'B' – Colonel Clausen
'C' – Colonel Mootz
'D' – Major-General Scheder (Luftwaffe)
'E' – Lieutenant-Colonel Römhild
'F' – Colonel Eder
'G' – Colonel Schäfer
'H' – Lieutenant-Colonel Rossbach
'Z' – Lieutenant-Colonel Seifert.[10]

The preparation of the defences presented a mammoth task. The Chief of Engineers, Colonel Lobeck, had only one engineer battalion at his disposal, so General Reymann, with Goebbels' permission, had two of the city's Volkssturm (Home Guard) battalions assigned to this role. The labour force itself was organized by Party officials, who, despite tremendous difficulties, still managed to muster about 70,000 people per day during the weeks preceding the attack. In addition to the Organization Todt (official civil engineering service) and Reichsarbeitsdienst (Labour Service) personnel, who were the only ones with proper tools and equipment for this work, soldiers, civilians, prisoners-of-war and slave-labour gangs were employed. Although the numbers may appear small in relation to the size of the population, it should be remembered that the city's many factories were being maintained at full production day and night until the very last minute. A major transport problem was caused by the lack of fuel; movement of the labour force depended largely upon the railways, which were constantly being disrupted by repeated air raids; and there were only horse-drawn wagons with which to move the sparse building materials. There was a drastic shortage of tools of all kinds, barbed wire, nails and anti-tank mines, and the time factor precluded the use of ferroconcrete in the construction of defensive positions. The shortage of supervisors with expertise in these matters led to some of the results being militarily useless, or even a handicap to their own troops. The greatest and best-qualified effort appears to have been expended in the preparation of 'Zitadelle' in the city centre, gradually diminishing in effectiveness toward the periphery, and to a great extent the quality of the troops initially assigned to these defences corresponded to this pattern.[11]

The Forward Defence Line had natural strength, but only normal field positions were constructed along it at critical points, and as these were eventually manned by Luftwaffe and Volkssturm units lacking the necessary arms or training for the task, no more than a token defence could be expected from them. Though the Oder Front troops might have put these facilities to better use, circumstances were to dictate otherwise.[12]

The obstacle belt consisted of a series of road-blocks at all road junctions on the route linking Schmöckwitz with Königs Wusterhausen and along Reichsstrasse 246 to Beelitz in the south, and on Reichsstrasse 273 from Strausberg through Bernau in the north. Each roadblock was covered by defensive positions intended to accommodate a Volkssturm platoon armed with infantry and anti-tank weapons, and all built-up areas between the obstacle belt and the Outer Defence Ring were also designated strongpoints to be defended by the local Volkssturm. However, because of the nature of the terrain, most of these positions could be easily bypassed and overcome at leisure.[13]

The first cohesive line of defence began at the city boundary with the Outer Defence Ring. This was some 60 miles round and obviously could not be manned effectively with the limited manpower available. In the north it followed the line of the Nordgraben, a water-filled ditch of little consequence, from Tegel harbour as far as Blankenburg, thus excluding all the northernmost suburbs. From there it curved around Hohenschönhausen, where it was bordered by a mass of sewage farms, down to the line of the S-Bahn, which it then followed through Biesdorf and Mahlsdorf to beyond the city boundary before cutting due south to the top of the Müggelsee. On the other side of the lake it crossed the wooded isthmus to the Dahme River, resuming at the eastern entrance to the Teltow Canal, which it then followed as far as the Wrede Bridge. It then followed the line Köpenicker Strasse/S-Bahn/

Wildmeisterdamm to the main lateral road connecting Buckow and Marienfelde, and on to the Teltow Canal again at the Eugen-Kleine Bridge. The line then continued westward protected by water as far as the Glienicker Bridge leading to Potsdam, and then turned due north by way of the Sakrower See and Gross-Glienicker See (lakes) to beyond Staaken, before turning east on the northern outskirts of Spandau to end on the Havel opposite the entrance to the Tegeler See.[14]

The alternative fallback positions in the west allowed a withdrawal across the Havel, should Gatow Airfield or Spandau have to be abandoned, and boats were placed in readiness for the evacuation of the Gatow garrison. In the east the fallback position followed the line of the Wuhle stream running northward from Köpenick. In the south the Teltow Canal served as a fallback position, as did the Hohenzollern Canal in the north.

The defences along the Outer Defence Ring consisted mainly of a single meagre fire-trench with a few covered positions built at intervals along it, but each road entering the city was strongly barricaded on this line and the barricades covered by defensive positions, including a few dug-in obsolete tanks. There was a continuous anti-tank ditch masking the southern and eastern suburbs, and 20 local artillery batteries were allocated in support of the Outer Defence Ring, plus some mobile elements of the Berlin Flak.

The Inner Defence Ring stretched for 30 miles and was a much stronger position, being based on the appreciable obstacle formed by the S-Bahn ring of railway tracks linking the city's mainline stations. This ring of several parallel tracks, sometimes running along deep cuttings, sometimes elevated on vast pylons or running along steep-sided embankments, provided a series of ready-made ramparts, anti-tank ditches or glacis, all of considerable width and giving good fields of fire to the defenders concealed in buildings along the inner perimeter. Again all the roads crossing this obstacle were strongly barricaded. They were covered by well dug-in anti-tank weapons or 88mm anti-aircraft guns, the latter being long famous for their effectiveness in the anti-tank role.[15]

The extent and complexity of defence arrangements within the sectors depended largely on the skill and ingenuity of the local commanders. The general scheme, which was achieved to a great degree, was to create barricades at all major road junctions and convert all strong buildings into fortified positions. At the same time the city's 483 bridges were prepared for demolition in two categories, the first category creating a maze-like approach to the city centre when eventually blown, the second category being left to the last minute.[16]

Preparations within the Inner Defence Ring were quite elaborate.

Barricades in the side streets allowed passage only to pedestrians, and those in the main streets were closed to vehicular traffic at night by means of movable sections. Machine-gun posts were prepared in cellars and upper storeys to cover these barricades, and holes were knocked through the dividing walls to allow covered passage from cellar to cellar. The generally shallow U-Bahn tunnels were also barricaded at intervals to prevent infiltration, and preparations were made for flooding some of them.

'Zitadelle' was particularly well prepared, and the arrangement at the Brandenburg Gate was said to be a model of its kind. Guns and tanks, including some powerful 'Tigers', were dug in to support the more important positions, and trenches were dug in the Tiergarten.

Communications proved a major problem in the conduct of the defence. The Luftwaffe Flak had their own communications system, as did the front-line units later involved within the city, but there were no radios available for the improvised garrison, which had to rely on the normal civilian telephone network and the use of runners for the passage of orders and information. This invariably led to poor co-ordination between sectors and units, lack of centralized control and consequently confusion everywhere and at all levels.[17]

The supply system was no less complicated. It was not until the beginning of April that Reserve Colonel von Hauenschild, who had been responsible for preparing Breslau as a 'Festung', was brought in to do the same for Berlin as Quartermaster on General Reymann's staff. There was no real problem about food, as there were ample stocks within the city for civilians and military alike, although regular distribution was soon disrupted by the fighting, but there was an almost immediate shortage of ammunition due to the three large depots in the outer suburbs being overrun at an early stage. The military authorities established ration, clothing and equipment stores in several U-Bahn stations, but would not make issues to the Party-sponsored Volkssturm, presumably because the matter had not been cleared at sufficiently high level. The Waffen-SS were well-supplied in all respects, but tended to hoard their supplies to the detriment of the other defenders. All organizations suffered from the common shortage of motor fuel.[18]

Thus the overall results were scarcely in keeping with the appellation 'Festung'. With adequate troops of the right calibre, General Reymann had a feasible outline plan for the defence of the capital, but the proper military facilities for developing the plan in depth simply did not exist any longer. However, the Nazi leadership had a completely different philosophy; Hitler's contention was that, if the Soviets succeeded in reaching Berlin, they should be forced to waste their strength in the city's ruins, much as von Paulus' 6th Army had done at Stalingrad. If this plan failed and the Soviets prevailed, the Germans would have shown themselves unworthy of their leadership and would deserve extinction, just as in nature only the strong survive.[19]

Adolf Hitler, Führer of the Third Reich and Supreme Commander of the German Armed Forces, had been installed in his new command bunker beneath the Old Reichs Chancellery in Wilhelmstrasse since 16 January 1945, although this was still a well-kept secret. His days of courting popularity with mass Party rallies and public appearances were long since over. He had not even visited a single German city to witness the effects of the Allied bombing, and when his special train necessarily had to pass through these areas the curtains were drawn to exclude such distressing sights. Nor, apart from a single visit to the CI Corps on 3 March 1945, had he made any front-line inspections for some considerable time. Secluded in his various remote command posts, he had become more and more removed from the reality of the world in which his subjects lived, suffered, fought and died unheeded.[20]

In an oppressive atmosphere of noisy air-conditioning and sweating concrete walls, with no distinction between night and day, Hitler's last headquarters suffered the serious defect of not being equipped with the normal communications facilities of the Führer Headquarters he had set up and occupied elsewhere in Europe during the course of the war. This was in part due to scale, for accommodation was extremely cramped in the Führerbunker itself, although more space could have been made available in the bomb-proof shelters beneath the New Reichs Chancellery building. However, the only communications facilities installed in the Führerbunker consisted of a one-man switchboard, one radio transmitter and a radio-telephone. The latter operated via an aerial suspended from a small but vulnerable balloon above the bunker to a relaying aerial mounted on the Funkturm (radio tower) near Adolf-Hitler-Platz (Theodor-Heuss-Platz).[21]

Meanwhile Hitler's courtiers kept up their internecine struggle with malicious gossip, slandering those absent and disguising the truth from each other. Despite Hitler's obvious deterioration, his presence overwhelmed reason and sane judgement in all of them, and his military staff were as obsequious as the rest.[22] Permanently with Hitler in the Führerbunker was Field Marshal Wilhelm Keitel, nominal Chief of the Oberkommando-der-Wehrmacht (OKW – Armed Forces GHQ) with his headquarters in Berlin–Dahlem, but in practice acting as Hitler's personal Chief-of-Staff and issuing orders in the Führer's name. The OKW Chief-of-Staff, Colonel-General Alfred Jodl, and the Chief-of-Staff of the Oberkommando-des-Heeres (OKH – Army GHQ), General Hans Krebs, were obliged to spend most of their time shuttling back and forth between the Führerbunker conferences and their own secret wartime headquarters in the vast bunkers known as 'Maybach

I' and 'II' respectively, some 20 miles south of the city at Zossen–Wünsdorf.[23]

The head of the Luftwaffe, the once flamboyant Reichs Marshal Hermann Göring, had been rightly blamed for its many shortcomings and was now a discredited figure, although he still occasionally attended conferences in order to display his loyalty to the Führer and to keep in with Martin Bormann, Hitler's secretary, whose scheming had assisted his fall from grace.[24]

It was inevitable under the Nazi system that various Party officials should intervene in the preparations for the defence of the city. The most important of these was Joseph Goebbels, who, like the other Party leaders, combined several titles and responsibilities acquired in the scramble for power. Although most commonly known for his role as Minister of Public Enlightenment and Propaganda, he remained the original Gauleiter of Berlin, and was now also Reichs Defence Commissar for Wehrkreis III (Berlin), giving him pleni-potential powers in the organization of the defence of the capital. It was to him that the Commander of the Berlin Defence Area was expected to report, not only for approval of his plans, but also for the necessary Party support to implement them.

Every Monday Goebbels held a Council of War in his office, which was attended by the military commanders, representatives of the Luftwaffe and Labour Service, the Mayor of Berlin, the Police President, various high-ranking SS and police officials, SA (Schützabteilung) Standartenführer Bock as commander of the city's Volkssturm, and representatives of the main Berlin industries. It appears that the efficiency he applied to his Propaganda Ministry was not so readily transferable, although the same disregard for reality pertained. He too gave out a constant stream of orders, interfering at all levels and in all directions in imitation of the Führer's own style. He would not countenance an evacuation of the civilian population, an idea which he regarded as unnecessarily alarmist, but neither did he make any provision for their needs in case of siege. However, he took a genuine interest in the military situation, frequently visiting the front and consulting with the field commanders on a far more realistic basis than Hitler did.[25]

One of Goebbels' responsibilities as Gauleiter was the raising of the Berlin quota of Volkssturm units as part of the overall concept for defence. The Volkssturm had originally been raised the previous autumn as a form of Home Guard, intended purely for local defence and fortification construction purposes, from men aged 16 years and over capable of bearing arms in an emergency but otherwise not physically fit for active service. The majority came from the upper age bracket and included many First World War veterans. They were organized into companies and battalions in their home districts, but with no set establishments, so that the Berlin battalions varied in strength from 600–1,500. Unit commanders were appointed by the Party, some being veterans with military experience and a strong sense of duty, others mere political warriors. The Wehrmacht had no responsibility for this Party-sponsored organization, which was meant to be armed, equipped and maintained entirely from local resources. The only common issue was an armband, uniforms being either varied (even captured British battledress being used) or non-existent.

There were two categories of Volkssturm, the first being those for whom there were arms, and the second intended as replacements for the first, but even then the issue of arms was varied to the extent of being farcical. It was reported in one battalion, for instance, that one company had been given only two rifles, another had received some Italian rifles with only a few rounds of ammunition, and a third some machine-guns and an old anti-tank gun, but only Italian rifles as personal weapons. However, there was a plentiful supply of Panzerfaust and Panzerschreck anti-tank weapons, although again distribution was most uneven. Training was conducted at weekends and in the evenings when there was no construction work to do, and some three-day courses were offered at SA camps, but no Volkssturm troops were trained up to the combat role that came to be expected of them as the enemy engulfed the homeland. This is not to say that some of the Volkssturm units committed to the Oder Front did not acquit themselves surprisingly well under the circumstances.[26]

The Commanding Officer of the 42nd Volkssturm Battalion later recounted:

> I had 400 men in my battalion, and we were ordered to go into the line in our civilian clothes. I told the local Party leader that I could not accept the responsibility of leading men into battle without uniforms. Just before commitment we were given 180 Danish rifles, but no ammunition. We also had four machine-guns and 100 Panzerfausts. None of these men had received any training in firing a machine-gun, and they were all afraid of the anti-tank weapons. Although my men were quite ready to help their country, they refused to go into battle without uniforms and without training. What could a Volkssturm man do with a rifle without ammunition? The men went home; that was the only thing we could do.[27]

Dr Johannes Stumm, who had been dismissed from the Berlin Police in 1933 by Göring for his anti-Nazi activities, and was later to become Police President under the Western Allies, also recounted:

> I was able to avoid joining the Volkssturm, into whose second levy I was later conscripted. I was to be entrusted with the command of a company

of the second levy of Volkssturm, although I had only served a few weeks as a driver with a motorised unit, was not a Party member, and had only been an NCO in 1917. I at first reported sick. On the 22nd April I received an order to muster the company and join the fighting, but I simply disregarded this; the company was thus saved from the fighting.[28]

Not all the Volkssturm were quite as badly equipped or as ineffective as indicated by these two examples. For instance, the mighty Siemens concern was able to field a reasonably equipped battalion under First World War veteran officers of 770 men, with three rifle companies, a support weapons company and an infantry gun company, which even received a modicum of training in the area it was expected to defend.[29] But this was an exception to the rule, and, on the whole, the remaining units of the Berlin Volkssturm constituted a most uncertain factor in the defence.

However, the Volkssturm did not represent the only resources upon which the Party could draw. Another important Party functionary was Reichs-jugendführer (State Youth Leader) Arthur Axmann, who had exhorted the children of the Reich in the March of that year: 'There is only victory or annihilation. Know no bounds in your love of your people; equally know no bounds in your hatred of the enemy. It is your duty to watch when others tire, to stand when others weaken. Your greatest honour is your unshakeable fidelity to Adolf Hitler.'[30]

The Hitlerjugend, originally incorporating all German youths aged 14 to 18, had taken an active part in the war effort throughout, particularly in civil defence, in which they had assisted as messengers and with salvage and relief duties. Then in 1943 the senior schoolboys had been sent to man the home defence anti-aircraft artillery in order to release experienced adult gunners for the front and to enable an increase in the home defence organization to meet the Allied air offensive. Now Axmann committed his charges as infantry, a criminal act further aggravated by the fact that the Hitlerjugend's age bracket had gradually dropped during the course of the war, and boys of 12 to 16 years of age were now expected to take up arms like men and risk dying either from enemy action or being hung from a lamppost as a deserter. Mixed with adult Waffen-SS and Wehrmacht troops, they fought with a fanaticism that appalled their opponents as much as did the callousness of their leaders. Needless to say, they were to suffer tremendous losses.[31]

Lothar Loewe relates his experiences:

On the 5th March the third wave of the German Volkssturm, males born in 1929, that is all 15 and 16 year-olds, members of the Hitlerjugend and leaders in the Deutschen Jungvolk, were called to arms. By chance I met up with an old school friend, Erhard Meissner, who as a second lieutenant was in charge of the basic training of 500 young flak assistants and Hitlerjugend at the Döberitz Training Area.

The flak assistants were drilled in the use of 88mm flak artillery pieces in the anti-tank ground-fighting role. We Hitlerjugend were to defend the capital Berlin as tank-hunting teams equipped with Panzerfausts and Italian submachine-guns. Combat-experienced NCOs conducted the training. The commander of our unit, which was called 'Fortress Anti-Tank Unit III Berlin', was Major Theodor Baechle, a highly decorated, solicitous officer, who was a priest in civil life.

On the 17th April our unit moved to Berlin. I and a comrade were allocated to Major Baechle's staff as runners. Our first command post was in the Reichs Weather Office at Tempelhof Airport.[32]

From his headquarters on the Kaiserdamm, but later withdrawing to a bunker in the Wilhelmstrasse, Axmann proceeded to organize the local Hitlerjugend units to take part in the defence of the city. The boys were issued with rifles, grenades and Panzerfausts, and then allocated by their companies either to the various Defence Sectors, to a special Hitlerjugend Regiment which was assigned to guarding the Havel bridges opposite Spandau on 23 April, or to the 'Axmann' Brigade, which appeared in the Strausberg area on 21 April, and included a tank-hunting group armed with Panzerfausts and mounted on bicycles for mobility.[33]

Girls were also expected to take part in the fighting with grenades and home-made Molotov cocktails, but no attempt appears to have been made to commit them by their Bund-Deutscher-Mädel (German Girls' League) units, although some are reported to have assisted in the defence of the Rotes Rathaus (Red Townhall) as messengers, etc. However, later in the battle, secretaries and other female staff from the various governmental departments were encouraged to join the mythical 'Mohnke' units as combatants.[34]

The Reichsführer-SS and Chef-der-Deutschen-Polizei (State SS and Police Chief) Heinrich Himmler, who was also Minister of the Interior, had several of his Allgemeine-SS and Waffen-SS units in the city. The Berlin-based elements of the 'Leibstandarte-SS Adolf Hitler' Panzergrenadier Division, which provided Hitler's ceremonial bodyguard, household guard and servants, was about 1,200 strong, some of whom were combat-experienced troops from the parent formation, and under the command of SS Major-General Wilhelm Mohnke, responsible for the defence of the Reichs Chancellery. From these and personnel of the 'Leibstandarte' Depot at

Spreenhagen, the 'Anhalt' Regiment of two battalions, named after its commander, SS Colonel Günther Anhalt was formed for the protection of 'Zitadelle'. A second regiment, also of two battalions, was formed from Allgemeine-SS personnel, but these appear to have been used only in the defence of their own establishments. Goebbels' propaganda added a mythical 2,000-strong 'Freikorps Adolf Hitler', consisting of volunteers rallying to the defence of their Führer from all over the country, and a 'Freikorps Mohnke' – 'Bring your own weapons' – but that was all sheer fantasy. The 'Anhalt' was responsible for the area west of the north–south line of Friedrichstrasse to inclusive the whole of the Tiergarten. When the 1st Battalion was removed on the evening of 23 April to form a counterattack reserve on Frankfurter Allee, this left only the 2nd Battalion to cover the whole of the regimental area, which meant a distribution as thin as two men in a foxhole every 50 yards throughout the Tiergarten, and a slightly stronger concentration where the bridges crossed the Spree.[35]

Other SS units were used as nuclei for the defence forces of the various sectors, and some SS and Feldgendarmerie (Military Police) personnel were employed for rounding up stragglers and deserters. The police and fire brigade services, all coming under Himmler's extensive empire, formed combat units to assist the defence, while at the same time managing to keep their normal services operating within the city as long as conditions allowed.

Also available to assist in local defence tasks were the Plant Protection Companies maintained by the larger industrial concerns, including the post office and the railways. These were recruited from old soldiers and armed only with rifles, and consequently were of limited combat value.[36]

One unusual aspect of the political influence on the conduct of the defence was the mixing of members of different organizations within strongpoints in the various sectors, so that SS, Wehrmacht, Volkssturm and Hitlerjugend literally fought side by side. This may have been of some value in bolstering the morale of the weaker elements, but must have made the command function even more difficult.[37]

The loyalty commanded by Hitler in his immediate entourage was most curiously displayed in the conduct of Albert Speer, Reichs Minister for Armaments and War Production. Hitler's architectural interests had cata-lyzed Speer's dazzling career under the Third Reich. First coming to Hitler's notice during the construction of the New Reichs Chancellery, which he was responsible for completing in record time, Speer soon became an intimate, working on Hitler's ideas for the grandiose transformation of Berlin and other pet projects until the course of the war caused them to be shelved. Then when Dr Fritz Todt, Minister of Armaments and Munitions, and head of the vast construction organization bearing his name, was killed in an air crash in February 1942, Hitler appointed Speer to succeed him, thus making Speer a leading member of the hierarchy overnight.[38]

Within a remarkably short time Speer's administrative methods achieved astonishing results in the increase of war production, despite the growing intensification of the Allied air offensive. However, although still personally spellbound by Hitler, Speer alone among the hierarchy was soon to perceive the extent of the dilemma in which Germany found itself. From the time of its inception in the summer of 1944, he constantly opposed Hitler's 'scorched earth' policy, for he saw that these orders for wholesale destruction would make it impossible for the countries concerned to recover after the war. By persuading local Party leaders and officials to refrain from carrying out these orders, which Hitler reiterated on 20 March and again on 4 April 1945, Speer achieved considerable success in both Germany and the occupied territories.[39]

According to his own account, in February 1945 Speer had gone so far as to plan the murder of Hitler by the introduction of poison gas into the Führerbunker's ventilation system, but was foiled by a screening chimney, which had just been built around the air intake after the accidental introduction of some smoke had revealed the flaw in the system. Although unaware of this plot, Hitler was not unaware of Speer's other activities and his lack of faith in ultimate victory, but seems to have chosen to ignore these treacherous aberrations, while at the same time taking steps to diminish Speer's influence.[40]

Then on 15 April Speer had contrived to appear at Colonel-General Gotthardt Heinrici's Army Group 'Weichsel' headquarters near Prenzlau during a visit by General Reymann to discuss the allocation of front-line troops for the city's defences. Heinrici was naturally concerned for the fate of the city, but had not been given any specific responsibility for it, nor was he aware that he was expected to part with any of his troops to Reymann. He was in any case fully opposed to the idea of exposing the population to the consequences of street-fighting should an attempt be made to defend the city in depth, and advised Reymann to confine his efforts to making a stand on the city boundary. If the Soviets succeeded in forcing his own troops from their positions along the Oder, Heinrici proposed drawing them aside from Berlin rather than getting them involved within the city.[41]

Speer had previously conspired with Heinrici to protect the Silesian industries and was now aware of the instructions received by Reymann to destroy all the bridges in the city. He had therefore brought along with him two technical experts to help plead his case: Langer, the city superintendent of roadworks, and Beck of the Reichsbahn (state railways). Together they explained that not only did the bridges carry pedestrian, vehicular and railway

26

traffic, but also the vital arteries of the city's gas, electricity and water supplies and the sewage system, whose severance would cause untold hardships to the inhabitants. Reymann was in a quandary over his duty to obey orders, but eventually agreed to Heinrici's recommendation to remove the explosive charges forthwith and not to blow any bridges except as required in the course of military operations. Thus, as a result of this meeting, only 127 of Berlin's 483 bridges were eventually destroyed by Reymann's engineers. Speer says that Langer and another city engineer, Kumpf, were active in preventing such demolitions, even during the fighting, and there is indeed other evidence of such activity having taken place.[42]

In the meantime the growing destruction of the city and a gradual reduction in living standards were becoming more and more apparent to the inhabitants when they emerged from their shelters in the brief intervals between air raids. With blocked streets, frequently severed electricity, water and gas mains, and other hindrances to normal life, even the basic essentials were becoming increasingly difficult to meet.

To add to these depressing factors came a stream of refugees from the eastern provinces, bearing tales of horror and spreading a haunting fear of the Soviets, who were being urged by Ilya Ehrenburg's manifesto to the Red Army to spare no one, even women and children, in their revenge. Yet the prevailing mood was nevertheless one of passive resignation, a kind of numbed acceptance of events and a refusal to believe in the imminence of catastrophe. No doubt the traditional docility of the Germans toward authority contributed something toward this apathy, but other factors also played a part. For instance, the population had yet to suffer from hunger; food rationing was adequate and distribution continued more or less regularly. In addition, all the semblances of public order were still in evidence: there were 12,000 police on duty in the city, the municipal transport and other services were still functioning, and the civilian defence organizations were as efficient as ever.[43]

To counter depression and defeatism there was an endless stream of propaganda from Goebbels' Ministry, which continued to hold out hope until the very end, while simultaneously threatening traitors and defeatists with the most dire penalties. Even the ruins were used to bear slogans such as: 'Our faith is in total victory' – 'Bolshevism is about to meet the most decisive defeat in history' – 'On the Oder will be decided the fate of Europe' – 'We will never surrender' – 'Berlin will stay German' – 'Break our walls but not our hearts'.

Beneath these smouldering ruins the man upon whom the entire situation hinged was making plans to meet the contingency of the Allied advances splitting the Reich in two. He issued a Führer-Order on 15 April announcing that in such an eventuality the struggle would be continued, with Grand

Admiral Karl Dönitz commanding the German forces in the north, and Field Marshal Albert Kesselring those in the south.[44] His staff were confident that Hitler was planning to move to Berchtesgaden, where he would conduct a stand from the so-called, but non-existent, 'Alpine Redoubt'. However, when his discreet and unassuming mistress Eva Braun suddenly moved into the Bunker from her apartment in the Chancellery on 15 April, declaring that she would remain with the Führer whatever happened, they took this as a strong indication that he intended staying in Berlin after all.[45]

3

THE RUSSIANS ARE COMING!

Late on 19 April Zhukov's forces finally broke through the German 9th Army's final lines of defence and the road to Berlin lay open before them. However, the troops were exhausted after the four-day battle that had cost them an enormous toll in casualties, including an admitted 33,000 killed, which is probably half of the actual total, and a quarter of their armour.[1]

The situation demanded a dramatic revision of Zhukov's original plans for taking Berlin. Colonel-General M.I. Katukov's 1st Guards Tank Army and the 8th Guards Army under Colonel-General Vassily Ivanovitch Chuikov would now continue as a combined force on the direct line along Reichsstrasse 1 to the city, and there swing south over the Spree and Dahme Rivers to encompass the southern suburbs along an arc extending from the Spree to the Havel. Although the original plan had been for Colonel-General S.I. Bogdanov's 2nd Guards Tank Army to provide the northern armoured pincer enveloping Berlin, the three component corps were now allocated individually to the three combined-arms armies in that sector. Major-General A.F. Popov's 9th Guards Tank Corps was given the task of pushing straight through to the Havel in support of Lieutenant-General F.I. Perkhorovitch's 47th Army, which was further reinforced by Major-General M.P. Konstantinov's 7th Guards Cavalry Corps and the 1st Polish Motorized Mortar Brigade of four regiments from Lieutenant-General S.G. Poplowski's 1st Polish Army's Reserve. Lieutenant-General S.M. Krivosheina's 1st Mechanized Corps and Major-General M.F. Teltakov's 12th Guards Tank Corps would approach the northeastern suburbs, acting as the spearheads of the 3rd and 5th Shock Armies respectively. The 2nd Guards Tank Army would then re-form with these two latter armoured corps to take over the northern arc of suburbs, while Colonel-General V.I. Kutznetsov's 3rd Shock Army took over the north-eastern and General N.E. Berzarin's 5th Shock Army the eastern suburbs respectively. It is clear that the armour set the pace for this next phase of the operation, with the exhausted combined-arms armies keeping up as best as

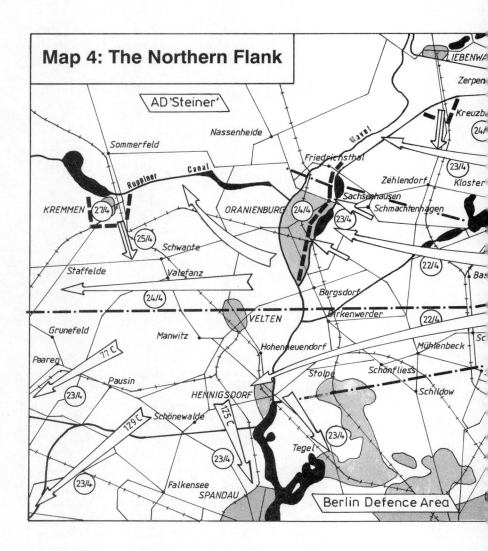

Map 4: The Northern Flank

AD 'Steiner'

LIEBENWA
Zerpen
Kreuzb.
24/
23/4
Kloster

Nassenheide
Havel
Friedrichsthal
Sommerfeld
Ruppiner
Canal
Zehlendorf
Sachsenhausen
Schmachtenhagen
KREMMEN 27/4
ORANIENBURG 24/4
25/4
Schwante
23/4
Staffelde
Valefanz
22/4
Bas
24/4
Borgsdorf
VELTEN
Birkenwerder
22/4
Grunefeld
Manwitz
Mühlenbeck
Sc
Paaren
77 C
Hohenneuendorf
Schönfliess
Stolpe
Schildow
Pausin
HENNIGSDORF
125 C
129 C
Schönewalde
23/4
23/4
Tegel
23/4
Falkensee
23/4
SPANDAU

Berlin Defence Area

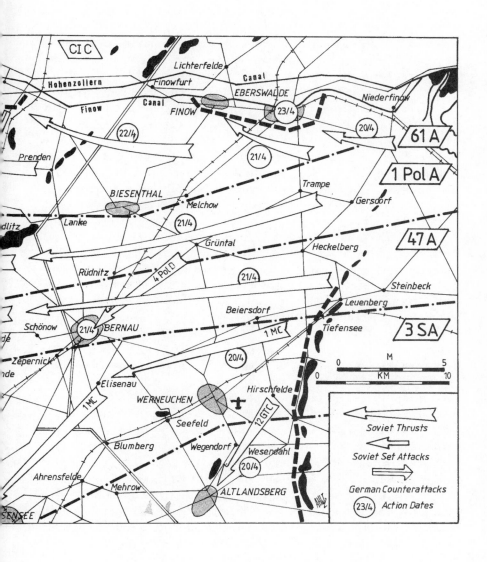

CIC

Lichterfelde
Hohenzollern   Finowfurt   Canal
Finow   Canal   EBERSWALDE   Niederfinow
Canal   FINOW   23/4   61 A
22/4   20/4
Prenden   21/4   1 Pol A
Trampe
BIESENTHAL   Melchow   Gersdorf
Lanke   21/4   47 A
adlitz   Grüntal   Heckelberg
Rüdnitz   4 Pol D   Steinbeck
21/4
Beiersdorf   Leuenberg
Schönow   21/4 BERNAU   1 MC   Tiefensee   3 SA
Zepernick   20/4   0   M   5
nde   0   KM   10
Elisenau   Hirschfelde
WERNEUCHEN   12 GTC
Seefeld
Blumberg   Wegendorf   Wesendahl
20/4
Ahrensfelde   Mehrow   ALTLANDSBERG
SENSEE

Soviet Thrusts

Soviet Set Attacks

German Counterattacks

23/4   Action Dates

they could.[2] With this group went some airfield construction and service units from Colonel-General S.I. Rudenko's 16th Air Army, who were to secure the airfields at Eberswalde, Werneuchen and Strausberg.[3]

The 12th Guards Tank Corps took Grunow on the morning of the 19th but their commander was wounded and the deputy commander of the 9th Guards Tank Corps, Colonel A.T. Shevchenko, was given temporary command in his stead.[4]

The 69th and 33rd Armies, commanded by Colonel-Generals V.Y. Kolpakchi and V.D. Svotaev respectively, together with Colonel-General A.V. Gorbatov's 3rd Army from Zhukov's second echelon, would converge on the remains of the 9th Army on the southern flank of the main thrust and destroy it.[5]

The primary objective was set as the Reichstag building, but only fate would determine which formation would actually take it, for all those surrounding the city, except the 47th Army, would be competing under front supervision.

As previously mentioned, Zhukov was aware that Stalin had given his rival Koniev permission to send his 3rd and 4th Guards Tank Armies toward Berlin on the night of 17 April, but still expected to have the city to himself, and part of Chuikov's task was to ensure this.[6]

Meanwhile Koniev's tank armies, backed by 75 per cent of Colonel General S.A. Krasovsky's 2nd Air Army's aircraft, continued to make steady progress northward, although not fast enough to satisfy Koniev who was still hoping to get into Berlin ahead of Zhukov. Apart from a few local Volkssturm units, there were no troops around to oppose the Soviets in this area and yet the 3rd Guards Tank Army, concerned about the enemy forces on its right flank, made only about 18 miles on the 19th, in comparison with the 31 miles made by Colonel General D.D. Lelyushenko's 4th Guards Tank Army.[7]

In order to protect the 3rd Panzer Army's southern flank from the threat posed by the Russian breakthrough, Heinrici decided to use SS General Felix Steiner's III SS 'Germanic' Panzer Corps Headquarters, which commanded the 3rd Panzer Army's reserve. He therefore ordered Steiner to move his headquarters forward to near Eberswalde and to take over the remains of the CI Corps and the 25th Panzergrenadier Division, with the task of holding the line of the Finow Canal. To supplement these meagre resources Heinrici ordered the 3rd Naval Division to come down by rail from Swinemünde on the Baltic Coast, and also assigned Steiner the 4th SS Police Grenadier Division, which was supposed to be forming in the area. Finally, he added all the odd units he could find, including some Luftwaffe battalions, some emergency units formed from clerks and storemen, and some local Volkssturm units. Steiner was immediately concerned with extending his front westward to keep pace with the Russian advance on the south side of the canal and in finding sufficient manpower to meet his task.[8]

On 20 April Hitler belatedly decided to make Army Group 'Weichsel' responsible for the defence of the capital by placing the Berlin Defence Area under its command. Heinrici immediately assigned the Area to the 9th Army, but General Busse argued the point and the order was rescinded, the Berlin Defence Area remaining directly under Army Group Headquarters. However, with the 3rd Panzer Army preparing to face up to the 2nd Byelorussian Front's offensive in the north and the remains of the 9th Army coiling back on themselves in the south, the only resources left to deal with this commitment were the LVI Panzer Corps, already fully stretched and in imminent danger of losing contact with the formations on either side.[9] In Heinrici's opinion, Hitler's instructions for the 9th Army to remain on the Oder had condemned it to extinction and he therefore decided to concentrate upon saving the 3rd Panzer Army from a similar fate, in essence leaving the problem of Berlin to General Weidling's LVI Panzer Corps.[10]

As a means of compensating for the depletion of the garrison, the 'Friedrich Ludwig Jahn' RAD Infantry Division of General Walter Wenck's 12th Army was reassigned to the Berlin Defence Area, but no one in Berlin seemed to know where the division was, or what it consisted of, and such was the state of communications that despatch riders had to be sent out to find it. Eventually the divisional headquarters were traced to a village north of Trebbin and General Reymann set out to visit them.[11]

The threat to the capital that night was sufficiently serious for Hitler to authorize the evacuation of various governmental departments to take place the following night by road, involving the use of much valuable transport and fuel. Advance parties had already reconnoitred a route west and south through the territory occupied by Wenck's troops. However, the Propaganda Minister had no intention of joining this exodus, and that evening, seemingly ignoring the gravity of the general situation, to which he merely made a passing reference, he broadcast his customary eulogy of the Führer on the eve of Hitler's birthday, just as he had done every year since 1933. Nevertheless, the Berliners were becoming increasingly uneasy as evidence of the true state of affairs percolated through to them.[12]

They had good reason, for Koniev's forces were approaching rapidly from the south against negligible opposition.[13] General Rybalko remained very concerned about his 3rd Guards Tank Army's vulnerability to flank attack, and kept dropping off road-blocks to seal off the Spreewald pocket, much to the annoyance of Koniev, who sent him the following signal:

> Comrade Rybalko, you are moving like a snail. One brigade is fighting, the rest of the army standing still. I order you to cross the Baruth/Luckenwalde line through the swamps along several routes and deployed in battle order. Report fulfilment. Koniev.[14]

With Koniev's exhortations urging them on, the 3rd Guards Tank Army succeeded in covering 37 miles on 20 April, taking Baruth during the course of the afternoon and almost reaching Zossen before disaster struck.[15] The leading brigade of the 6th Guards Tank Corps ran out of fuel and was then destroyed piecemeal by Panzerfausts.[16]

This occurred close to the 'Maybach' bunker complex, where the bulk of the OKW and OKH staff had anxiously been awaiting permission to evacuate all day. The camp guard company, together with six to eight tanks from the nearby Wünsdorf training establishment, had been sent to block the crossroads at Luckau. By 0600 hours that morning, however, they were already reporting being bypassed by Soviet armour, and by nightfall the 20 survivors of the 250-strong unit were back in Zossen, apparently unaware of the cause of the delay in the Soviet advance. This, presumably, had been due to the intervention of local Volkssturm or Hitlerjugend units. Permission was then received from the Führerbunker to evacuate but, before leaving, Lieutenant-General August Winter, Jodl's deputy, addressed the assembled staff on the occasion of Hitler's birthday and for the first time openly admitted that the war might end badly for Germany. The staff then packed in such haste that there was no time to destroy any of the documents and equipment left behind, and the Soviets were able to take over these comprehensive items intact next day.[17]

On the left flank the 4th Guards Tank Army came up against some resistance in the Jüterbog–Luckenwalde area but were still able to cover 28 miles in daylight, and one group pushed on through the night for a further 21 miles until they reached the southern obstacle belt of the Berlin defence system.[18]

That evening General Reymann returned to Berlin with the news that the 'Friedrich Ludwig Jahn' RAD Infantry Division, while still forming up on the parade ground at the Wehrmacht's main ammunition depot at Jüterbog that day, had been surprised and scattered by Soviet tanks. Some of the men from the two regiments had been saved but nearly all the artillery had been lost and the divisional commander, Colonel Klein, had been captured while trying to re-establish contact with the missing third regiment. Shortly afterward General Krebs telephoned through instructions to send this division together with the 'Wünsdorf' Tank Unit to drive back the enemy spearheads approaching Berlin from the south. These Führerbunker orders, committing the remains of two badly shattered regiments and a handful of tanks that had already been destroyed to repulse two tank armies, Reymann could only ignore, and he ordered the survivors back to Potsdam.[19]

Meanwhile the centre and right of the 1st Byelorussian Front was also on the move. The northern flank hastened to assume their role in support of the 2nd Guards Tank Army's thrust with the advancing combined-arms armies. In the centre the 1st Guards Tank Army moved cautiously ahead of the 8th Guards Army, only too well aware of the effectiveness of the hand-held anti-tank weapons liberally supplied to the German infantry, which continued to exact a heavy toll.[20] The LVI Panzer Corps managed to delay the Soviets along the city's Forward Defence Line in a desperate bid to maintain contact with the 9th Army on their southern flank in accordance with Heinrici's instructions. Nevertheless, they could not possibly cover the whole of the exposed front, their left flank stopping short of Werneuchen in the north, and the 2nd Guards Tank Army had little trouble in overcoming the Volkssturm and Luftwaffe units they encountered on the main line of advance.[21]

The 1st Mechanized Corps pushed on as far as Elisenau, just south of Bernau, that day, and the 12th Guards Tank Corps formed up in the wood southwest of Tiefensee and attacked toward Werneuchen, Hirschfelde and Wegendorf, breaking through to Alt Landsberg that night. Meanwhile the 32nd Rifle Corps of the 5th Shock Army took Strausberg, which was to house Marshal Zhukov's headquarters for the remainder of the operation. Neither the Forward Defence Line nor the obstacle belt was able to check the Soviet advance.[22]

From Map 4 it can be seen how the armoured spearheads cleared the way for the combined-arms armies without heeding the planned boundaries. In similar manner the 4th Polish Infantry Division, operating on the southern flank of the 1st Polish Army, was to clear Bernau itself for the 47th Army next day (21 April).[23]

Progress was sufficient on 20 April to enable the long-range artillery of the 79th Rifle Corps and the 1st Battalion, 30th Guards Artillery Brigade, of the 3rd Shock and 47th Armies respectively, to fire the first salvoes into the city perimeter in what was more of a defiant propaganda exercise than a tactical measure. However, railway engineer units were hard at work extending and preparing the main line from Küstrin to take some heavy siege artillery that could fire shells weighing half a ton each.[24]

Colonel-General Heinrici spent most of the day personally trying to restore order in the Eberswalde area, where there was the utmost confusion among the units scattered by the Soviet breakthrough. The belt of woodland south of the Finow Canal was swarming with disorganized troops but by nightfall he had established some form of front along the line of the autobahn, although it could be regarded as only a temporary expedient. He appealed to the OKH for troops to hold the line of the Havel between Oranienburg and Spandau as a fallback position and was allocated the 'Müller' Brigade, consisting of a few understrength infantry battalions from the Döberitz Training Area, for this purpose.[25]

The 2nd Byelorussian Front had started their assault across the west branch of the Oder with an hour-long artillery and aerial bombardment that morning, but it was bad flying weather with poor visibility, much to the advantage of the defence. Only Colonel-General P.I. Batov's 65th Army managed to establish a bridgehead of reasonable size that day, the 49th and 70th Armies making little progress in what were extremely difficult circumstances.[26]

Hitler rose at 1100 hours on 20 April and throughout the day received congratulatory calls from his court on the occasion of his 56th birthday. Among those who came to pay tribute to their Führer were Goebbels, Grand Admiral Dönitz, Speer, von Ribbentrop, Göring, Axmann and Himmler, as well as members of his staff, such as Field Marshal Keitel, Generals Jodl, Krebs and Koller, and the diligent Bormann. Some of the foreign diplomats remaining in the city also called to pay their homage to him. At one stage in the afternoon he climbed the steps to the Chancellery garden to review a small parade of representatives of the Hitlerjugend, Waffen-SS 'Frundsberg' Division and the Kurland Army, after which he gave a small speech on the theme of 'fighting on' that surprisingly evoked none of the customary enthusiastic applause expected on such occasions.[27]

At the Waffen-SS 'Leibstandarte-SS Adolf Hitler' barracks in Lichterfelde, SS Major-General Wilhelm Mohnke held a parade in honour of Hitler's birthday, after which the band was reassigned as a mortar platoon under SS Sergeant-Major Willy Rogmann in support of the SS 'Anhalt' Regiment.[28]

At noon the Americans added their salute to the occasion with an air raid by 299 B-17 bombers lasting two hours and conducted from such a height that the city's flak could not reach them. To Keitel, Dönitz and their wives, watching from a garden in Dahlem, it seemed as if the silver bombers were on parade, dropping their bombs in perfect unison. The raid left Berlin stunned and silent in its desolation, with the gas, electricity and sewage services once again disrupted, and water now available only from the street pumps, so that queuing for water in the open was to become a necessary hazard for survival during the rest of the battle. After the bombers had gone, some low-flying 'Mosquitos' of the Royal Air Force pestered the flak defences until dusk, when the Red Army Air Force made a short raid. That night the British made their last attack on the city and were followed in the morning by a final attack from the American 8th Army Air Force. From then on the sky above Berlin was to be dominated by the Soviets.[29]

During the afternoon of 20 April, Field Marshal Keitel's private aircraft also took off from Tempelhof with his wife, Frau Jodl, Lieutenant-General Winter and Dr Rudolf Lehmann (head of the OKW's legal department), bound for Prague where a staff car was waiting to take them on to Obersalzberg. The aircraft was back in Berlin by the evening, awaiting instructions for the anticipated evacuation of other Nazi leaders.[30]

The last big war conference took place in the Führerbunker at 1600 hours that day, and was attended by all the dignitaries assembled for Hitler's birthday. It began with the usual briefing on the war situation, Krebs covering events on the Eastern Front for the OKH and Jodl covering the rest for the OKW. It was a gloomy account at best, with the Soviets and Americans closing in from east and west, the British about to enter Bremen and Hamburg in the north, and the Allied armies in Italy already in the Po Valley. They all looked to their Führer for guidance.[31]

From arrangements made ten days previously, when an advance party had been sent to Bavaria to prepare the Berghof for Hitler's arrival, it was generally expected that he would leave Berlin either that night or the following night.[32] At the conference, Göring, Goebbels, Himmler, Bormann and Krebs all urged Hitler to leave the city before it was too late, but he gave no positive response. Instead he repeated his instructions of 14 April to the effect that, in the event of Germany's being split in two, separate commands would be established in the north and south of the country to continue the struggle under Grand Admiral Dönitz and Field Marshal Kesselring respectively.[33] On this occasion he formally transferred authority over the armed forces in the north to Dönitz but omitted to do the same for Kesselring in the south, which led them to believe that he still intended taking command of the mythical 'Alpine Redoubt' himself. He went on to authorize von Ribbentrop to try to open negotiations with the Anglo-Americans, using Sweden as an intermediary, unaware that

Himmler had already been having private talks with Count Folke Bernadotte on these lines, using Jewish lives as his bargaining point.[34]

Having taken their leave of Hitler, the Party elite, armed with special passes, began making their exodus from Berlin by road and air, their staff cars mingling with the trucks loaded with the files and office equipment of the various government departments on the move. Grand Admiral Dönitz headed north for Plön to establish his headquarters there.[35]

Himmler went to his castle at Ziethen to continue his treasonable plotting,[36] and Speer to Hamburg, where he secretly recorded a speech with the connivance of the city Gauleiter, Erich Kaufmann. The speech was to be broadcast in the event of the death of either himself or Hitler and was in fact broadcast on 3 May, exhorting the people not to despair, but to keep going and salvage as much as they could. Kaufmann's complicity in this matter resulted from his disillusionment with the Party leadership, following Hitler's refusal to visit the city and commiserate with the survivors after the terrible air raids of July 1943, in which 30,000 inhabitants died and three-quarters of the city was destroyed.[37]

Göring made a final call at the Führerbunker at 0100 hours to say farewell, and then was caught in an air raid on his way to Werder and forced to take cover in a public shelter, where his relief at being able to get away expressed itself in good-humoured jokes against himself. At the Luftwaffe Headquarters in Werder he met up with the convoy of trucks carrying the personal treasures he had saved from 'Carinhall', his favourite residence on the Schorfheide just north of Eberswalde, before blowing it up.[38] He left the headquarters compound at the head of his convoy in such haste that he did not even bid farewell to his saluting Chief-of-Staff, Lieutenant-General Koller, who, together with Major-General Eckhardt Christian at the Führerbunker, was to represent him in his absence.[39]

Meanwhile General Busse was trying to cover the exposed northern flank of his truncated 9th Army as best he could. The Soviet thrust toward Fürstenwalde threatened the rear of the 169th and 712th Infantry Divisions which, with the Frankfurt Garrison, were still trying to hold on to their forward positions. He had only the remains of the 'Kurmark' and SS 'Nederland' Panzergrenadier Divisions, the latter having been cut off from the LVI Panzer Corps in the battle for Müncheberg, to cover this exposed rear, which now hinged on the 156th Infantry Division's position at Lietzen, and to counter the Soviet thrusts on his front.[40] Inevitably, the three infantry divisions began to reel back to the southwest as the situation deteriorated rapidly, the Panzergrenadier divisions fighting to keep the escape routes open over the Spree east of Fürstenwalde. In order to cover the Spree west of this point, part of the 32nd SS '30 Januar' Grenadier Division was pulled out of the line to establish a screen from Fürstenwalde to the Müggelsee along the Oder–Spree Canal/Spree River barrier.[41]

That same night 713 bombers of the 18th Air Army and Po-2s of the 16th Air Army bombed German positions north and northeast of the city, softening them up for the advancing ground forces.[42]

4

ENCIRCLEMENT

During the early hours of 21 April, a small nucleus of personnel from Zossen reported in by telephone from Wannsee in southwest Berlin and were directed to establish temporary headquarters for the OKH at the Luftwaffe Academy at Gatow and for the OKW at the barracks in Krampnitz nearby. The main body headed south for Obersalzburg and later in the day had the misfortune to be attacked by some of their own aircraft, who mistook the convoy for a column of Soviet tanks.[1]

That same morning, the 2nd Guards Tank Army crossed the autobahn ring on the northeast side of Berlin, brushing aside the opposition, and advanced toward the city on a broad front. The 12th Guards Tank Corps' component brigades advanced with the 48th Guards Tank Brigade on the axis Mehrow/Ahrensfelde/Hohenschönhausen; the 66th Guards Tank Brigade on the axis Eiche/Marzahn; the 49th Guards Tank Brigade on the axis Hönow/Kaulsdorf; and the 34th Motorized Rifle Brigade swung around through Dahlwitz to attack through southern Kaulsdorf into Lichtenberg. A counterattack of battalion size supported by 12 tanks was beaten back at Hönow, and by the evening the 12th Guards Tank Corps and 32nd Rifle Corps of the 5th Shock Army were firmly established in the suburb of Hohenschönhausen. Similarly on their northern flank the 1st Mechanized Corps was established in the suburb of Weissensee with troops of the 3rd Shock Army. The Soviet troops easily submerged the small pockets of resistance that had been set up by local Volkssturm detachments in accordance with the original defence plan, and a platoon screening the 3/115th Siemensstadt Volkssturm Battalion's position in Kaulsdorf was taken without a fight when elements of the 26th Guards Rifle Corps unexpectedly entered Hellersdorf at 2200 hours.[2] In several places they came across groups of houses flying the white flag and nowhere was there any serious opposition. A witness from one of the outmost suburbs related:

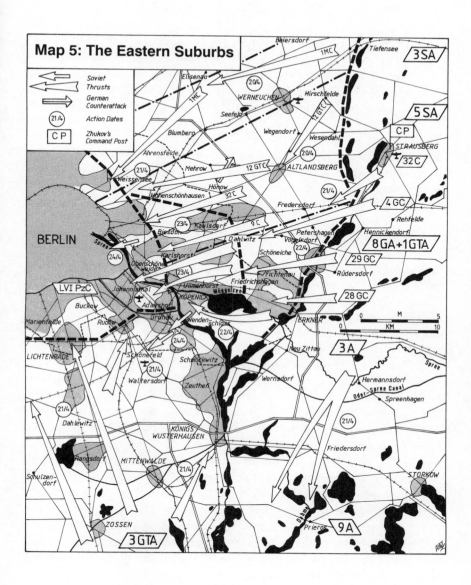

Map 5: The Eastern Suburbs

Soviet Thrusts

German Counterattack

(21/4) Action Dates

CP Zhukov's Command Post

Twelve assault tanks appeared, flanked left and right by infantry, approximately one company, armed with submachine-guns and spraying the walls of the houses whilst moving from door to door at the double. They were followed by anti-aircraft guns. Behind these assault troops came carts drawn by two or four horses, containing food and ammunition as well as loot.[3]

That evening the Soviet troops were briefed on the severe kind of fighting they could expect to encounter in the more densely built-up areas of Berlin, and preparations were made to adapt to this kind of warfare. For General Berzarin of the 5th Shock Army the personal good news was his promotion to Colonel-General.[4]

It is not proposed to expound here on the atrocities that followed the fighting. On this subject all accounts are agreed without exception; the ransacking of cellars and shelters, the summary executions, immediate looting and the rape of women, from young girls to the very oldest and infirm, were a standard corollary to all the fighting in the city. These facts were known to all the defenders and in several accounts mention is made of the demoralization caused when they heard the screams of the women being raped at night. Ilya Ehrenburg had written in his manifesto to the Red Army: 'Kill! Kill! None of the Germans are innocent, neither the living nor those not yet born! Follow the advice of Comrade Stalin and wipe out the Fascist Beast in his lair for ever! Break the proud racial pride of the German women brutally! Take them in just revenge.'[5] Although this policy had been revoked on 14 April, it still represented the basic attitude of the Soviet soldier toward the German population.

The 8th Guards and 1st Guards Tank Armies, which were advancing westward in the Rüdersdorf–Erkner area, now received orders to swing southwest so as to approach the city from the south and southeast. However, these orders took some time to implement, for the troops were already fighting in built-up areas and it was not easy to extricate them. The nature of the terrain with the many lakes and waterways in this particular area not only helped to concentrate the defence but also channelled the lines of approach, while the built-up areas were seen to absorb troops like sponges.[6]

The inefficiency of the Nazi Party apparatus in dealing with defensive measures at this stage is exemplified by the experience of four of the Volks-sturm battalions based on the Reichssportfeld, next to the Olympic Stadium. Late on the 20th they received orders to embus at 0300 hours next day to move to Grünheide, east of Berlin, where they were to take up defensive positions. The city buses detailed to convey them failed to arrive, having been sent to the dropping-off point in error. It was 1600 hours before the battalions could depart in their assigned transport. When they eventually arrived at their destination, they found no one waiting for them and no orders for their deployment, as they took their first casualties from Soviet bombers.[7]

The LVI Panzer Corps had been forced back into the Rahnsdorf–Neuenhagen area by the Soviet advance, losing contact with the parent 9th Army in the process, and during the course of the 21st was obliged to withdraw even further to the line Köpenick/Marzahn. General Weidling's headquarters in Kaulsdorf apparently made no attempt to get in touch with the Führerbunker in compliance with the Führer-Order of 21 January (Appendix 4), although they should have been able to do so on the normal civilian telephone network had they so wished. 'Seydlitz-Troops' had been particularly active during the withdrawal in disseminating false orders for the troops to reassemble at Döberitz and other locations outside the city, and the rumour then spread that the corps had withdrawn to Döberitz, west of Berlin. When General Busse and Hitler heard of this that evening, they both ordered Weidling's arrest and execution.[8]

Meanwhile Weidling was having disciplinary problems of his own with SS Major-General Joachim Ziegler, who was apparently piqued at having to serve under a Wehrmacht commander and unilaterally wanted to pull his SS 'Nordland' Panzergrenadier Division out from the LVI Panzer Corps' left flank and rejoin Steiner's command. Weidling suspended him from duty but Ziegler was able to resume command next day when the division was ordered back to Berlin without reference to the corps commander.[9]

The extraordinarily chaotic atmosphere that prevailed at the senior German command level at this stage comes out quite clearly from the various exchanges recorded between senior officers on 21 April. Disruption of communications contributed to the chaos, but could not be held responsible for the air of fantasy and sheer lack of realism that dominated proceedings and resulted in decisions and orders, which were then enforced under penalty of death.

Before the noon conference Hitler formally placed SS Major-General Mohnke in command of the central government area, which included the Reichs Chancellery and Führerbunker. However, the overall command of 'Zitadelle' remained that of Lieutenant-Colonel Seifert.[10]

At 1130 hours the Russian siege and heavy field artillery started shelling the city centre, causing considerable alarm, as it introduced a new dimension of horror and discomfort to life. The fairly regular pattern of air raids, which hitherto had enabled people to go about their business between alerts, had ended. Shells arrived without warning, sending shrapnel tearing along the streets and creating havoc. More buildings collapsed, streets were torn up and old debris churned over by the force of the explosions. In the affected areas, the central districts in particular, people were obliged to take to the shelters permanently, emerging only occasionally for vital supplies of food and water. Only the main flak-towers had their own water supplies; elsewhere the plumbing had already been shattered by the bombing, the toilets no longer functioned and people had to relieve themselves wherever they could in the densely packed shelters, adding a nauseating stench to the already appalling conditions. For food and water people had to risk their lives queuing in the streets.

The solid fuel stocks at the city's power stations being almost exhausted, the authorities were obliged to shut down the factories to conserve enough electricity for lighting and essential services. Cooking by electricity was now forbidden under pain of death.[11]

When the firing started Hitler telephoned General Karl Koller at Werder asking the Luftwaffe to locate and destroy the guns concerned. He would not believe Koller when the latter reported back that the flak-towers were already engaged with enemy batteries firing from the eastern suburb of Marzahn. The towers counted over 500 incoming shells that day, mainly from what they suspected were 152mm guns with a range of nine miles.[12]

In the afternoon Hitler telephoned Koller again asking for details of Luftwaffe operations south of Berlin, but Koller could only reply that communications with the operational units were now so unreliable that they would have to wait until the next 24-hour report arrived to get the information. Shortly afterward Hitler telephoned again to complain about the failure of some jet fighters to arrive from Prague and was told that the German airfields were now so closely invested by enemy aircraft that it was often impossible to take off.[13]

Field Marshal Schörner arrived in Berlin that day in time for the afternoon war conference. He briefed Hitler on his Army Group 'Mitte' whose counter-attack against Koniev's southern group was delaying Soviet progress toward Dresden to such an extent that Koniev had sent his new Chief-of-Staff, Colonel-General I.E. Petrov, to put some more zest into the operation.[14]

Another caller during the course of this conference was General Wenck, commander of the 12th Army covering the line of the Elbe, who had come to report the XXXIX Panzer Corps' progress in the Harz Mountains, unaware that as he spoke they were being eliminated in the forlorn attempt to rescue elements of the 11th Army trapped there.[15]

During this conference Hitler looked for some means of stemming the Soviet advance. First he decided to pull back the LVI Panzer Corps into the city, not realizing that they were already fighting on the city boundary (they had been out of touch since 2000 hours the previous evening), and to get them to link up with Steiner's group in the north. He then seized on Steiner's name, for Steiner had conducted a successful counterattack against the 1st Byelorussian Front in Pomerania in February, and perhaps could do the same thing again. All available resources would be allocated to him, forming Army Detachment 'Steiner', which would mount an attack southward from Eberswalde next day in conjunction with an attack northward by the 9th Army, thus nipping off the head of Zhukov's advance. It was emphasized that the matter was to be pursued with the utmost vigour and that the Luftwaffe were to support the operation with every aircraft still capable of taking to the air. The orders to Steiner concluded:

> It is expressly forbidden to fall back to the west. Officers who do not comply unconditionally with this order are to be arrested and shot immediately. You, Steiner, are answerable with your head for the execution of this order. The fate of the Reichs capital depends upon the success of your mission.
>
> Adolf Hitler[16]

None of those present dared raise any objections to this plan, and the next 24 hours were spent in frenzied activity. The bulk of the manpower came from the Luftwaffe, who found 12–15,000 men from their ground services in the northern region, regrouping them by their companies and battalions into larger formations under the command of Luftwaffe General Johannes Stumpff. Other units were formed from cadets, railway troops, the Berlin Fire Brigade, police, Volkssturm and even convicts. Thus the manpower equivalent of about one and a half infantry divisions was raised virtually overnight, but of course lacking in the necessary training, cohesion, communications, heavy arms or equipment for the intended role. The Motor Transport Department was given the task of getting them into position, but at first there was considerable confusion on this point, as Steiner's location and requirements were unknown to the Berlin-based organizers. Eventually Steiner was located at Oranienburg and the troops sent off to the Finow Canal, using fuel requisitioned from vital airfield supplies.[17]

In typical fashion Steiner received his orders direct from the Führerbunker, bypassing Army Group 'Weichsel', to which he was accountable. He was appalled at what was expected of him and the type of troops allocated for the task, and immediately telephoned Army Group Headquarters to report his dilemma. Of all the troops assigned to him, only those Heinrici had previously transferred from the 9th Army were in any way capable of mounting a military operation. Moreover, the remnants of the 5th Light, 25th Panzergrenadier and 606th Infantry Divisions were already fully committed along the line of the Finow Canal and could not be redeployed until relieved by the 3rd Naval Division, which had been delayed by air attacks on the railways and had yet to arrive from the coast. The so-called 4th SS Police Grenadier Division so far amounted to only two unarmed battalions.

When Krebs eventually briefed Heinrici on Steiner's mission by telephone, Heinrici took the opportunity of once more asking him to impress upon the Führer the urgent necessity of withdrawing the 9th Army from its present position without further delay. Zhukov's southern thrust toward Königs Wusterhausen had already isolated the 9th Army from the city, and should Hitler continue to refuse this request, Heinrici asked to be relieved of his command. He said that he would rather serve as a simple Volkssturm soldier than continue to bear the responsibility for ordering them to hold on any longer. Krebs merely replied somewhat stuffily that the Führer alone took responsibility for his orders. Shortly afterwards Heinrici was informed that his Chief-of-Staff, General Eberhart Kinzel, was to be replaced by a Major-General Ivo-Thilo von Trotha, generally believed to be a Nazi, but who had in fact previously served under Heinrici in the same capacity.[18]

That evening scouts of the 3rd Guards Tank Army reached Königs Wusterhausen from the south, thereby effectively completing the encirclement of the 9th Army, although as they were on the other side of the water complex from the 8th Guards Army, the troops of the two Soviet fronts apparently remained unaware of the proximity of each other. The orders from Moscow were to have the 9th Army surrounded by the 24th,[19] so Marshal Koniev ordered forward the balance of the 28th Army to seal off the Spreewald pocket in place of the 13th Army, which he wanted for other tasks. His orders to the 28th Army, which was allocated all the front's transport for the move, included placing two infantry divisions in the Baruth area as a counterattack force in case of an attempted breakout. The screening force was to block off the exit routes with strong defences against tanks and infantry to thwart any possible breakout to the west or southwest. Koniev was also very conscious of the vulnerability to attack from the 9th Army of his main communications route, the Dresden–Berlin autobahn.[20]

To comply with Moscow's instructions, Marshal Zhukov moved the bulk of the 69th Army from its ineffective deployment on the Oder and despatched it with the 3rd Army from his reserve to apply pressure on the 9th Army from the north, while at the same time protecting his southern flank. By the evening of the 21st the Soviets had a bridgehead across the Spree west of Fürstenwalde in the area where a part of the 32nd SS '30 Januar' Grenadier Division were hastily trying to establish a defensive screen.[21]

General Busse's Spreewald concentration also became a focus of attention for Air Chief Marshal Novikov, who devoted a large part of the resources of the 2nd, 16th and 18th Air Armies to the harassment of the 9th Army pocket around the clock, with as many as 60 to 100 aircraft at a time.[22] With the 9th Army were tens of thousands of refugees from the eastern provinces who had been camping out in the woods since their arrival in the winter, their numbers now augmented by inhabitants of the combat zone that had fled their homes. Although there was sufficient food for everyone, communications rapidly deteriorated, and troops and civilians became hopelessly mixed in their predicament. Ammunition and fuel were in particularly short supply and when the artillery ran out of shells on the 21st, General Heinrici advised General Busse to find some means of disengaging from the enemy and to forget Hitler's orders about holding on to the Oder.[23]

At 2030 hours Hitler called General Koller to say that the 'Hermann Göring' Field Division stationed at 'Carinhall' was to be sent to the front at once. From 'Carinhall' Koller established that in fact only one battalion of the division remained there. When he reported this to Hitler, he was abruptly told to assign the battalion to Steiner's command and then was cut off. At this stage Koller knew nothing about either Steiner or his mission, although presumably Major-General Christian had represented the Luftwaffe at the meeting in the Führerbunker when Hitler issued the relevant orders. Koller therefore telephoned the 'Hermann Göring' Field Division, which was able to give an outline of the plan, together with the information that Steiner had last been seen in Schönwalde that afternoon accompanied by only one staff officer.[24]

Koller then tried to get information from the Führerbunker, eventually contacting Krebs. While he was asking where he was to despatch the men he was supposed to be mustering for Steiner, Hitler broke into the conversation with, 'Do you still doubt my orders? I thought I had made myself quite clear. All Luftwaffe forces north of the city are to join Steiner and take part in a ground attack. Any commander that holds his men back will pay for it with his head within five hours. You are responsible with your life for seeing to it that every last man gets into battle!' Krebs then added that the attack would be from Eberswalde southward and that Koller was to throw in every man he had.[25]

Next, Koller telephoned the OKW to see if they had any more information to offer but they had none, promising to contact him as soon as they had found Steiner, whom they believed to be based in Oranienburg.[26]

Then Colonel Count Nicolaus von Below, Hitler's Luftwaffe aide-de-camp, called with orders for air activity to be concentrated on the gap in the 4th Panzer Army's line between Cottbus and Spremberg and for the 'Spremberg' unit to be supplied by air. Once again no one knew exactly where or what the 'Spremberg' unit was.[27] In fact, the 5th Guards Army had completed mopping up the Spremberg area that day, and within 24 hours the 3rd Guards Army, with powerful artillery and air support, were to do the same to the Cottbus area.

At about midnight Koller spoke with Hitler again, saying that he could not possibly air-supply a unit whose location was unknown, and then went on to say that the Luftwaffe men he was assembling for Steiner's operation were both untrained and insufficiently armed for ground combat. Surprisingly, Hitler did not take umbrage at these remarks, but expressed optimism about the outcome of the operation, adding: 'You will see: the Russians are about to suffer the bloodiest defeat of their history at the gates of Berlin!'

Eventually, uncertain of what to do for the best, Luftwaffe contingents were sent to both Oranienburg and Eberswalde in the hope that at least some would arrive at the right place in time.[28]

That night over 700 aircraft of the 16th and 18th Air Armies attacked targets in the northern outskirts of Berlin in preparation for the 2nd Guards Tank Army's operations the next day.[29]

On the morning of 22 April the four Reichssportfeld Volkssturm battalions discovered that their route back to Berlin had been blocked by the Soviets taking Erkner behind them. During the course of the day they found themselves caught up in the general retreat, conducting a fighting withdrawal from Grünheide southwest toward the bridge over the Dahme at Smöckwitz. Casualties were heavy and the units became hopelessly split in the confusion, but they knocked out four tanks and noted that the accompanying Soviet infantry were reluctant to expose themselves to their rifle fire.[30]

The day began with a distinct aura of optimism in the Führerbunker. Hitler kept asking for news of Steiner's attack, but there had been a total disruption of communications over the past 24 hours and any news that did arrive was uncertain and contradictory.[31]

At 1100 hours General Heinrici telephoned General Krebs to say that unless the 9th Army was allowed to withdraw it would be split in two by nightfall. This time his words must have had some effect, for at 1450 hours Krebs telephoned back with permission for the Frankfurt-an-der-Oder garrison to abandon the city and fall back on the 9th Army, thus allowing some adjustment to the latter's over-extended disposition.[32]

At this stage the 9th Army's northern flank was still firm from Frankfurt-an-der-Oder to a bridgehead north of Fürstenwalde. From there it followed the line of the Spree to a point north of Prieros, where it cut down to the chain of lakes, with strong road-blocks across the Berlin–Frankfurt autobahn. On gaining control of the V Corps, General Busse had immediately ordered them to leave only a light screen in the Neisse positions and to establish a line of defence from north of Lübben to Halbe. He had also taken their 21st Panzer Division under direct command of Army Headquarters and sent it to establish a line of defence along the chain of lakes between Teupitz and Königs Wusterhausen, but it had since been driven back from there to the other chain of lakes between Teupitz and Prieros, where they held out against all further attacks.[33]

Hitler's orders for the 9th Army, which were received by Heinrici at 1720 hours, were to hold on to the existing line from Cottbus to Fürstenberg, and from there curve it back via Müllrose to Fürstenwalde. At the same time a strong front was to be established between Königs Wusterhausen and Cottbus, from which repeated, vigorous and co-ordinated attacks in co-operation with the 12th Army would be made on the deep flank of the enemy attacking Berlin from the south.[34]

However, General Busse had already started making preparations for the breakout suggested by Heinrici. The redisposition of the V Corps was part of his plan. As soon as the Frankfurt garrison withdrew into his lines, the V and V SS Mountain Corps would start a simultaneous withdrawal from their Oder–Neisse positions in two bounds back either side of Friedland to the line Straupitz/Beeskow/the junction of the Spree and the Oder–Spree Canal.[35]

Meanwhile, Steiner, as he had explained to Army Group Headquarters the previous day, as yet had no means of implementing Hitler's ambitious instructions and remained primarily concerned with meeting the initial commitment of covering the 3rd Panzer Army's southern flank. The pressure from Zhukov's northern flank group and their air support caused him to evacuate his own headquarters northward out of Oranienburg during the day, when the town suddenly became part of the front line. Not only did he have to concern himself with the defence of Oranienburg but also with preparations for the extension of his flank westward along the Ruppiner Canal, for, although the town had some natural strength from its canals as a defensive position, the promised 'Müller' Brigade had failed to appear from Döberitz and the line of the Havel south of the town remained unmanned.

Marshal Zhukov naturally expected the Havel to prove a major obstacle in the path of his northern encircling thrust. His northern flank group, having recovered from its bad start, was pushed hastily forward to keep abreast of this thrust and to support the main crossing with diversionary attacks. Spearheaded by the 9th Guards Tank Corps and the 47th Army's 125th Rifle Corps, the armoured thrust led through Zepernick, Schönlinde, Mühlenbeck and Schönfliess, then on to the bridge at Hennigsdorf. Meanwhile the 1st Polish Army had cleared the centre strip between Biesenthal and Bernau, their 4th Infantry Division having taken Bernau to ease the 47th Army's passage, and passed on to close up to the canal in front of Oranienburg. The 61st Army on the extreme northern flank cleared the south side of the line of the canals, but also had to contain the bridgehead at Eberswalde and the two minor ones at Zerpenschleuse and Kreuzbruch.[36]

On the night of 22/23 April, supported by artillery, rocket-launchers and bombing attacks from the air, the 1st Polish Army attacked Oranienburg, while the 61st Army attacked across the Oder–Havel (Hohenzollern) Canal between Friedrichsthal and Kreuzbruch. Unexpectedly, the main crossing by the 47th Army at Hennigsdorf met with only light resistance and the armour were able to cross the bridge there without much difficulty. The spearhead was closely followed by the 7th Guards Cavalry Corps, who were to be used extensively in the scouting role in the next phase of the operation.[37]

Steiner was under considerable pressure around Oranienburg and was forced to commit the two newly arrived battalions of the 3rd Naval Division to assist in the defence of the town. These two units were the only ones to get through from the coast. Steiner had hoped to use them to relieve his combat-experienced troops at the eastern end of the line, which he badly needed if he was to mount the counterattack demanded by Hitler.[38] A member of the Oranienburg Hitlerjugend described his experiences a few days later:

> Our leader and the police fetched us from our homes and we had to assemble in the SS barracks and at the Schlossplatz. Then we were divided by our companies and attached to the SS and the Volkssturm. We first saw action to the northeast of the town. Most of us were killed by infantry fire, because we had to attack across open fields. Then the fighting in the town; two days of it. In two days and two nights Oranienburg changed hands four times. That finished another part of us. Then the Russians started bombarding

the town with Stalin-Organs, and when we wanted to give up and go home, we were stopped and made to join the escape across the canal. My platoon leader, who refused, was strung up on the nearest tree by some SS and an SA man, but then he was already 15 years old.[39]

The spearheads of both the 3rd and the 5th Shock Armies seem to have spent the day of the 22nd preparing themselves for the street-fighting role that was to follow. Their artillery shelled the city, but little attempt was made at further penetration from these initial entry points. That evening, their shepherding role completed, the 2nd Guards Tank Army's 1st Mechanized and 12th Guards Tank Corps pulled out in a wide flanking march around the northern suburbs that brought them to their allotted sectors for the envelopment of the city. To assist in the forthcoming role, the 11th Tank Corps, which originated with the 8th Guards Army but had been transferred to the 1st Guards Tank Army for 'Operation Berlin', was redirected to the support of the 5th Shock Army that night.[40]

Meanwhile, early on the 22nd, the 3/115th Siemensstadt Volkssturm Battalion had its baptism of fire. The battalion had been incorporated into Major Funk's three-battalion 57th Fortress Regiment in Defence Sector 'A', and was occupying the positions it had prepared during the past two months immediately north of the Kaulsdorf and Mahlsdorf S-Bahn stations. This was in the centre of the regiment's line, with a Wehrmacht battalion on the left and the 'Warnholz' Police Battalion on the right. At daybreak some Soviet tanks and infantry were seen forming up near Hellersdorf and by 0900 hours four of these tanks had approached and, after destroying two 20mm flak positions in their path, were attacking the battalion's two forward companies. The regiment then sent forward four SPGs with some reserve infantry from the 3/121st Volkssturm Battalion for the 3/115th to mount a counterattack. This was duly carried out successfully and with comparatively few casualties but, while it was still in progress, orders were received for the battalion to pull out of Kaulsdorf, as the battalions on either side had already withdrawn, leaving the 3/115th vulnerable. (Apparently the anti-tank barrier in front of the police battalion had been opened at first light to enable the recovery of damaged German tanks involved in the Hönow counterattack the previous day, and some Soviet tanks had taken the opportunity of slipping through the gap unnoticed, thus turning the position.) The withdrawal at 1300 hours involved destroying the heavy weapons, and the battalion was now reduced to 500 rifles and two light machine-guns (LMGs). The battalion then took up positions near Friedrichsfelde-Ost S-Bahn station, where its neighbours

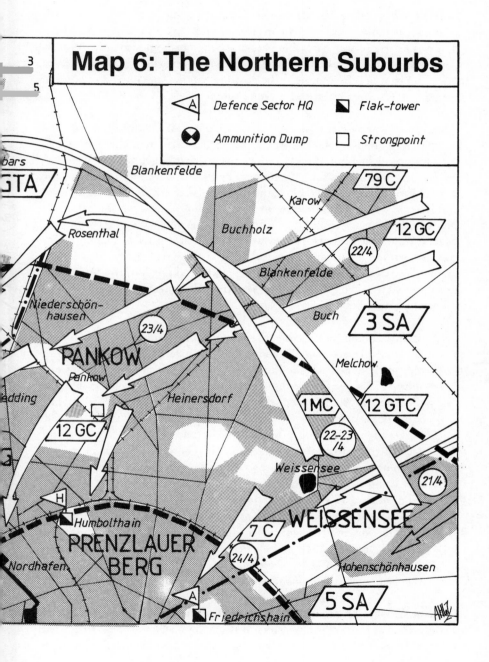

Map 6: The Northern Suburbs

Legend:
- Defence Sector HQ
- Ammunition Dump
- Flak-tower
- Strongpoint

GTA

Blankenfelde

Karow

79 C

Buchholz

12 GC

22/4

Blankenfelde

Rosenthal

Buch

3 SA

Niederschön-
hausen

23/4

Melchow

PANKOW

Pankow

Heinersdorf

1 MC

12 GTC

adding

22-23
/4

12 GC

Weissensee

21/4

H

Humbolthain

WEISSENSEE

PRENZLAUER
BERG

7 C

Nordhafen

24/4

Hohenschönhausen

A

5 SA

Friedrichshain

were elements of Captain Schweickart's 1st Parachute Officer School, with whom the battalion was to remain in close association for the rest of the battle. The Soviet troops were pressing hard from the north and east, their scouts penetrating as far as the battalion command post, from where they were driven off with pistol fire. By midnight the position had become untenable and the battalion was ordered to withdraw once more.[41]

That same day the 8th Guards and 1st Guards Tank Armies entered the southeastern suburbs of Dahlwitz, Schöneiche, Fichtenau and Rahnsdorf, their leading elements getting as far forward as Friedrichshagen and Wenden-schloss on either side of the Müggelsee. The enterprising 269th Guards Rifle Regiment of Major-General G.J. Pankov's 88th Guards Rifle Division crossed two rivers that day. First they swam across the Spree to reach the peninsula between the Müggelsee and the Dahme in the morning and then they found boats at Wendenschloss, which they were able to use to cross the Dahme under cover of darkness and so establish themselves in Grünau and Falkenberg before dawn next day.[42] The resistance encountered north of the Müggelsee was minimal following the withdrawal of the LVI Panzer Corps, as was later related by a member of the local forces:

> After the middle of February, Sergeant-Major Gümpel and ten men from the Field Replacement Battalion of the Grünheide Administrative Unit were made responsible for directing the construction of fortifications east of Friedrichshagen and to the north of the Müggelsee, a sector about three kilometers in width. Manpower was recruited from the local Friedrichs-hagen population and from workers in the local factories, as many as 500 workers per day being provided. A continuous trench was dug and permanent emplacements prepared. The construction of shelters was begun under the supervision of an expert from Friedrichshagen but none were completed before the fighting began. It had been planned to occupy the position with a force of 250 men, comprising elements of the Field Replacement Battalion and Volkssturm. With the approach of the Russians the force holding the position disintegrated and the position was left virtually unmanned. Only the battalion commander and about 25 men offered resistance. The defence was quickly overcome, after which Sergeant-Major Gümpel and his men were tasked with rounding up stragglers.[43]

General Weidling summoned his divisional and regimental commanders to a conference at Corps Headquarters in Kaulsdorf, where he told them that General Busse had threatened to have him shot if he failed to link up with the 9th Army, and that Hitler had threatened him with the same fate if he did not go to the defence of the city. They all agreed that to go into the city would mean the end of the corps, and decided that they should try to hold on to their present positions in the southeastern suburbs to enable the 9th Army to withdraw in their direction.[44]

Marshal Koniev's armour made rapid progress on 22 April, the lack of natural obstacles and a widely scattered and uncoordinated defence all contributing toward its success. The southern obstacle belt and the scanty city perimeter defences with their Volkssturm and Hitlerjugend defenders were easily overcome, the tanks bypassing the barricades, infiltrating the built-up areas, silencing any resistance they encountered and pounding on down the main roads as fast as they could. They were closely supported all the while by powerful air-strikes, having completely outstripped their ground support.[45]

In the 4th Guards Tank Army's sector, the 5th Guards Mechanized Corps began forming a protective screen along the line Beelitz/Treuenbrietzen/Kropstädt, where they would be reinforced by the bulk of the 13th Army, whose 6th Guards Rifle Division reached Jüterbog that day. The 6th Guards Mechanized Corps reached Beelitz that evening and rested prior to pushing on further to link up with the 47th Army in the encirclement of the city and to probing toward Brandenburg. On their right, the 10th Guards Tank Corps swept through Saarmund and Schenkenhorst to seal off the approaches to Potsdam at Caputh and Babelsberg by the evening, Army Headquarters being established in the village of Schenkenhorst.

The 3rd Guards Tank Army had fought throughout the previous night, forcing the Notte Canal near Zossen. During the course of the 22nd they fanned out to advance on Berlin along a broad front. By evening the leading elements of the 7th and 6th Guards Tank Corps had reached the Teltow Canal at Stahnsdorf and Teltow respectively, while on the right the 9th Mechanized Corps, having crossed the autobahn ring at 0900 hours, was well into the southern suburbs of Lichtenrade, Marienfelde and Lankwitz by nightfall.

A French prisoner-of-war saw them arrive:

> At midday on that Sunday, the 22nd April 1945, the sky was a lovely cloudless blue and the sun bathed us in its spring warmth. A peaceful calm reigned in Stalag III-D-500, only broken by the familiar sounds of comrades preparing their food.
>
> At about 1630 hours the first fighting started in our area. Six Russian aircraft circled and machine-gunned from a low altitude. No defence activity spoilt their evolutions during the 20 minutes of their appearance.

Soon we could pick out quite clearly the crackle of machine-guns or automatic weapons perhaps ten kilometers south of the camp. Several German soldiers fled toward the city along the Berlin–Wittenberg railway tracks that passed close by. Then some bullets whistled over the camp.

The Volkssturm company based on the camp had left that morning. No German defence existed near us, except that some 500 meters away a tank buried up to its turret in the road alongside a synthetic rubber factory assured some resistance. A section of young boys normally billeted at Lankwitz occupied the factory with the task of putting up a defence. Within a radius of three kilometers there were three of these tanks with only their turrets serviceable, that could enfilade the streets with their anti-tank guns. Barricades made out of tree trunks stacked one and a half meters high and one meter wide cut the roads leading to the city. One of these tree-trunk barricades was opposite our camp on the Heinersdorf–Lichterfelde road.

At about 1700 hours the first Russian appeared. He was walking straight ahead, stooped and with his machine-gun at the ready, advancing along the ditch bordering the road. He did not pay the least bit of attention to the camp. I think they were like that all along the front, with one man every 20 to 50 meters, each man in sight of the others.

I could not see more because of the bushy terrain. He passed our camp unconcernedly, then engine noises announced the presence of tanks nearby. When they reached the barricade several bursts of machine-gun fire were directed at the disinfection building belonging to our camp and which was normally occupied by three Germans. This fire was not returned. The tanks went round the barricade, passing between the trees bordering the road and coming into our sight. They were two tanks of about 30 tons each, well rounded and of an imposing mass, each armed with a machine-gun and a light cannon. They were directed by a Russian or Ukrainian prisoner-of-war sitting on the top. No shots were fired into our camp.

A single Russian got down from one of the tanks, abandoning his advance, and interested himself in our camp, a revolver in his hand. I led him to the German shelters, where only one sentry was on duty at the entrance. He dropped his rifle and raised his arms. The Sergeant-Major responsible for the Russian prisoners-of-war, who had lately shown himself full of solicitude for them, came out of the shelter bare-headed. No hurt or harm was done to them. The Russian ordered them to leave the camp. They quit happily, but no doubt uneasily.

The gun in the German tank turret then fired two or three shells into the building that normally housed the Germans. One shell went into a window-frame, making a hole in the woodwork and breaking two or three panes of glass. Four Russians crept up cautiously, quickly spotted the turret, and in an instant set up three mortars in the ditch bordering the road and fired at top speed for five minutes.

Peace then returned. The camp gates were closed again and a guard placed to prevent anyone going in or out. The tanks followed the road slowly without making a noise. They did not fire, nor did they meet with any resistance. Ten minutes later a light gun appeared in front of our camp drawn by a kind of jeep, something like one of our 37mm anti-tank guns. It did not intervene, moving on again.

At 1730 hours we were liberated. About ten Russians at the most came into sight without bothering themselves about us. The French flag flew at our gate.

Until 1900 hours no further troop movements were seen. The first Soviet officer then appeared at the gate. Night was beginning to fall. He was dressed in black overalls and appeared to have come on foot, as no vehicle had stopped in front of the camp. He asked to see us and urged us to leave the camp for the wise precaution that the number of Russian troops was insufficient to stop a German counterattack and we stood the chance of being recaptured.

In this camp there were also many Russian prisoners. All were quickly incorporated into the Soviet units and took part in the battle after simply being given a submachine-gun or rifle.[46]

The same sort of treatment was experienced in all the prisoner-of-war camps, the local knowledge of ex-prisoners being used to guide the combatants and, later on, the looters. As for the Allied prisoners, most were invited to leave the battlefield and head for camps further to the rear. This usually involved long journeys on foot before reaching the extremely badly organized repatriation centres.[47]

The 'Skorning' Combat Group, formed from the 2nd Battalion, 60th Fortress Regiment, a Volkssturm Company, an artillery battery and other minor units, all under the command of Lieutenant-Colonel Wolfgang Skorning and deployed along the southern defence boundary between Marienfelde and Buckow, came under mortar fire when Soviet scouts came up Reichsstrasse 96 and encountered the mines laid in front of the anti-tank barriers there, but some Soviet tanks managed to break through on the right flank, where the 'Krause' Battalion had failed to close the anti-tank barriers. These tanks were later hunted down by a unit of the 'Skorning' Combat Group on the street known as Alt Mariendorf, three kilometres to the rear. That night most of a Luftwaffe interpreter company that was under command of the Combat Group deserted to the Soviets with their commander.[48]

On the night of 22 April Marshal Koniev ordered the 3rd Guards Tank Army to prepare to attack across the Teltow Canal on the morning of 24 April. To assist them in this operation, he assigned them additional infantry in the form of the 128th Rifle Corps from the 28th Army and the artillery reserves from the 5th Guards Army, who were ordered to travel only by night to avoid detection. The artillery formations concerned were the 10th Assault Artillery Corps, and the 25th Assault and 23rd Anti-Aircraft Artillery Divisions. Air support was to be provided by the 2nd Fighter Corps. In the meantime the 3rd Guards Tank Army was to secure the suburb of Buckow on their right flank and to try to establish contact with the 1st Byelorussian Front, whose troops were expected in that area.[49]

Koniev had beaten Zhukov to the southern suburbs of Berlin, but he needed the day of 23 April to amass sufficient strength for his attack on the city proper next day, which he intended supervising in person. A major threat to his lines of communication having been removed with the elimination of the Cottbus stronghold, the 3rd Guards Army was ordered to turn its attention to the western flank of the German 9th Army.[50]

The daily conference in the Führerbunker took place at 1500 hours with only Bormann, Keitel, Jodl and Krebs in attendance. Shortly after it began shells started falling in the area of the Chancellery up above. The generals drew out the briefing for as long as possible, but when Hitler realized that Steiner had not yet even issued orders for the attack he was supposed to have led that day, he flew into a terrible rage, raving about betrayal, cowardice, ignorance and corruption destroying all that he had done and planned for the Third Reich and the German people. Eventually he recovered sufficiently to declare his intention to remain in Berlin to the bitter end. All attempts to dissuade him failed, even pleas by telephone from Dönitz and Himmler. Finally he announced that he would take personal charge of the defence of the city, saying: 'I order an immediate radio proclamation to the people of Berlin of my resolve to remain with them to the end, whatever may happen.'[51]

Hitler then withdrew to his private quarters, leaving the others to discuss the import of his decision with the rest of his staff. The whole affair had been so emotional that they found it difficult to assimilate, and now they had to make up their minds whether to leave or stay. Meanwhile, Hitler telephoned Goebbels and invited him to move into the Führerbunker with his family. Goebbels agreed and he and his wife and six children arrived soon afterward from the Propaganda Ministry across the street. They discussed the situation together and both Goebbels and his wife said that they would stay and commit suicide rather than be captured. Frau Goebbels added that she would first poison the children and remained adamant on this point, despite Hitler's objections.[52]

Hitler then went through his papers. Those items he wished to preserve for posterity were packed in metal boxes, and the rest were burnt by his aide-de-camp in the Chancellery garden. Meanwhile some 40 members of the Chancellery staff had decided to take advantage of the opportunity to leave for Berchtesgaden, and these, together with the documents, were assembled and driven out to various airfields around the city, from where they were flown out that night. This operation, organized by Hitler's personal pilot, General Hans Bauer, was known as 'Seraglio'. Nine of the ten aircraft used reached Munich safely, although the departure of one aircraft from Gatow was delayed by the baggage-loaders scattering the luggage all over the tarmac in protest against this privileged evacuation. The one carrying Hitler's documents crashed, killing all but the rear-gunner.[53]

At 1900 hours Hitler summoned Keitel and Jodl for another conference, at which he formally announced his intention of committing suicide in the event of the city falling to the Soviets, rejecting their protestations. Accustomed to the immovability of his decisions once they had been made, they then asked for his final orders, but Hitler replied that he had no further orders to give them and referred them to the Reichs Marshal. This dismayed them, for not only did this statement constitute an abdication of his authority and responsibility with regard to the armed forces still fighting elsewhere, but they were fully aware that Göring was now generally regarded as an object of ridicule. When they told Hitler that no one would fight for Göring, Hitler commented that it was no longer a question of fighting, but of negotiation, for which Göring was best suited.[54]

However, Hitler had not given up all hope for, prompted by his generals, he then turned to his maps and began discussing possible means of saving the situation. It was agreed that the 12th Army had nothing to fear from the Americans, who clearly had no intention of crossing the Elbe, and therefore they could afford to turn their backs on the river and march to the relief of Berlin. Simultaneously the 9th Army could send their strongest infantry division westward to meet up with the 12th Army, mopping up any enemy formations encountered on the way, and then make a joint thrust on the capital. Field Marshal Keitel would deliver the orders to Wenck in person, while Jodl would see to the organization of the OKW staff at Krampnitz in preparation for their move to Plön, where they would serve both Dönitz and Hitler.

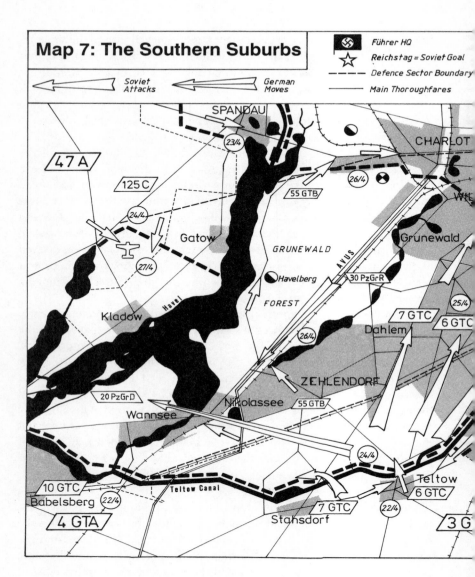

Map 7: The Southern Suburbs

Führer HQ
Reichstag = Soviet Goal
Defence Sector Boundary
Main Thoroughfares

Soviet Attacks
German Moves

SPANDAU
23/4
CHARLOT

47 A

125 C
26/4

55 GTB
Wt

24/4
Gatow
GRUNEWALD
Grunewald

AVUS

27/4
Havelberg
30 PzGrR

Kladow
Havel
FOREST
25/4

7 GTC
6 GTC
Dahlem

26/4
ZEHLENDORF

20 PzGrD
Nikolassee
55 GTB

Wannsee
24/4

10 GTC
Teltow
Babelsberg
22/4
Teltow Canal
6 GTC

4 GTA
7 GTC
22/4
Stahsdorf
3 G

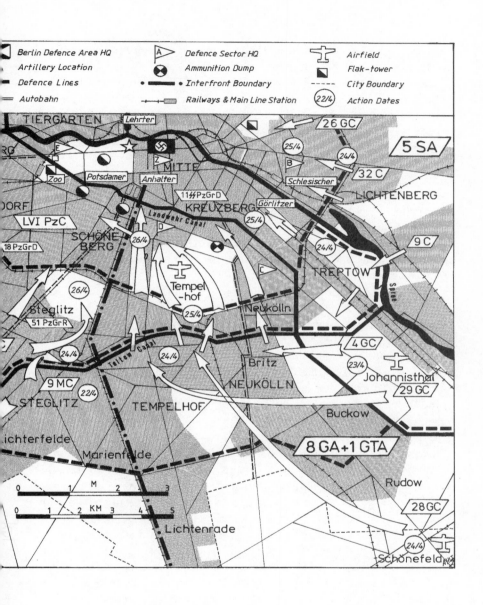

Legend:

- Berlin Defence Area HQ
- Artillery Location
- Defence Lines
- Autobahn
- Defence Sector HQ
- Ammunition Dump
- Interfront Boundary
- Railways & Main Line Station
- Airfield
- Flak-tower
- City Boundary
- 22/4 Action Dates

TIERGARTEN
Lehrter
26 GC
25/4
5 SA
E
Z
B
24/4
MITTE
32 C
Zoo
Potsdamer
Anhalter
Schlesischer
LICHTENBERG
DORF
11 SS PzGrD
KREUZBERG
Görlitzer
LVI PzC
Landwehr Canal
25/4
9 C
D
SCHÖNE-
BERG
26/4
24/4
TREPTOW
18 PzGrD
C
Spree
Tempel
-hof
26/4
Steglitz
25/4
Neukölln
51 PzGrR
4 GC
24/4
Teltow Canal
24/4
23/4
Johannisthal
9 MC
22/4
Britz
29 GC
STEGLITZ
TEMPELHOF
NEUKÖLLN
Buckow
ichterfelde
8 GA+1 GTA
Marienfelde
Rudow
0   1   M   2   3
0   1   2 KM 3   4   S
28 GC
24/4
Lichtenrade
Schönefeld

General Krebs would remain as Hitler's military adviser. The conference broke up at about 2000 hours.[55]

The departure of Keitel and Jodl left only General Krebs and his aide, Major Bernd Freiherr Freytag von Loringhoven, representing the General Staff in the Führerbunker, so Cavalry Captain Gerhard Boldt was summoned from the OKH at Krampnitz to assist with the preparation of situation reports for presentation to Hitler.[56]

At about 2300 hours SS Lieutenant-General Professor Karl Gebhardt, Himmler's personal physician and his nominee for the vacant post as head of the German Red Cross, arrived at the Chancellery to receive confirmation of his appointment. He brought with him the offer of Himmler's 600-man guard battalion, which Hitler gladly accepted, assigning them to the 'Zitadelle' force. Gebhardt then offered to arrange the evacuation of the remaining women and children from the bunker, but Hitler said that all those now remaining were doing so of their own free will.[57]

Hitler's decision to assume personal command of Berlin's defence relieved Army Group 'Weichsel' of the responsibility, and Goebbels took advantage of the opportunity to have Lieutenant-General Reymann, whom he regarded as somewhat lacking in spirit, removed from his appointment to take command of the Potsdam Garrison, and to have a Colonel Ernst Kaether appointed in his place. Kaether had made a name for himself as a regimental commander on the Eastern Front and had since held the appointment of Chief-of-Staff to the Wehrmacht's chief National Socialist Officer, or political commissar. However, Kaether's tenure of office in the rank of lieutenant-general was to be brief, for he was wounded on the second day.[58]

Reymann left by car for Potsdam and found the Avus racetrack section of the autobahn crowded with vehicles of all kinds as people sought to leave the city by the only route still open to them. In the distance he could hear the sound of tanks in action, and it was obvious that even this route would soon be closed. His command in Potsdam was called Army Detachment 'Spree', although it was no more than a weak corps of two infantry divisions, including the remains of the 'Friedrich Ludwig Jahn' RAD Infantry Division. Helped by the terrain, for Potsdam is virtually an island surrounded by vast expanses of water connected by rivers and canals, Reymann was able to maintain an effective defence, even when completely surrounded, and despite enemy penetrations into the town itself, until the 28th, when an avenue of escape was opened for them by the 12th Army.[59]

One of the people to leave Berlin that day was Beate Uhse, then a Luftwaffe pilot in an air-delivery squadron, who had flown into Gatow the day before in an Arado 66, with the object of rescuing her two-year-old son and his nanny from their home in Rangsdorf. However, when she returned to Gatow with them, she found that the Arado had been destroyed. Fortunately she then encountered an aircraft mechanic she knew, who told her of a twin-engined five-seater aircraft, a Siebel 104, belonging to some general, that was in a hangar there. She managed to persuade the colonel in charge of the airfield to let her have some fuel for it to enable her to return to her squadron at Barth, and flew out at 0555 hours that morning with her son, the nanny, the mechanic and two wounded soldiers, arriving safely at Barth an hour later.[60]

5

SIEGE PREPARATIONS

The night of 22/23 April marks an important stage in the development of the battle, when both sides found themselves obliged to reappraise the measures required to deal with the situation. The Soviets had had their first experience of what the next phase of the operation would entail and needed to reorganize their forces accordingly. Belatedly the Germans had to adapt to the implications of a siege.

In the city Goebbels' propaganda efforts produced a noticeable stiffening of the defence.[1] To back up his words, teams of Feldgendarmerie, police and SS, assisted by Party members and cadets from the police and SS schools, set up roadblocks in the suburbs and city centre to check for deserters and prevent the population from fleeing. They also searched cellars and shelters, querying the identity of the occupants and arresting suspects. Some civilians became so afraid of these visits that they even refused shelter to wounded combatants. Those unfortunate enough to be found wanting usually received a short parody of a trial and were promptly hanged from a nearby lamppost and adorned with labels such as:

> 'I have been hanged because I was too much of a coward to defend the Reichs capital.'

> 'I was hanged because I was a defeatist.'

> 'I was hanged here because I did not believe in the Führer.'

> 'I am a deserter: because of this I will not see the change in destiny.'

> 'All traitors will die like this one.'

However, these measures still did not prevent several thousand deserters from going into hiding until they were found and taken prisoner by the Soviets.[2]

Goebbels appreciated that the people needed more than just exhortations

64

and discipline to keep going, so his staff were tasked with providing something upon which they could base their hopes. It was thus decided to treat the announcement that General Wenck's army was marching to the relief of Berlin as an accomplished fact, and tracts addressed to Wenck's troops were deliberately released in Berlin, as if in error, with the following text:

FÜHRER-ORDER – 23 April 1945

To the Soldiers of Wenck's Army!

An order of immense importance has removed you from your combat zone facing the enemy in the west and set you marching eastward. Your task is clear. Berlin must remain German. The objectives given you must be achieved whatever the circumstances, for operations are in progress elsewhere to inflict a decisive defeat on the Bolsheviks fighting for the capital and from this the situation in Germany will change completely. Berlin will never capitulate of Bolshevism!

The defenders of the capital have found renewed courage with the news of your rapid progress, and are fighting with bravery and determination in the certainty of soon hearing your cannon. The Führer has summoned you, and you have gone forward into the attack as in the days of conquest. Berlin awaits you! Berlin encourages you with all the warmth of her heart.[3]

This hope in Wenck's army, and the news that Hitler was directing the battle in person, gave heart to many and was the theme for newspaper articles that continued to appear until 28 April. Encouragement also came from outside the city: a British correspondent based in Sweden reported in the *Daily Mail* of 24 April a broadcast by Radio Hamburg:

'Hitler is with you!' [repeated several times] 'Hold out, Berliners! The reserves of the Reich are on their way. Not just the reserves of a fortress, but the reserves of our great Reich are rolling toward Berlin. The first reinforcements arrived in the early hours of today, anti-tank gun after anti-tank gun, tank after tank, rumbled through the streets in long columns. The troops that man them understand the gravity of the hour.'

Then came the report of a front-line reporter: 'Approaching Berlin I can see huge fires in the centre, and hear the boom of the Russian artillery. Grenades and shells whistle through the air. Flames light up the night. the guns are rumbling in this hellish battle. Our Führer is under shellfire.'

'Up Berliners, and rally round the Führer!' shouted another spokesman. 'As a tower of strength he is amongst us at this critical hour in the history of the Reichs capital; those who desert him and his city are swinish cowards.'

Said another speaker: 'Berlin trusts the Führer! Berlin fights on, though the hour is grave!'

With words and effects such as these the population and the soldiers were encouraged to continue their resistance to fate at the behest of leaders who had long since lost any contact with reality. Even Field Marshal Keitel, who was to spend the next few days touring the battle area visiting units and headquarters, attempting to organize and encourage relief operations, remained insensible and impervious to the evidence of his own eyes as to the truth of the situation.[4]

Keitel reached General Wenck's headquarters in the woods east of Magdeburg with some difficulty at about 0100 hours on 23 April. Wenck's 12th Army, whose boundary extended from the junction of the Havel and Elbe Rivers in the north to below Leipzig in the south, at its strongest contained the following formations:

1. XXXIX Panzer Corps under Lieutenant-General Karl Arndt, which remained under command only from the 21st to the 26th April. Formed earlier in the month with the 'Clausewitz' Panzer, 'Schlageter' RAD, 'Potsdam' and 84th Infantry Divisions, it had been sent into the Harz Mountains to support the 11th Army and was virtually destroyed within five days, but by the time it was transferred to the newly formed 21st Army on the 26th it had been reconstituted to consist of:

'Hamburg' Reserve Infantry Division (2 regiments)
'Meyer' Infantry Division (2 regiments)
84th Infantry Division (3 battalions)
'Clausewitz' Panzer Division (3 battalions)

2. XXXXI Panzer Corps under Lieutenant-General Rudolf Holste, which was based near Rathenow, and consisted of miscellaneous units, some of which had survived the Rhine battles, including:

'von Hake' Infantry Division (2 regiments)
199th Infantry Division (1 regiment [ex Oslo])
'V-Weapons' Infantry Division (6,000 men)
two anti-tank brigades

3. XX Corps under Lieutenant-General Carl-Erik Koehler, which was originally responsible for containing the minor American bridgeheads near Zerbst and consisted of:

'Theodor Körner' RAD Infantry Division
'Ulrich von Hutten' Infantry Division

'Ferdinand von Schill' Infantry Division
'Scharnhorst' Infantry Division

4. XXXXVIII Panzer Corps under General Maximilian Freiherr von Edelsheim, which constituted the Army Reserve near Coswig, and consisted mainly of miscellaneous units culled from the Leipzig and Halle areas, including the 14th Flak Division, most of whose guns were static.[5]

Keitel first briefed Wenck on the general situation as he knew it, and then gave him Hitler's orders for the 12th Army. Keitel waited for Wenck to draft out his orders, as he wanted to take a copy with him back to the Führerbunker and he also wanted to deliver the orders to General Koehler's XX Corps, who were to provide the bulk of the attacking force. At dawn he reached one of the latter's infantry divisions, which was already preparing for the operation, and addressed the assembled officers.[6]

What Keitel failed to realize was that Wenck, unlike his immediate superiors, had formed a very clear appreciation of the situation and had no illusions about the future, which he saw as a simple choice between captivity in either the east or the west. There was no doubt in his own mind which was the more preferable, and he regarded his primary task as that of holding the door open for a general exodus from what would become the Soviet Zone of Occupation. He was already doing all that he could to facilitate the passage of refugees through his lines, including giving them food. He therefore interpreted his instructions as enabling him to attempt the rescue of the tens of thousands of men and women trapped with the 9th Army and helping them to escape across the Elbe with his own troops. He certainly had no intention of allowing his forces to become engulfed in Berlin in pursuit of a hopeless cause.[7]

Wenck was fortunate in that many supply barges from all over the country had been trapped and stranded in his sector, so that he had no shortage of supplies, including motor fuel. Although he dutifully reported all this, no attempt was made by the OKW to have this windfall distributed.[8]

Keitel went on to call on Lieutenant-General Holste, whose XXXXI Panzer Corps, being the weakest of Wenck's formations, was to be detached from the 12th Army to continue surveillance on the line of the Elbe west of Berlin. However, during the course of their discussion Holste agreed with Keitel that the Americans apparently had no intention of crossing the river.[9]

By 1100 hours Keitel was back in Krampnitz, where he conferred with Jodl and had a brief rest before they set off for the Chancellery together. At the afternoon war conference Keitel reported to the Führer on his trip and Krebs announced that the 12th Army was already on the move. Hitler asked if the 9th and 12th Armies had established contact yet, but there was no information available on this point and Krebs was directed to tell the 9th Army to get on with it. Before leaving, Keitel again tried to persuade Hitler to leave Berlin without success.[10]

This conference clearly illustrates the fantasy world in which Hitler and his staff operated and which Keitel did nothing to dispel. He must have been fully aware that neither army was ready to act immediately and yet said nothing to this effect. In fact, Wenck did not expect to be ready until 25 April, by which time his formations would be redeployed for the attack and he hoped to have recovered some of his armour from west of the Elbe to assist him. In the meantime Wenck was acutely conscious of the threat from the southeast, where the 1st Ukrainian Front was making rapid progress in his direction.

When Keitel and Jodl returned to Krampnitz there were rumours of Soviet cavalry patrols heading south across the Döberitz Training Area. Much to Keitel's annoyance, the camp commandant had already ordered the destruction of the vast ammunition dump in his charge containing Berlin's reserves but for which there were no guards available. Keitel set off westward to see what he could do to expedite the relief operation, and shortly afterward Jodl was obliged to evacuate the OKW headquarters to one of Himmler's bases at a camp hidden in the woods at Neu Roofen, a small village between Rheinsberg and Fürstenberg about 50 miles to the north of Berlin and behind the still relatively intact 3rd Panzer Army.[11]

Keitel found Wenck still trying to recover some of his armour from west of the Elbe, and his other units hastily preparing for the forthcoming offensive. At midnight on 23 April Keitel was back in Holste's headquarters, where he gave the orders for the XXXXI Panzer Corps to ignore the Elbe Front and concentrate on protecting Wenck's northern flank in his drive on Berlin.[12]

In the meantime some reinforcements had got through to the city, although by no means on the scale or with the equipment indicated in the Radio Hamburg broadcast. Grand Admiral Dönitz ordered a battalion of sailors to be flown in on the night of the 25/26 April. This 'Grossadmiral Dönitz' Battalion consisted of a headquarters, three companies of naval trainees and one of officer cadets, under a Commander Franz Kuhlmann. The individuals had been rounded up that afternoon, formed into their companies and provided with basic equipment before being flown during the night in five Ju 352 transports from Tutow, near Greifswald, to Gatow, where only two of the aircraft are known to have landed, while a third is said to have crash-landed, possibly on the East–West Axis airstrip. Kuhlmann and his 80 or so sailors then marched off to the Heerstrasse, where they were picked up by a convoy of trucks and taken to the cellars of the Foreign Office on Wilhelmstrasse to await assignment. Next day three Fw 200s or Ju 290s took off from Rerik with about 15 armed sailors each from the Radar Training Establishment at Fehmarn aboard, only one of which reached Gatow.[13]

Presumably, it was at this stage that the orders for blowing the city's bridges were issued. Not all the bridges were destroyed immediately, some being retained as reserve demolitions, such as the Frey Bridge on the Heerstrasse and the Mussehl Bridge over the Teltow Canal, but access from one part of the city to another was severely curtailed. As Speer had warned, the blowing of these bridges also disrupted the city's surviving main service arteries, the most serious result being the lack of drinking water at a time when the air was constantly filled with smoke and dust.

Some wagons of arms and ammunition that had arrived by rail during the previous two or three days were unloaded by civilian labour and distributed among the population on Goebbels' orders amid considerable confusion. The Volkssturm units of the inner districts were kept busy improving their fortifications.[14]

The northern and eastern suburbs were evacuated as far as it was possible and the inhabitants willing but, as the last escape routes were cut off in the west, the refugees had to find shelter elsewhere in the city as best they could. Among them were deserters from the Volkssturm and Wehrmacht, looking for civilian clothes and a place to hide until the fighting was over. The streets became littered with military vehicles, trucks, field-kitchens, ambulances, gun-limbers, etc., all mixed up with farm carts and even prams abandoned by the refugees. All were immobilized through lack of fuel or the disappearance of their owners.[15] Dr Hans Fritzsche, a senior radio commentator, who was to become involved in the surrender negotiations a few days later, described the scene:

> One could already see many shell craters on the Unter-den-Linden, and as one went further eastward the noise of battle increased. Fresh debris and broken electricity cables littered the dead streets. Here and there some women threaded their way along, sheltering from building to building, whilst little groups ran alongside the walls clutching their wretched belongings.
>
> Even Alexanderplatz was empty and abandoned, except at the entrance to the big concrete shelter, which was packed tight with human beings. A member of the Volkssturm, wearing a brassard but without even a rifle, told me that the shelter could take several hundred people, but was in fact packed with thousands of them living in intolerable conditions.
>
> Further off the sounds of battle resounded and fires flared in the dusk.

In Danziger Strasse there were only two soldiers armed with Panzerfausts, but the adjacent streets were littered with destroyed vehicles and the bodies of dead soldiers and civilians.[16]

The possibility of the enemy infiltrating by means of the U-Bahn and S-Bahn tunnels had been considered at the Führerbunker, and orders had been issued stopping traffic through these tunnels on the 21st so that barricades could be set up at various points. As the lines ran under the Spree and the Landwehr Canal, consideration was also given to the deliberate flooding of these tunnels as a defensive measure. The Waffen-SS staff responsible for 'Zitadelle' took over the plans and control installations and began their preparations for flooding in a somewhat one-sided altercation with the railway engineers, who were primarily concerned with the safety of the thousands of people sheltering in the tunnels and underground stations. There were also four hospital trains filled with wounded and attendants, and another four trains reserved for civilian casualties, parked in the S-Bahn tunnel between Potsdamer Platz and the Unter-den-Linden. One civilian engineer tried to stop the boring of holes for demolition charges near the Spree embankment and was shot for his pains.[17]

The LVI Panzer Corps Headquarters moved across the Spree and the southern branch of the Teltow Canal during the night of 22/23 April into the suburb of Rudow. Sometime on 23 April, General Weidling's Chief-of-Staff, Lieutenant-Colonel Theodor von Dufving, telephoned his old friend from their cadet days, Colonel Refior, to ask for news. Refior was surprised when von Dufving told him that the corps was seeking to rejoin the 9th Army and had no intention of defending the capital, but enabled von Dufving to re-establish contact with the 9th Army Headquarters. General Weidling then spoke to the Chief-of-Staff, Colonel Hölz, who gave him orders to secure the 9th Army's northern flank. From another source Weidling learnt that a general had been sent to Döberitz to arrest him on Hitler's instructions, so he tried to contact Krebs for an explanation. Eventually he was summoned to report to the Führerbunker at 1800 hours, where he saw Krebs and General Burgdorf, who received him most coolly at first, but once they had heard his account they agreed to put his case to the Führer immediately.[18]

Weidling then told them that he was moving his corps south toward Königs Wusterhausen that night in support of the 9th Army in accordance with General Busse's instructions, but Krebs said that these orders would have to be cancelled as the LVI Panzer Corps was needed in Berlin. Weidling saw Hitler shortly afterward and was shocked by the latter's appearance and obvious deterioration. When he emerged from this interview, Krebs informed him that, with immediate effect, he was to take over the defence of the southeastern and southern Defence Sectors 'A' to 'E' on the arc Lichtenberg/Karlshorst/Niederschöneweide/Tempelhof/Zehlendorf.[19]

Weidling therefore decided to set up his command post in the administrative buildings at Tempelhof Airport and ordered his formations to disengage from the enemy and redeploy in the defence of the city as follows:

1. 9th Parachute Division to Lichtenberg ('A').
2. 'Müncheberg' Panzer Division to Karlshorst ('B').
3. SS 'Nordland' Panzergrenadier Division to Tempelhof ('D').
4. 20th Panzergrenadier Division to Zehlendorf ('E').
5. 18th Panzergrenadier Division in reserve just north of Tempelhof Airport.
6. Corps Artillery to concentrate in the Tiergarten.[20]

All but the 'Müncheberg' Panzer Division, which was caught up in a fierce tank battle around Rudow, were able to disengage and redeploy as instructed during the night of 23/24 April. Then at 1100 hours the following morning Weidling was summoned to the Führerbunker once more and told by Krebs that he had so impressed the Führer the previous evening that it had been decided to appoint him overall Commandant of the Berlin Defence Area forthwith. Major-General Werner Mummert of the 'Müncheberg' Panzer Division would relieve him as Corps Commander.[21]

Weidling's request to have sole authority for the issue of orders for the defence of Berlin was ignored; he would be directly responsible to the Führer. Consequently the same profusion of orders emanating from Hitler, Goebbels and other lesser Nazi dignitaries was to continue to confuse the defence. In any case it was too late to rectify the damage already done by the muddled system of command. The Sector Commanders were now fully involved with the enemy and, for lack of co-ordinating instructions, had to decide for themselves where they would make a determined stand with their severely limited resources. They simply did not have the manpower to implement the full concept of General Reymann's original plan. Some tried to hold on to the perimeter and interim strongpoints, while others fell back rapidly to positions covered by the canals or the Inner Defence Ring. In all cases they were handicapped by poor communications both vertically and laterally. This was further aggravated by the difficulties of movement now that many of the bridges had been blown and the streets were under shell-fire and no longer being cleared of debris, so that for a messenger to travel a few hundred yards could sometimes take hours.[22]

Weidling moved his command post to the Berlin Defence Area Head-quarters on the Hohenzollerndamm and tried to appraise the situation in which he now found himself. He decided that his first priorities were:

1. To re-site his headquarters more centrally, either at the flak-control tower in the Tiergarten, or at the Bendlerstrasse. He eventually chose the latter for its proximity to the Führerbunker and because of the overcrowding of the former.
2. To use his corps's communications units to bolster the defence communications system.
3. To augment the Berlin Defence Area Headquarters staff with officers from the corps's staff.
4. To completely reorganize the Defence Sector staffs.[23]

The staff responsibilities were split under two Chiefs-of-Staff, Lieutenant-Colonel Theodor von Dufving of the LVI Panzer Corps being responsible for all military matters, and Colonel Hans Refior for liaison with the civilian authorities as a natural continuation of his previous role as Chief-of-Staff to the Defence Area Commander. Fortunately, Weidling, Refior and von Dufving knew each other well from previous military service, the latter having also been at Staff College together. Refior was exhausted and had all but lost his voice from the stress of dealing with the endless telephone calls from Party officials.[24]

It was not possible to establish exactly what forces Weidling had at his disposal under his new command, as no one had the chance to take stock. However, rough estimates place the strength of the LVI Panzer Corps as 13–15,000 men, the equivalent of two divisions, the Waffen-SS forces under SS Major-General Mohnke as about 2,000 men, and the remaining miscellany of units as equating to some two to three divisions, a total of four to five divisions in all, with about 60,000 men and some 50–60 tanks.[25] Of this force only the LVI Panzer Corps formed a cohesive and reasonably equipped entity, the component formations being as follows:

1. 18th Panzergrenadier Division, which was still relatively intact under Major-General Josef Rauch.
2. 20th Panzergrenadier Division, which was severely reduced and whose commander, Major-General Georg Scholze, was to commit suicide a few days later.[26]
3. Major-General Werner Mummert's 'Müncheberg' Panzer Division, of which only one-third survived the Rudow battle to take part in the defence of the city.

4. 9th Parachute Division under Colonel Harry Herrmann, which had taken considerable punishment in the battle for the Seelow Heights, and was thus severely reduced in effectiveness.
5. SS 'Nordland' Panzergrenadier Division, which was still in reasonable shape, although its commander, SS Major-General Ziegler, continued to be troublesome and was shortly to be replaced.

For artillery, Weidling had at his disposal the integral units of the 18th, 20th Panzergrenadier and 'Müncheberg' Panzer Divisions, the city's flak batteries, and some locally raised units under the garrison's artillery commander, Lieutenant-Colonel Edgar Platho. The local artillery consisted of seven light and seven heavy batteries of foreign guns manned by Volkssturm and soldiers of all arms, but few gunners, and a further six batteries of German guns which Platho had assembled from dismantled exhibits in the local ordnance training establishments.[27] The foreign guns were limited to about 100 rounds per battery and all the crews lacked training. Colonel Hans-Oskar Wöhlermann, the commander of the LVI Panzer Corps' artillery, who remained Weidling's artillery chief, related:

> In the afternoon I contacted the artillery commander of the Berlin Defence Area, Lieutenant Colonel Platho, who was stationed in a flak-tower (in the Tiergarten). At the same time I inspected various strongpoints, a difficult task in that mass of debris, and also several batteries that had been placed in position in the meantime. Altogether four artillery regiments had been posted in the various divisional sectors of Berlin but, as far as I can remember, there were only some eight to ten motorized units. In addition we had the guns of our four divisions (LVIth Panzer Corps) and of the 408th Volks Artillery Corps, though what few guns we had left were almost useless for lack of ammunition. Had I not been born a Berliner and known the places like the back of my hand, I should have found it impossible to site the batteries in the very short time I had been given. As it was, I knew where to go without having to bother too much with the map. As most of our guns were low-firing there were not many places to chose from; the Tiergarten and some of the larger squares, such as Lützowplatz, Belle-Alliance-Platz (Mehringplatz), the Lustgarten, Alexanderplatz, etcetera, and the railway cuttings between the Potsdamer and Anhalter stations in the centre of the city. We also placed a few mortars on Belle-Alliance-Platz, Lützowplatz and Steinplatz, and guns on the railway tracks. Toward evening I visited a 15cm battery in the Botanical Gardens near my Berlin apartment.[28]

Shortage of ammunition was common to all the field units, supply being a matter of chance or relying on the ingenuity of the unit commander, although there were in fact ample supplies of standard German ammunition within the city. Large depots existed at three locations, one in the Jungfernheide Volkspark next to the Siemensstadt complex, one in the Grunewald near the War Academy site (now buried under the Teufelsberg) and one in the Hasenheide Volkspark next to Tempelhof Airport. There was also a smaller one in the Tiergarten. The three main depots had been stocked to 80 per cent capacity before the fighting and measures taken to secure the stocks against dissipation to other fronts. On the approach of the Soviets two-thirds of the Jungfernheide depot's stores were evacuated to the Grunewald but, in the event, all three depots were quickly overrun.[29]

The miscellany of units on the ground meant that the Soviets were often able to bypass the more effective units, isolating them and reducing them at leisure, and it was later noted that they seemed to pick on the weaker Volkssturm units for attack, although in fact it was Party policy, and widely practised, to mix the different types of combatants into composite units. Nevertheless, Weidling kept his LVI Panzer Corps units intact for use on the 'fire brigade' principle.[30]

For the Soviets, adjustment to the new circumstances mainly entailed reorganizing their forces for the street-fighting role, and the co-ordination of the various arms into combat teams in the style previous tried out by the 8th Guards Army. It was decided to utilize the artillery resources left over from the initial phase of the operation to augment the integral artillery formations, allowing the divisional and corps artillery to be split into small detachments and allocated to individual combat teams, while the army and front artillery took over the counter-bombardment role and harassed the central districts.[31]

A particular problem arose in the joint 8th Guards Army and 1st Guards Tank Army sector as they entered the street-fighting phase. Marshal Zhukov's orders of 18 April concerning co-operation had not been fully implemented for lack of opportunity, but now suddenly the units of the two armies found themselves chaotically entangled with each other in the narrow streets and something had to be worked out quickly. Although they appear to have co-operated efficiently together thereafter, the relationship remained somewhat strained, and it obviously could not have been easy for one army commander to subordinate himself to the other without some feeling of resentment that would have continued down the chain of command.[32]

In order to facilitate air support, Air Chief Marshal Novikov established two air control centres, the principal one being based on the headquarters of the 16th Air Army under the Deputy Commander, General S.A. Senarov, east of Berlin, and a secondary one in the north under General B.K. Tokarev, responsible for controlling the ground-attack operations. All air units and individual aircraft operating over Berlin had to keep in touch with these centres and could attack targets only with their permission. There was such a pall of smoke hanging over the city that these measures were imperative. Observers stationed on the rooftops directed the aircraft to their targets with the aid of radio, light and rocket signals.[33]

The combat teams generally consisted of a platoon of infantry, one or two tanks, some sappers, some man-pack flame-throwers, a section of anti-tank guns, and two or three field guns, usually 76mm, but sometimes even 150mm guns or 203mm howitzers were used in this role when particularly strong positions had to be attacked. In this direct support role the guns advanced with their teams, firing over open sights at ranges of up to 400 yards down the axis of the streets. They would set themselves up under cover of smokescreens, or would fire at the blank walls of buildings to raise clouds of dust for the same purpose. At these ranges the gunners inevitably took casualties from infantry fire, and it was a particularly trying time for their observers with the leading infantry, who frequently needed relief from the strain and fatigue of their role.

For the mass artillery the main problem was finding sufficient open space to operate from, and in some places the guns were packed so close together it seemed that their wheels must be touching. The Katyusha rocket-launcher units found a solution to their problem by dismantling the frames from the truckbeds and reassembling them on convenient rooftops. All these artillery concentrations were protected by a profusion of anti-aircraft guns.[34]

A pattern emerged by which all the artillery combined in a massive hour-long bombardment of the day's targets first thing every morning. This was first experienced at 0515 hours on 24 April and gradually increased in intensity as more guns were brought into play on subsequent days. At night the shelling did not actually stop but diminished considerably.[35] The effects of deliberate, concentrated and sustained artillery bombardment were particularly severe in comparison to that previously produced by Allied bombing raids, reducing building after building to swathes of churned-up rubble. Some of the avenues leading into the city centre became corridors of destruction as the Soviet guns literally blasted a way through for their combat teams. As Colonel-General Berzarin was later to comment: 'The Allies dropped 65,000 tons of bombs – we fired 40,000 tons of shells in two weeks!' One of the German combatants related:

Gradually we lost all human appearance. Our eyes burned and our faces were lined and stained with the dust that surrounded us. We no longer saw the blue sky; everywhere buildings were burning, ruins falling, and the smoke billowing back and forth in the streets.

The silence that followed each bombardment was merely the prelude to the roar of engines and the clank of tracks heralding a new tank attack.[36]

For several days the Soviet pressure on the city remained very uneven as the various formations closed in to take up their positions around the defence perimeter and adjusted themselves to the new fighting conditions.[37]

6

ENCIRCLEMENT COMPLETED

On 23 April the 3rd Panzer Army was still desperately holding on to its Oder positions, although hard-pressed to do so. It was obvious to Colonel-General Heinrici that General von Manteuffel's troops could not hold out much longer, and he was in fact planning their withdrawal to the other side of the Elbe to enable their surrender to the Western Allies. On their southern flank Steiner continued to hold the line of the canals but the outflanking of Oranienburg meant that he had quickly to man the line of the Ruppiner Canal at the expense of the town, whose fall was imminent. Nevertheless, that day, Heinrici received orders from Field Marshal Keitel, on behalf of the Führer, for Steiner to mount an immediate attack southward to relieve the pressure on Berlin and to sever Zhukov's thrust across the Havel. He was promised reinforcements in the form of the 7th Panzer and 25th Panzergrenadier Divisions, neither of which was yet available, and in any case the latter was coming from the eastern end of his own line, where he had been given permission to abandon the Eberswalde bridgehead. At the same time the XXXXI Panzer Corps of Wenck's 12th Army was ordered to block the Soviet advance westward.[1]

The force that crossed the Havel at Hennigsdorf on the night of 22/23 April consisted of the 47th Army with the 9th Guards Tank Corps of the 2nd Guards Tank Army and the 7th Guards Cavalry Corps under its command. This force had the dual task of completing the encirclement of the city and of providing a protective screen for the operation as far west as possible. The 9th Guards Tank Corps appears to have been shared out in brigade groups among the rest of the force, whose main body advanced nearly 15 miles to reach the outskirts of Nauen on 23 April. The 125th Rifle Corps, supported by the 50th Guards Tank and 33rd Guards Mechanized Brigades, closed up to the defences of Spandau and Gatow Airfield, but made no attempt to penetrate the town that day. The 77th Rifle Corps' 328th Rifle Division, supported by the 65th Guards Tank Brigade, headed south to link up with

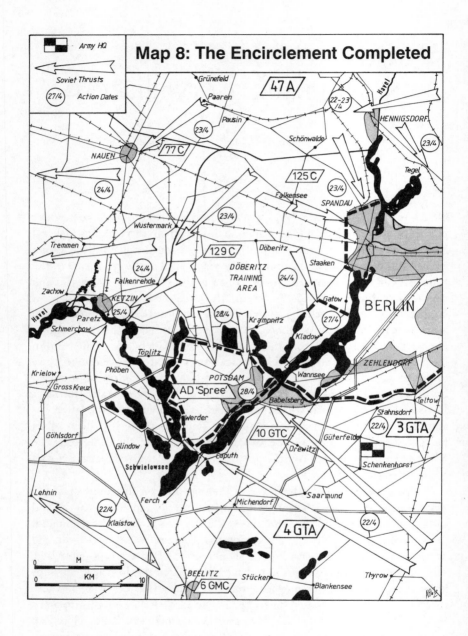

Map 8: The Encirclement Completed

Army HQ

Soviet Thrusts

27/4   Action Dates

Grünefeld

47 A

22-23/4

HENNIGSDORF

Paaren

Pausin

Schönwalde

23/4

23/4

Tegel

NAUEN

77 C

125 C

24/4

Falkensee

23/4

SPANDAU

Wustermark

23/4

Döberitz

Tremmen

129 C

Staaken

DÖBERITZ
TRAINING
AREA

24/4

24/4

Falkenrehde

Gatow

Zachow

KETZIN

28/4

Krampnitz

27/4

BERLIN

Paretz

25/4

Kladow

Schmerchow

Havel

Töplitz

ZEHLENDORF

Krielow

Phöben

POTSDAM

Wannsee

Gross Kreuz

AD 'Spree'

28/4

Babelsberg

Teltow

Stahnsdorf

22/4

3 GTA

Werder

Göhlsdorf

10 GTC

Güterfelde

Glindow

Drewitz

Schenkenhorst

Schwielowsee

Caputh

Lehnin

22/4

Ferch

Michendorf

Saarmund

4 GTA

22/4

Klaistow

M   5

BEELITZ

Stücken

Thyrow

KM   10

6 GMC

Blankensee

AH

the 4th Guards Tank Army, while the cavalry fanned out between these main groups, scouring the countryside for signs of resistance. It was their appearance on the Döberitz Training Area that caused the hasty evacuation of the OKW from Krampnitz.[2]

During the course of 23 April the encircling formations worked their way slowly into the northern and eastern suburbs, gradually accustoming themselves to the circumstances and learning the techniques of street-fighting from practical experience. Of course, these suburbs did not have the solid blocks of multi-storeyed structures common to the older parts of the city, and therefore did not present exactly the same kind of problems that were to be encountered later. For the most part these suburbs consisted of orderly groups of one- and two-storeyed houses set in individual gardens. There were also many garden colonies to be found among these suburbs, allotments belonging to city apartment-dwellers who had constructed small summer houses and huts for their weekend leisure, and many of these were now permanently occupied as a result of the bombing. It was too early in the year for there to be vegetation of any significance except at bush level, but the density of the suburbs was sufficient to conceal from the air those defence locations not indicated by the scars of trench systems or barriers across important road junctions, which could be expected to be defended.

The Soviets advanced cautiously, but not always wisely. Mistakes were made by both sides. Chuikov writes of tank commanders sending their tanks through the streets in columns, only to be blocked in at either end by flank attacks and then destroyed piecemeal by Panzerfausts and Panzerschrecks.[3]

The Germans, firm believers in the doctrine that attack is the best means of defence, even used their *ad hoc* units in repeated counterattacks that only sapped their morale and strength uselessly against the more experienced Soviet troops, when fighting from behind cover would have been more effective with such inexperienced resources.

The Outer Defence Ring at Tegel was held by a Plant Protection Battalion, whose commander, a Major Schwark, later reported:

> The position sector was bounded on the left by the northern tip of the Tegeler See, from where it extended to the right along the Tegeler Run, also called the Nordgraben. This ditch held very little water and was more a line on which to build fortifications than an actual obstacle itself. The position consisted of a shallow fire trench without barbed wire or mines.
>
> The Battalion Commander had been familiarized with the terrain and had participated in two map exercises. The position was occupied by the

Plant Protection Battalion, which comprised four understrength companies armed with rifles, hand grenades and a few Panzerfausts. Most of the men were veterans of World War I, and because of their service with plant protection units were accustomed to order and discipline. The Russians avoided a frontal attack, using infiltration instead, especially at night. Such tactics were aided by the poor visibility afforded by the terrain. Particular trouble was caused by roof-top snipers in front of and behind the German lines. Nevertheless it was still possible to keep the men together. When the battalion was almost surrounded after three days of fighting, it withdrew and occupied a new position in the Wittler Bakery plant, where the writer was seriously wounded.[4]

This unit was fortunate in that the 1st Mechanized Corps, in coming down through Hermsdorf, Waidmannslust and Wittenau, had bypassed them, and their assailants appear to have been a detachment of the 47th Army detailed to secure the Hennigsdorf crossing-point by clearing the area down as far as Tegel. Further east the 12th Guards Tank Corps swept down through Lübars, Blankenfelde and Rosenthal, where its arrival was described by a witness:

Rosenthal was taken after an artillery barrage, followed by an advance of tanks supported by helmetless infantry, excellent fighters. As soon as they arrived the men dug individual foxholes and took care of their wounded and their weapons. No uniforms to speak of. Then the looting and the rape. No discipline for most of the troops, as admitted by several Soviet officers, but this was only after the fighting was over.[5]

The 12th Guards Tank Corps pushed on, working its way through Reinickendorf District with the 79th Rifle Corps of the 3rd Shock Army on its left flank in Niederschönhausen.

The 12th Guards Rifle Corps' experience in Pankow, as recounted by a member of the Volkssturm opposing them, seems fairly typical:

We were in two companies [formed by the auxiliary police] of about 45 men armed with Italian rifles. On the 23rd the Russians appeared in the houses and gardens in Breite Strasse opposite Pankow townhall. House to house fighting lasted until four Russian tanks advanced to within 400 meters of us along Breite Strasse. Two were put out of action by an infantry NCO with a Panzerfaust, and the others turned back.

A counterattack was then mounted by combatants from the police, auxiliary police and Hitlerjugend, but this failed. Our losses amounted to 40 per cent and, as we lacked both food and ammunition, on the 25th we pulled back to Charlottenburg, where I was allowed to go as I was over 60 years old.[6]

Evidently, infantry–tank co-operation had yet to be perfected by the Soviets in this case, but the unskilled defenders stood little chance when used in the open against them. However, a nucleus of resistance was to remain in Pankow until the very end of the battle and appears to have been centred around an air raid bunker.

The 7th Rifle Corps at Hohenschönhausen was still not ready to move, but the 5th Shock Army closed up to the fallback position in Defence Sector 'A', taking Kaulsdorf and Biesdorf without difficulty. The 9th Rifle Corps on its right flank started moving in a southwesterly direction and took Karlshorst with its engineer training barracks. Colonel Shishkov's 301st Rifle Division captured the Rummelsburg power station not only intact but operating – which delighted his superiors and brought him the award of the Order of Suvarov.[7]

Immediately to the south of them the 4th Guards Rifle Corps of the 8th Guards Army took the industrial suburb of Oberschöneweide and prepared to cross the Spree to Johannisthal 'island'. That evening the Dnieper Flotilla arrived to assist both them and the 9th Rifle Corps of the 5th Shock Army with their impending river crossings, the intention being to place the 8th Guards Army, with the 1st Guards Tank Army under command, and the 9th Rifle Corps supported by an armoured brigade, in a position to attack Berlin from the south.[8]

In the early hours of the 23rd the 29th Guards Rifle Corps took intact the railway bridge leading south across the Spree into Adlershof and promptly began moving across to the west bank. During the day the 39th Guards Rifle Division cleared Köpenick with its bridges across the Spree and the Dahme, thereby ensuring the two armies' communications routes through this area. Consequently by the day's end the left flank corps, the 28th Guards Rifle Corps, was concentrating in the Grünau–Falkenberg area below the southern spur of the Teltow Canal, the 29th Guards Rifle Corps was on the central 'island' facing Johannisthal Airfield, and the 4th Guards Rifle Corps was still on the east bank of the Spree.[9]

That night the Military Council of the 1st Byelorussian Front called for an all-out effort to speed up the fall of Berlin. They were way behind schedule, Stalin was pressing them and Zhukov must have been apprehensive about the progress of Koniev's forces.[10]

The 3rd Guards Tank Army spent 23 April regrouping south of the Outer Defence Ring between Stahnsdorf and Lichtenrade, allowing the main body to catch up with the leading troops. The presence of Koniev's troops was still apparently unsuspected by Zhukov, although Air Chief Marshal Novikov and his staff must have been fully aware of their location. There was still little to oppose them, as Volkssturm Lieutenant von Reuss reported:

> Preparations for the defence of the Teltow Canal included the construction of works along the northern bank and the organization of a bridge demolition team. A fire trench was laid out at a varying distance from the canal and machine-gun emplacements were established 500–600 meters apart. Each emplacement was connected with a protected shelter by means of a communication trench.
>
> The trenches led partly through marshy terrain and interfered greatly with troop movements. A machine-gun emplacement protected with concrete slabs was constructed in the ground of an asbestos factory. There were no artillery emplacements to the rear, although two anti-aircraft guns had been brought into position. A rocket-launcher had also been set up.
>
> The only complete unit that figured in this sector was the Kleinmachnow Volkssturm Company, which was joined by a few stragglers from the Wehrmacht.
>
> The platoon was armed with only one machine-gun of Czech manufacture, which went out of action after having been fired only once. In addition there were rifles of various foreign makes, including even some Italian Balilla rifles.

The Lieutenant went on to say that the neighbouring Volkssturm platoon packed up and went home for the night after their first encounter with the enemy, returning in the morning to continue the fight![11]

On the extreme right, Soviet troops broke through a Volkssturm battalion's positions and reached the Teltow Canal in Britz, obliging the German defence in Marienfelde and Mariendorf to withdraw to the line of the canal.[12]

However, Marshal Koniev's estimation of his opposition was 15,000 men at 1,900 per mile, 250 guns and mortars, 130 tanks and armoured vehicles, and 500 machine-guns.[13] To counter this he was amassing some 3,000 guns and mortars to cover his attack lines along the canal, giving an extraordinary density of 1,050 guns to the mile. In addition, a large number of guns of all calibres were allocated to the direct-fire role in support of the crossing and follow-through. Koniev's main problem was the nature of the obstacle before him; his infantry could easily swim the canal under the covering fire available, but once across they would need armoured support. New bridges could not be built under these circumstances and they would have to rely on the few remaining standing.[14]

During the day elements of the 128th Rifle Corps of the 28th Army continued to arrive to take part in the operation, but one of them, the 152nd Rifle Division, was caught up near Mittenwalde in what was thought to be a breakout attempt by the 9th Army but which may well have been the 21st Panzer Division's redeployment. Whatever the cause, the division was still fighting in the Mittenwalde area that night and does not appear to have rejoined its parent formation for another day or two. The two other corps of this army, the 3rd Guards and 20th Rifle Corps, were also heading north toward Berlin, but were diverted to assist with the encirclement of the 9th Army.[15]

The 4th Guards Tank Army continued closing in on Potsdam and closing the gap with the 47th Army, but made no attempt to cross the line of the Havel, which seems to have been their operational boundary. The 6th Guards Mechanized Corps alone pushed on westward from Beelitz toward Brandenburg and Paretz, taking Lehnin that day.[16]

By the end of 23 April the 13th Army had almost reached the Elbe at Wittenberg. Koniev decided to detach its 350th Rifle Division to the 4th Guards Tank Army to assist with the screening of Potsdam, and to take over its reserve corps at Luckau as his Front Reserve and locate it at Jüterbog, where it would be more centrally placed to meet anticipated contingencies.[17]

Further south the bulk of the 5th Guards Army closed up to the Elbe around Torgau on a wide front that day. Koniev decided to leave only the 34th Guards Rifle Corps in that area to await the arrival of the Americans on the opposite bank, and pulled back the 32nd Guards Rifle and 4th Guards Tank Corps into the second echelon prior to striking a counterblow at the German forces on the southern flank. The latter had now penetrated some 20 miles toward Spremberg, splitting the 52nd and 2nd Polish Armies and creating havoc in their rear areas.[18]

Although he had just sufficient troops to cope with this emergency in the south, it is clear that Marshal Koniev's forces were extremely finely stretched at this stage. His active northern front extended in a great loop from Cottbus in the east to Wittenberg in the west, via Berlin, Potsdam, Brandenburg and Beelitz, and had only a very small reserve in the centre to counter the viable threat posed by the German 9th and 12th Armies. In addition to these problems, he was also responsible for the 6th Army, which was not actually involved in the Berlin operation but impatiently besieging Breslau way behind his lines in Upper Silesia.[19]

It is therefore even more remarkable that he should personally concentrate solely with the key members of his front staff on the 3rd Guard Tank Army's penetration of Berlin and the race for the Reichstag.

Meanwhile the Nazi leaders continued to play out their heedless melodrama. On the 23rd General Koller arrived at Berchtesgaden and briefed Göring on the general situation and the events in the Führerbunker of the previous day, stressing that Hitler had apparently abandoned leadership of the government and armed forces and had said that Göring should sue for peace. Koller urged Göring to act, but Göring was reluctant to do so, as he had been out of favour for some time and thought that Bormann might well have been chosen to take over from Hitler. However, Göring had been nominated Hitler's successor in the Law of Succession of 1941, and Lammers, head of the Reichs Chancellery, advised him that this law was still valid. Eventually it was decided to send the following signal to Hitler in code:

> Führer!
>
> In view of your decision to remain at your post in the fortress of Berlin, do you agree that I take over, at once, the total leadership of the Reich, with full freedom of action at home and abroad, as your deputy, in accordance with the decree of 29 June 1941? If no reply has been received by 2200 hours I shall take it for granted that you have lost your freedom of action, consider the conditions of your decree as fulfilled and act for the best interests of our country and our people. You know what I feel for you in this gravest hour of my life. Words fail me to express myself. May God protect you and speed you here quickly in spite of all. Your loyal,
>
> Hermann Göring[20]

When the signal arrived at the Führerbunker, Bormann deliberately kept it to himself for two or three hours until he could catch Hitler in a nervous, irritable mood. He then showed the signal to the Führer, suggesting that Göring was trying to seize power for himself. Hitler flew into a rage and denounced Göring as a traitor. He then sent two signals to Göring, one forbidding him to take any action, and a second ordering him to resign from all his posts if he wished to avoid trial for treason. Separate orders were sent to the SS guards, placing Göring and his staff under house arrest.[21]

A surprise witness to Hitler's rage and the drafting of these signals was Albert Speer, who had flown into Gatow that evening, and then flown on by Fieseler 'Storch' to land on the East–West Axis airstrip by the Brandenburg Gate. Speer had come for the curious reason of confessing to Hitler all that he had done to obstruct the 'scorched earth' policy – an act which could well have cost him his head, but which only evoked from Hitler an unusually mild response under the circumstances, for he told Speer that all was forgiven and forgotten.[22]

In another conversation later that evening, Speer tried with Bormann and Ribbentrop to persuade Hitler to leave Berlin, but Hitler refused, saying, 'I shall not go out of the bunker to meet my death at the barricades, for I should risk being wounded and taken alive by the Russians. I shall shoot myself here with my own revolver. My body must not fall into enemy hands; they would have be sure to use it for propaganda. I have made arrangements for it to be burnt.'[23] Speer stayed until 0400 hours on the morning of 24 April before flying out again the same way he had come eight hours earlier.[24]

On 24 April Steiner at last managed to launch simultaneous attacks southward from his minor bridgeheads at Kreuzbruch and Zerpenschleuse, using a total of seven battalions. It was a feeble gesture when measured in terms of Hitler's expectations, but little short of miraculous under the circumstances. These twin attacks caught the 61st Army by surprise, and both groups were able to advance about four miles, as far as the villages of Zehlendorf and Klosterfelde respectively, before the Soviets rallied and drove the survivors back to the canal. The Luftwaffe supported this operation in accordance with Hitler's instructions, and also attacked the long lines of vehicles backing up the 47th Army's advance westward, but the Soviets had established good ground-to-air liaison with their own air force and were able to call in superior numbers to drive off the German aircraft before too much harm was done.[25]

The 47th Army continued exploiting further to the west and south, with the 76th and 60th Rifle Divisions of the 125th Rifle Corps attacking Spandau simultaneously from the north and west, while the 175th Rifle Division concentrated on Gatow Airfield. Goebbels' propaganda had been effective, and they met determined resistance everywhere. Although they used heavy fire support, their progress was slow and costly. A French prisoner-of-war gave the following account of an attack on a barricade outside the Schultheiss Brewery in the northern part of the town:

> The roadblock's defenders were bombarded by heavy mortars set up in some ruined houses nearby. Then the Russians set up a 75mm or 105mm gun several hundred meters from the barricade.
>
> The Russian gunners were extremely exposed and, at the cost of several casualties, succeeded in getting some shots on the target, destroying the barricade and killing a number of Germans.

Then the Soviet infantry, about a hundred strong, charged in screaming, quickly swamped the remaining defenders, opened the barrier and regrouped on the street corner opposite the brewery.

German losses were increased by the bitterness of the Soviet soldiers, who seemed to be drugged, and rarely took prisoners. We found numerous German corpses, civilians and soldiers, when we were able to get out of the brewery.[26]

At the end of the day, the Soviet penetration of Spandau had failed to dislodge the defence, and the situation was so confused that they appear to have withdrawn to safer lines for the night and called for aircraft to bomb the town.[27]

The situation at Gatow Airfield was somewhat different. It was an important Luftwaffe establishment, in which were based the Officer Training, Engineering and Staff Academies, whose remaining students participated in the defence of the airfield. Major Komorowski, who commanded a composite battalion on the Outer Defence Ring here, reported:

The battalion, as part of a regiment, defended a section of the first position located along the western perimeter of Gatow Airfield, which was to be protected against attack from the west. If the position were lost, the troops were to cross the Havel in boats lying in readiness, in order to occupy the second position on the east side of the lake.

The position consisted of a well-built, continuous trench. The battalion was composed of construction and Volkssturm troops, none of whom had any combat experience. They were armed with captured rifles and a few machine-guns, and only had a limited supply of ammunition. The infantry were supported by an 88mm anti-aircraft battery and a heavy infantry gun platoon, although the latter unit had never fired its weapons. Support was also received from the Zoo Flak-tower. On the evening of the first day of battle all the Volkssturm troops deserted, and the gap was filled by recruiting stragglers. In two days of fighting all the defenders were either killed or captured.[28]

Despite the fighting, the airfield remained in operation until actually overrun, as we shall see.

During the day the garrison's last reinforcements to come by road arrived. SS Major-General Dr Gustav Krukenberg brought in some 350 volunteers, mainly French, from his old command, the SS 'Charlemagne' Panzer-grenadier Division. This division had just been disbanded in the interest of questionable future loyalty, now that General de Gaulle, as Head of State, was fielding a proper national army against the Germans. The survivors of this formation had been offered the choice of either being employed on construction work or volunteering for the last-ditch stand in Berlin, and it was the latter that he brought with him. Krukenberg himself, a superb commander of mercenaries, came in response to General Weidling's request for someone to replace the troublesome Ziegler. When they found their route from Nauen blocked at Wustermark, Krukenberg took them by a roundabout route on country roads. Near Ketzin they saw Soviet infantry converging on them cautiously from north and south, but were able to get through unscathed by holding their fire and keeping the enemy in doubt as to their identity. At Falkenrehde some Volkssturm blew the canal bridge as they arrived, mistaking them for Soviets, thus obliging them to continue their journey on foot. On their way via Krampnitz, Gross Glienicker and Pichelsdorf, they came across no defenders except three Hitlerjugend boys armed with Panzerfausts and riding bicycles. They passed through the still unmanned roadblocks on the Frey Bridge, where the Heerstrasse (East–West Axis) crosses over the Havel, and arrived at the Olympic Stadium at 2200 hours. Presumably the Soviets must have pulled back for the night from their attack on Gatow Airfield, as otherwise Krukenberg's group would have run into the fighting there.[29]

On 24 April, the 1st Mechanized Corps and the 12th Guards Tank Corps continued their movement south, crossing the Jungfernheide to close up to the line of the Hohenzollern Canal during the course of the afternoon. Under the cover of the woods lining the north bank they quickly prepared a crossing operation, which took place that evening, and by nightfall several combat groups had established themselves on the edges of Siemensstadt, the big modern industrial suburb founded by the Siemens Company.[30]

The 79th Rifle Corps of the 3rd Shock Army was not so lucky, for, having come through the southern part of Reinickendorf and swung as far west as the deserted Luftwaffe 'Hermann Göring' Barracks before turning south for the Hohenzollern Canal, it came under heavy fire from the direction of Plötzensee Prison and the Westhafen warehouses, and was unable to effect a crossing that day.[31]

The 12th Guards Rifle Corps began working its way down through the old working-class district of Wedding, with its enormous tenement block complexes, each a mass of connecting courtyards. An improvement in tactics is indicated in the following eye-witness account of events in Müllerstrasse: 'A dozen tanks penetrated our street in the direction of the townhall. Infantry slipped through in the same direction, covering each other. They were on

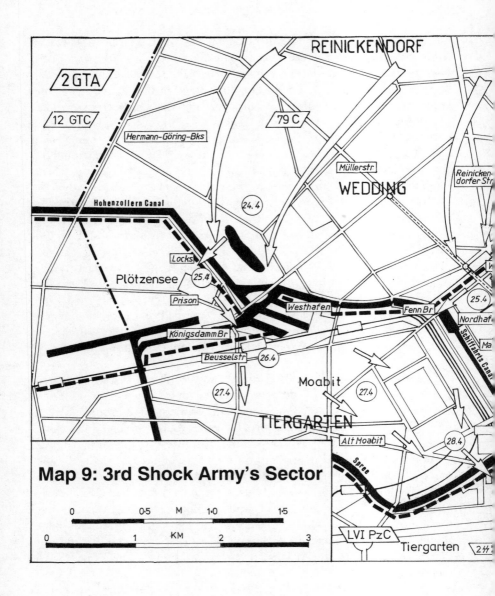

Map 9: 3rd Shock Army's Sector

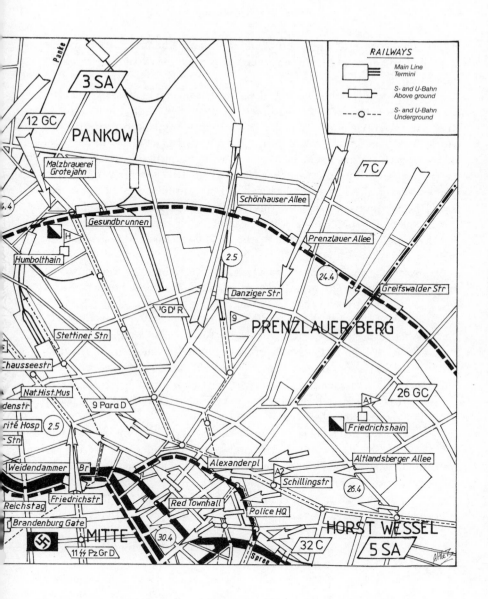

RAILWAYS

Main Line
Termini

S- and U-Bahn
Above ground

S- and U-Bahn
Underground

3 SA

12 GC

PANKOW

Panke

Malzbrauerei
Grotejahn

Schönhauser Allee

7 C

Gesundbrunnen

Prenzlauer Allee

Humbolthain

H

2.5

24.4

Danziger Str

Greifswalder Str

'GD'R

9

PRENZLAUER BERG

Stettiner Stn

Chausseestr

Nat.Hist.Mus

26 GC

denstr

9 Para D

A1

rité Hosp

2.5

Friedrichshain

Stn

Altlandsberger Allee

Weidendammer

Br

Alexanderpl

A2

Schillingstr

26.4

Friedrichstr

Red Townhall

Police HQ

HORST WESSEL

Reichstag

Brandenburg Gate

MITTE

30.4

32 C

5 SA

11 ∅ Pz Gr D

Spree

either side of the street and about 20 meters apart. The firing stopped after about half an hour and the soldiers then went from house to house searching the cellars.'[32]

Where the main roads from Tegel (Müllerstrasse) and Pankow (Reinickendorfer Strasse) converged at Wedding S-Bahn station on the Inner Defence Ring, the Soviets encountered fierce resistance from well-prepared positions, which held them up for a while until the strong Soviet artillery support was able to overwhelm the defence. However, the units on the 12th Guards Rifle Corps' left flank came up against the Humboldthain flak-tower position, which could not be reduced so easily. An arc of railway cuttings forming a dry moat across the northern approaches to this position, plus the framework of streets around the park behind, all helped to keep the attackers at bay. The position had therefore to be contained and bypassed, and so remained in action until the very end of the battle.[33]

Wolfgang Karow, an infantry NCO on leave in Berlin, had been mustered into an *ad hoc* unit based on the Humboldthain flak-tower only the previous day, and gave the following account of activity on 24 April:

> We first came under fire from the Hertha BSC football ground, sat fast and then pushed off to Bellermannstrasse [all within a kilometre of the flak-tower], where we took over an apartment block. We had to get the occupants out of the cellars to unlock their apartment doors for us. The other side of the street was already occupied by the Russians, and a brisk exchange of fire was opened up between us.
>
> Our Lieutenant and combat team leader was a good comrade. We knew as well as he did that this was 'five minutes to midnight' and that the war would be over in a few days. His orders were therefore considerate, and he was careful not to take risks with anyone unless it was necessary.
>
> So we pulled out, quit the apartment block and made for Humboldhain Flak-tower. There we were put into reserve and were able to get to know the interior of this vast bunker. We experienced the violent shaking when all eight 125mm anti-aircraft guns fired a salvo at the Russians, feeding them a violent form of respect.
>
> The artillery fire was particularly fierce against the walls of the bunker since their infantry could not get in. The brave gunners were being killed mercilessly at their posts, and they were nearly all young Flak Auxiliaries, 14- to 16-year-olds. These brave youngsters continued to serve their guns fearlessly, and several were felled before our eyes.
>
> An assault group was formed from our reserve combat team, and I also belonged to it. We were ordered to try and get some sweets from the

Hildebrandt Chocolate Factory in Pankestrasse, which was nearby in no man's land, so we put on some large Luftwaffe rucksacks and set off. We arrived without any trouble, but then had to detain an NSDAP (Party) official, who tried to prevent us entering at gunpoint. We were able to fill our rucksacks with chocolates and return to the bunker without suffering any casualties, and were warmly received by our comrades.[34]

The 7th Rifle Corps advanced through Prenzlauer Berg District, which was similar in character to Wedding, working its way down the two main roads leading into Alexanderplatz (Prenzlauer Allee from Blankenburg and Greifswalder Strasse from Weissensee) and through the Inner Defence Ring without encountering any serious opposition.[35]

The 26th Guards and 32nd Rifle Corps of the 5th Shock Army, strongly supported by armoured elements, continued their advance astride Frankfurter Allee on the East–West Axis and cleared the Schlachthof (Abattoir) complex just inside the Inner Defence Ring, which does not appear to have presented much of a problem to them. One of the units opposing them was the 3/115th Siemensstadt Volkssturm Battalion, whose two remaining companies had been tasked with defending the Zentral-Viehhof (Central Stockyard) part of the Schachthof (Abattoir) complex immediately south of the Storkower Strasse S-Bahn station, to which the stockyard was connected by a footbridge across the railway tracks forming the Inner Defence Ring. Although the position looked easy enough to defend, heavy Soviet tanks had already occupied the garden colonies opposite and Soviet infantry had penetrated the abattoir complex before the Volkssturm battalion arrived. As this situation was revealed at daylight, the Volkssturm had quickly to adopt an all-round defence. More Soviet troops then crossed the footbridge with some heavy weapons, forcing a wedge between the two companies, which then also came under heavy mortar fire. That afternoon the battalion had to withdraw once more, this time to Samariterstrasse, either side of Rigaer Strasse, from where heavy Soviet traffic could be seen on Frankfurter Allee.[36]

However, Soviet progress became uneven when those units that came under fire from the Friedrichshain flak-tower were brought to an abrupt halt, as was the case with those advancing along Frankfurter Allee. Progress along this main artery was henceforth marked by the systematic destruction of every building, and it was along this avenue that the most damage appears to have been caused. The 5th Shock Army had been sent 2,000 railway wagons of ammunition for its 2,000 guns and mortars of over 80mm calibre, and General Berzarin had given orders not to spare it.[37]

The third component of the 5th Shock Army, the 9th Rifle Corps, crossed

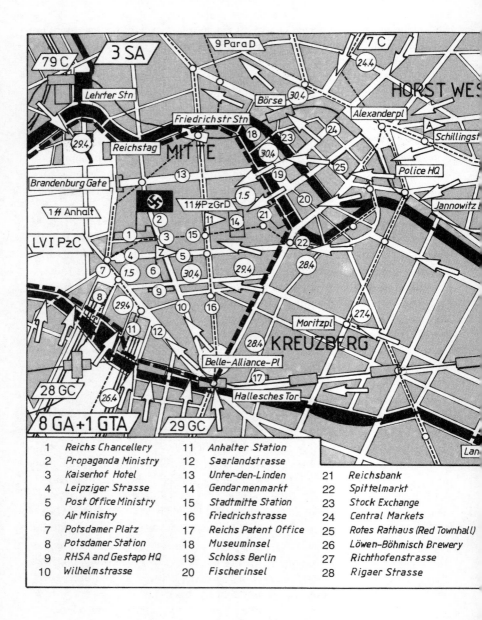

1	Reichs Chancellery	11	Anhalter Station	
2	Propaganda Ministry	12	Saarlandstrasse	
3	Kaiserhof Hotel	13	Unter-den-Linden	21 Reichsbank
4	Leipziger Strasse	14	Gendarmenmarkt	22 Spittelmarkt
5	Post Office Ministry	15	Stadtmitte Station	23 Stock Exchange
6	Air Ministry	16	Friedrichstrasse	24 Central Markets
7	Potsdamer Platz	17	Reichs Patent Office	25 Rotes Rathaus (Red Townhall)
8	Potsdamer Station	18	Museuminsel	26 Löwen-Böhmisch Brewery
9	RHSA and Gestapo HQ	19	Schloss Berlin	27 Richthofenstrasse
10	Wilhelmstrasse	20	Fischerinsel	28 Rigaer Strasse

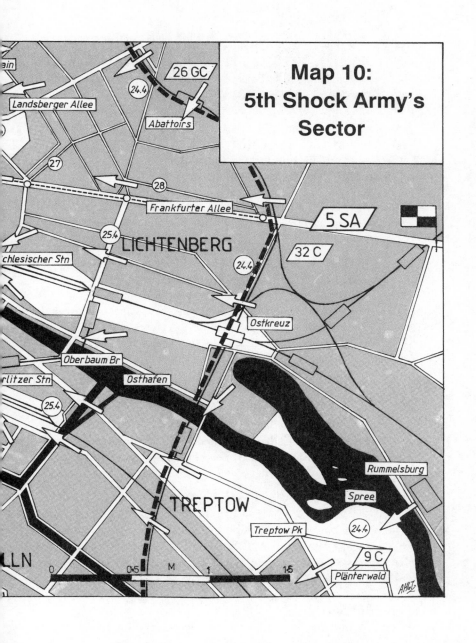

Map 10:
5th Shock Army's
Sector

26 GC

24.4

Landsberger Allee

Abattoirs

27

28

Frankfurter Allee

5 SA

25.4

LICHTENBERG

32 C

chlesischer Stn

24.4

Ostkreuz

Oberbaum Br

rlitzer Stn

Osthafen

25.4

Rummelsburg

Spree

TREPTOW

24.4

Treptow Pk

9 C

LLN

0   0·5   M   1   1·5   Plänterwald

AHG

the Spree into Treptow Park during the early hours of the morning, assisted by part of the 1st Brigade of the Dnieper Flotilla. Ten craft, described as semi-hydrofoils, had been delivered to Berlin by road, and these, together with 50 pontoons, 180 large and 70 small inflatable boats, were used to get 16,000 men, 100 guns and mortars, 27 tanks and 700 supply trucks across the Spree under fire.[38]

According to Soviet accounts the river crossing was opposed in strength, which was the result of the engineer battalion of the SS 'Nordland' Panzergrenadier Division coming to the support of the local defence.[39] The 9th Rifle Corps spent the rest of the day clearing Treptow 'island', being reinforced by the 220th Tank Brigade, and we have the following account of its activity on its southern flank on the road linking the 'island' to Britz:

> The defence was the work of the Volkssturm and some SS, using snipers. The Russians did their mopping up very cautiously and burnt with petrol all the houses from which they had been fired upon. Here the Russians used the following tactics; by day aircraft flew over the buildings where resistance was suspected and where they had spotted snipers posted on the roofs, dropping small-calibre bombs, or possibly clusters of hand grenades. Simultaneously the tanks advanced, slowly opening a passage with their fire. Behind the tanks came the infantry, usually about 30 to 40 men armed with submachine-guns. Behind the assault troops came other shock troops, who searched the houses to left and right. As soon as a cellar or building had been visited, the assault troops passed on, leaving one or two sentries.
>
> In Baumschulenstrasse there were one or two machine-guns, manned by two men, firing toward the station, and one or two armoured cars were dodging about in one of the sidestreets. These two pockets of resistance held up the Russian advance for about four hours.[40]

The 8th Guards Army, with the 1st Guards Army under its command, and therefore Marshal Zhukov's strongest striking force, was busy that day side-stepping to the west to get into position to attack Berlin from the south. However, their plans were unexpectedly modified as the result of a surprise encounter, which must have created a tremendous upheaval at Front and Army command levels. In the early hours of the morning some of Chuikov's troops traversing Schönefeld Airfield came across several tanks from the 3rd Guards Tank Army, thus linking up with the 1st Ukrainian Front. According to Chuikov, Zhukov did not apparently learn of this encounter until the evening and then acted disbelievingly, insisting that Chuikov send officers to discover what units of the 1st Ukrainian Front were involved, where they were located and what their objectives were.[41]

If, as it appears, this was Zhukov's first intimation of Koniev's participation in the battle for the city itself, we can imagine the consternation this report must have caused. Apart from the blow to Zhukov's pride, this incident clearly demonstrates the lack of communication among the Soviet leaders and their continuing mutual distrust. Having had his hand revealed, Stalin then laid down the interfront boundaries, which were to run from Lübben through Teupitz, Mittenwalde and Mariendorf to the Anhalter Railway Station. Within the city, this meant the line of the railway leading north from Lichtenrade.

Koniev was obviously aware of the GHQ order laying down the new interfront boundaries on the night of 22 April, when he issued his orders for the attack across the Teltow Canal and for the 71st Mechanized Brigade to cover the right flank and establish contact with the 1st Byelorussian Front. The boundary line, when extended beyond the Anhalter Railway Station, passed well to the east of the Reichstag, giving him the opportunity of reaching it first from the south. Somehow this GHQ order had been withheld from Zhukov, although it was effective from 0600 hours (Moscow time) on 23 April, and his balance of forces and reported reactions to the news of this encounter on Schönefeld Airfield clearly demonstrate how unprepared he was for this eventuality.[42]

Significantly Chuikov states, '... the 8th Guards Army, in whose front of advance formations of the 1st Guards Tank Army were also operating, was diverted by order of the Front Commander to the northwest – against the central sector of Berlin'.[43] This diversion led to the 28th and 29th Guards Rifle Corps wheeling right through Rudow, Buckow and Lichtenrade into Mariendorf, and closing up to the line of the Teltow Canal on the 24th, while the 4th Guards Rifle Corps crossed the Spree to clear the Königsheide part of Johannisthal 'island' before taking up position in Britz that evening. Co-operation with the 1st Guards Tank Army units was improved (Chuikov's choice of words does not indicate a happy relationship), and the night generally spent in preparing for next day's attack across the canal.[44]

The 3rd Guards Tank Army's assault across the Teltow Canal began with a 55-minute bombardment at 0420 hours on the 24th, each of the three corps having an attack line of about one mile. On the right flank in Lankwitz the attack by the 9th Mechanized Corps and 61st Guards Rifle Division had some initial success, but was then beaten back by German tanks and infantry, and their bridgehead eliminated with heavy loss. However, in the centre at Teltow, the 6th Guards Tank Corps' operation went well. Leading elements of the 22nd Guards Motorized Rifle Brigade went across the canal first in wooden boats or scrambled over the remains of a destroyed bridge. They established themselves on the opposite embankment and were joined by the rest of the brigade at 0500 hours. The 48th Guards Rifle Division then followed and enlarged the bridgehead. By 1100 hours the engineers had their first bridge ready to get guns and tanks across, and by the end of the day the corps had penetrated some one and a half miles, securing the southern half of Zehlendorf. Nearby, on the left flank at Stahnsdorf, the 7th Guards Tank Corps also succeed in establishing a small bridgehead, but against such fierce opposition that it was decided not to try to expand it further after the already partially destroyed bridge over the canal finally collapsed.[45] Koniev, who was directing the operation in person, did as he had done at the crossing of the Upper Spree and channelled all three corps through the successful bridgehead, even ordering the 10th Guards Tank Corps of the 4th Guards Tank Army to get its right wing across the same route to cover its attack on Potsdam.[46]

The resistance encountered at the Teltow and Stahnsdorf bridgeheads was due to the support provided to the local defence by the remains of the 20th Panzergrenadier Division, later followed by the arrival of elements of the 6,000 strong 18th Panzergrenadier Division, which still had two 'Tigers', 20 Panzer IVs and 25 APCs. The latter division was tasked with covering the Teltow Canal as part of an arc extending from the Anhalter Railway Station to the Olympic Stadium, with its 30th Panzergrenadier Regiment based in Dahlem, the 51st in Schöneberg, and the 118th Panzer Regiment in reserve. During the fighting the 20th Panzergrenadier Division, now down to only 92, all ranks, was driven back on Wannssee 'island', where it was effectively isolated from the rest of the defence, although it continued to preoccupy the 10th Guards Tank Corps until the very end of the battle. (Part of the latter division had become separated from the rest and re-formed on 25 April as a Panzer Brigade at Wutzetz, west of Fehrbellin, from where they became involved in the retreat of the 3rd Panzer Army.)[47]

In their advance on Potsdam the 10th Guards Tank Corps took the eastern suburbs without difficulty but found all the bridges leading across the Havel into the main part of the town had been destroyed. The 6th Guards Mechanized Corps continued its advance and penetrated the eastern suburbs of Brandenburg, taking the prison and releasing some prominent German communists incarcerated there.[48]

In the south the 13th Army reached Wittenberg on the Elbe that afternoon but ran into the encamped 'Ulrich von Hutten', 'Theodor Körner' and 'Scharnhorst' Infantry Divisions, which reacted so violently that Koniev was led to believe that Wenck's 12th Army was launching its anticipated counterattack, and therefore called in part of the 5th Guards Mechanized Corps and the 1st Air Attack Corps to assist. In fact, General Wenck was not yet ready to launch an attack, but the news of the fighting caused some concern in the 4th Guards Tank Army.[49]

Meanwhile, there was a surprise development in the 33rd Army's sector, whose bridgehead had been firmly contained by the V SS Mountain Corps since the beginning of the operation against all attempts to break out. That morning the 2nd Brigade of the Dnieper Flotilla laid a smokescreen across the Oder opposite Fürstenberg (Eisenhüttenstadt) and supported an attack by marine infantry and some troops of the 33rd Army on the town. The withdrawal of the V SS Mountain Corps had already begun, so presumably there could not have been much resistance, if any, to this assault.[50]

On 24 April Colonel-General A.V. Gorbatov's 3rd Army of the 1st Byelorussian Front linked up with the 1st Ukrainian Front's 28th Army at Teupitz, thereby completing the encirclement of the 9th Army in accordance with Stavka orders. Also that day the 2nd Air Army moved all but its bomber bases forward across the Neisse, the bombers still having ample range capacity for their operations in support of the 1st Ukrainian Front.[51]

Further south the intervention of the 5th Guards Army group under Koniev's Chief of Operations, General V.I. Kostylyov, who, in addition to the Chief-of-Staff, had been sent to resolve the situation, succeeded in checking Field Marshal Schörner's disruptive drive toward Spremberg. However, several more days of hard fighting were to ensue before the Germans were driven back. Lieutenant-General V.K. Baranov's 1st Guards Cavalry Corps took no part in this episode, for they were engaged on strictly private cavalry business. That day they reached the Elbe and prepared to make a foray across to recover the entire stock of one of the largest pedigree stud farms in the Soviet Union that had been removed from the Northern Caucasus by the Germans in 1942. The mission had been initiated by the famous Marshal Budyonny, an old friend of Stalin.[52]

As already mentioned, General Weidling's redeployment of the LVI Panzer Corps into the city the previous evening had helped to bolster the pitifully weak defence structure that he had found there upon taking up his new appointment. The 20th Panzergrenadier Division having been caught off balance and forced back on to Wannsee 'island', the 18th Panzergrenadier Division had to be taken out of reserve to replace it in the southwestern suburbs. This division established itself behind the chain of small lakes that extend from the Wannsee part of the Havel near Nikolassee toward the Westkreuz S-Bahn Station at the northern end of the Avus. This meant that it was in thick woods, completely outside the built-up area, but the divisional headquarters were collocated with the Defence Sector's in the flak-control tower in the Tiergarten. The 9th Parachute Division was sent to support the northern sectors and based itself on the Humboldthain flak-tower, from where it made a most useful contribution in blocking the 12th Guards and 7th Rifle Corps of the 3rd Shock Army. The 'Müncheberg' Panzer Division was assigned to assist with the defence of Tempelhof Airport but, being the only armoured formation, inevitably lost some of the few remaining tanks to other areas in difficulties, and the 11th SS 'Nordland' Panzergrenadier Division moved into Neukölln and the eastern end of Kreuzberg.[53]

Hopeful rumours continued to circulate, and Second-Lieutenant Walter Kroemer, a liaison officer on the staff of the 'Müncheberg' Panzer Division, recorded in his diary: 'News and rumours come from the Air Ministry of a successful attack toward Berlin by Wenck. Wenck's artillery can be heard on the Havel. Another army is breaking through to us from the north.'[54]

As we know, Wenck's army had yet to make a start and Steiner's seven battalions had been routed, but, in any case Weidling's staff were already secretly working on a plan to break out to west on the following lines:

    a. *A Spearhead* of all available tanks and the bulk of the divisions.

    b. *A Führer Group* with Hitler and the other VIPs from the Führerbunker, protected by one division.

    c. *A Rearguard* of one reinforced division.[55]

Late that evening, Hitler made some command decisions that showed that he had completely recovered from his breakdown of 22 April. He drafted an order for publication the next day that read:

1. The OKW is responsible to me for the conduct of all operations.
2. It will issue orders in accordance with my instructions, which I shall transmit through the OKH Chief-of-Staff now with me.
3. Command Staff 'A' under Grand Admiral Dönitz will not assume its function until notified.
4. The main task of the OKW is to re-establish broad contact with Berlin by attacking from the southwest, northeast and south, thus bringing the battle for Berlin to a victorious conclusion.

Hitler was to remain Supreme Commander, while Command Staff 'B' was given to Lieutenant-General Winter (not to Field Marshal Kesselring as previously considered) and would be directly subordinate to the OKW. These decisions, which ended the illogical OKW/OKH split of responsibilities, were greatly to Jodl's satisfaction as he had been trying to achieve this for some time, particularly as it made him, as OKW Chief-of-Staff, virtual head of the armed forces.[56]

That evening Colonel-General Ritter von Greim, commanding the 6th Air Fleet based on Munich, received orders from Hitler to report in person to the Führerbunker. He was puzzled by these instructions as he had not heard of Göring's disgrace, and first telephoned Koller, whom he knew to be at Berchtesgaden. Von Greim then decided that he should consult with Koller in person before attempting the hazardous flight to Berlin, but was unable to get away until the following morning, as continuous enemy attacks on his airfields were preventing aircraft from taking off.[57] That same evening Field Marshal Keitel revisited the XXXXI Panzer Corps, where General Holste blamed the tardiness of his redeployment to the east on the lack of transport.[58]

Back in Berlin General Weidling did his best to improve the existing defence structure by sacking incompetent commanders and reducing the number of Defence Sectors, but could do little that was effective at this late stage. Most of the remaining military and governmental establishments closed down, sending their personnel into the line to assist with the defence of 'Zitadelle'. The 5,000 boys of the Hitlerjugend Regiment, commanded by Obergebietsführer Dr Schlünder, with a few experienced officers and NCOs, were sent to hold the two southernmost of the three bridges leading over the Havel into Spandau with the primary aim of keeping the route open for Wenck's army's entry into the city.[59]

The Soviets appointed Colonel-General Nikolai Erastovitch Berzarin, commanding the 5th Shock Army, Soviet Commandant of Berlin and Commander of the Berlin Garrison. In Hermsdorf they set up their first civil administration with a German mayor.[60]

It will be noted that the Soviet encirclement of the city still contained many gaps. Despite their numbers, depleted though they had been in the fighting so far, the sheer size of the city made complete peripheral control impossible at this distance from the city centre. For instance, the 3rd Shock Army's three corps appear to have fought their battles in isolation from each other. The 79th Rifle Corps was separated from the rest by the Schiffahrts Canal, and there was a considerable gap between the 7th Rifle Corps advancing on the Alexanderplatz defences and the 12th Guards Rifle Corps in the centre. The latter seem to have adopted their normal open-country tactics in this situation, using the S-Bahn ring as a firm base-line from which to strike out at the enemy, in this case concentrating their efforts on the right wing down the Chaussee-strasse axis. This left a considerable area of no man's land for the antagonists to move around in, as we shall see, and one Soviet group claims to have penetrated as far as the Unter-den-Linden and held out for a week in sight of the Brandenburg Gate, well inside 'Zitadelle'.

7

THE NOOSE TIGHTENS

On the morning of 25 April, Colonel-General Heinrici visited General von Manteuffel, whose 3rd Panzer Army was now strained to breaking point trying to hold the 2nd Byelorussian Front on the Oder. He then went on to the headquarters of the 25th Panzergrenadier Division, where he found Colonel-General Jodl trying to persuade Steiner to launch an immediate attack for the relief of Berlin. Both Keitel and Jodl were primarily concerned with the relief of the capital and the rescue of Hitler, and were counting on the 3rd Panzer Army to hold firm in order to enable Steiner to attack southeast toward Spandau. Steiner was decidedly reluctant, producing many reasons why he should not comply immediately, much to the annoyance of the OKW leaders. He still had to receive two of the formations promised him: the 3rd Naval Division, which was strung out along the railway line from Swinemünde, and the 7th Panzer Division, which had arrived by sea from Danzig only a few days previously and was stuck in its assembly area near Neubrandenburg for lack of transport and fuel. The fall of Oranienburg had not affected the main issue, and Steiner was doing well, and all that could reasonably be expected of him under the circumstances, in holding the line of canals securing the 3rd Panzer Army's exposed southern flank and keeping both the 61st Army and the 1st Polish Army at bay.[1]

The lack of realism displayed by the OKW leaders was in direct contrast to the views of the generals in the field, evoking this comment from Heinrici:

> To get to their new command post from Berlin, Keitel and Jodl had passed interminable columns of fugitives and broken units during the night, and had been mixed up with them again during the course of the morning. During this journey they had probably seen for the first time the true picture known to every combatant, whether at the front or the rear. If their eyes had not been completely closed to the truth, they would undoubtedly have come to the conclusion there and then that the war had inexorably reached its end.[2]

Upon his return to his headquarters there was an urgent call from von Manteuffel reporting that the Soviets had breached his lines south of Stettin. Heinrici promptly authorized withdrawal in accordance with a detailed plan he had worked out previously, but not conveyed to the OKW, and specifically ordered the abandonment of the Stettin Festung. This was all done without reference to the OKW, although he immediately gave instructions that they were to be informed of his decisions, and 48 hours were to pass before a scandalized Keitel received the message.[3]

Some good news for Heinrici that day was the information that Colonel Biehler's Frankfurt-an-der-Oder Garrison had at last succeeded in breaking through to the 9th Army, a full three days after receiving Hitler's permission to do so. General Busse could now attempt his breakout to the west. His 'Kessel' (pocket) was now being harassed day and night from both land and air, and it was time to act if the people in his charge were to have a chance of escaping either death or capture at the hands of the Soviets.[4]

Busse ordered an immediate breakout spearheaded by Colonel Hans von Luck's Battle Group, based on his 125th Panzergrenadier Regiment, whose orders were:

> Tonight at 2000 hours you will attack with your battle group and all available armoured vehicles allocated to you westward over the Dresden–Berlin autobahn with the aim of reaching the Berlin–Leipzig autobahn in the Luckenwalde area in the rear of the 1st Ukrainian Front attacking Berlin. The breakout point is to be kept open to enable the following elements of the 9th Army to reach the west on foot. This is not open to the civilian population; thousands of refugees would hamper the operation.[5]

Simultaneously, the Pipkorn Battle Group, led by SS Colonel Rüdiger Pipkorn and consisting of the remains of his 35th SS Police Grenadier Division and elements of the 10th SS Panzer Division, were to strike out westward from Schrepzig, north of Lübben, their common goal being the road junction immediately north of Baruth from where a road ran to Luckenwalde.

The rest of the 9th Army was organized for the breakout as follows:

XI SS Panzer Corps
Facing the breakout line near and north of Halbe with all the remaining armoured vehicles.
V Corps
Supporting the breakthrough and covering the southern flank.

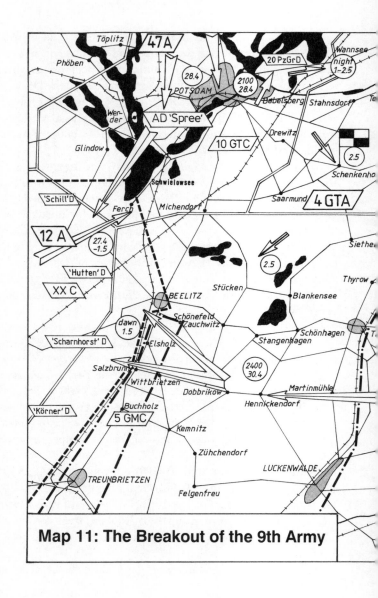

Map 11: The Breakout of the 9th Army

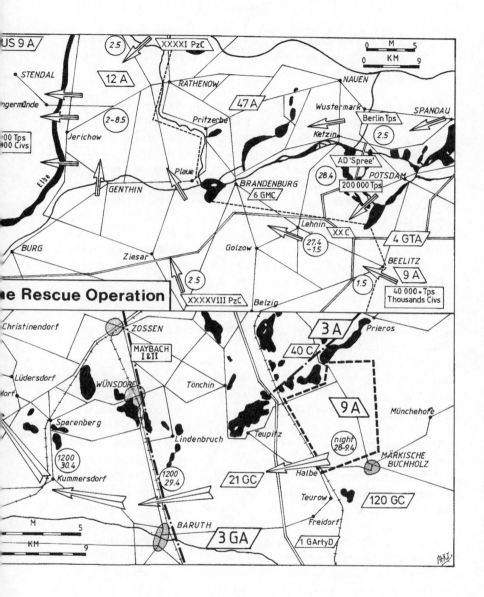

V SS Mountain Corps
Covering the breakout from the east and north, thereafter covering the rear of the breakthrough.

Von Luck's Battle Group struck at the junction of the 3rd Guards and 28th Armies, quickly overrunning the Soviet forward positions and crossing the autobahn. Before midnight they had reached the northern outskirts of Baruth, where fierce opposition was encountered on the parallel north–south lines of Route 96 and the railway. The Pipkorn Battle Group was severely mauled by flank attacks on its way west, and only a few tanks appear to have reached Baruth, where Pipkorn and von Luck joined forces. The Soviets had 'Stalin' tanks, some of them dug-in, and put up such a fierce fight that the Germans rapidly ran out of ammunition and fuel. Von Luck reported the hopelessness of the situation to General Busse by radio, but the latter ordered him to fight on. Von Luck then ordered his troops to try to fight their way out in small units, but decided that he would return to the cauldron to report with his adjutant and liaison officer rather than be accused of cowardice. Pipkorn was killed in the action and von Luck captured early on 27 April while still making his way back. Some of his men actually reached the Elbe, but most were either killed or captured.[6]

Fifty years later a former Red Army Corporal, Zvi Harry Glaser, described how his rifle section, part of the 438th Rifle Regiment of the 129th 'Orel' Rifle Division of the 3rd Army, had taken up defensive positions in open ground at the east end of Halbe. Some white flags were seen at the edge of the woods nearby and, as a German speaker, he was sent forward to negotiate, but before he had gone halfway the flags disappeared. This was apparently the work of 'Seydlitz-Troops' who had been about to organize a surrender and then were stopped and executed by Waffen–SS or other loyal troops.

German tanks and infantry then conducted an attack that forced the Soviets out of the village by nightfall. Glaser's battalion spent the next day recovering and, having received reinforcements, returned in preparation for a dawn attack to recover the village with the support of some 'Katyusha' multiple-barrelled rocket-launchers and T-34 tanks.

Early the following morning the 'Katyushas' softened up the German positions for ten minutes, then Glaser's section climbed on to the leading tank, which took them toward the woods where the remains of the pocket were concentrated, stopping 100 metres short to avoid being hit by Panzerfausts. The section then jumped off and charged forwards. A few gunshots were all the resistance that was encountered from the remaining German soldiers. One was shot, the others dropped their weapons and raised their hands. Further on a whole mass of Germans stood up with raised hands, obeying the order for the prisoners to assemble in groups. Another part of the same platoon as Glaser's section was responsible for capturing Colonel von Luck that morning.[7]

The 25th also saw the historic link-up of the Soviets and the Americans on the Elbe, when the 5th Guards Army's 58th Guards Rifle Division encountered patrols from the 69th Infantry Division of the American 1st Army near Torgau. Germany was thus split horizontally in two, but when Hitler learnt of this meeting and that the Soviets had apparently hesitated before stopping their advance, he concluded that discord reigned among the Allies and predicted an early outbreak of hostilities between the Anglo-Americans and the Soviets.[8]

At noon that day General Weidling issued his revised command organization instructions for the defence of the city, which were based on the deployment of the LVI Panzer Corps already effected.[9] The Defence Sectors were to be grouped and commanded as follows:

'A' and 'B' (East)
    Major-General Mummert, now nominal Corps Commander.
'C' (Southeast)
    SS Major-General Ziegler of the SS 'Nordland' Panzergrenadier Division.
'D' (astride Tempelhof Airport)
    Colonel Wöhlermann, the Corps Artillery Commander.
'E' (Southwest and Grunewald Forest)
    Commander 20th Panzergrenadier Division but, due to the developments previously referred to, the same day replaced by Major General Rauch of the 18th Panzergrenadier Division. (Two days later the 20th Panzergrenadier Division was transferred to Army Detachment 'Spree'.)[10]
'F' (Spandau and Charlottenburg)
    Colonel Eder.
'G' and 'H' (North)
    Colonel Herrmann, Commander 9th Parachute Division.
'Z' ('Zitadelle')
    Lieutenant-Colonel Seifert.

Despite General Weidling's nomination as Defence Commandant, the division of responsibility on the ground was not as clear-cut as appears above. The basic problem lay with relationships between the Wehrmacht and the

Waffen-SS, which were often hostile. Lieutenant-Colonel Seifert was responsible for 'Zitadelle', but within that sector SS Major-General Mohnke was responsible directly to Hitler for the defence of the Reichs Chancellery, his command including the SS 'Anhalt' Regiment, the other *ad hoc* SS regiment previously mentioned and those elements of Commander Kuhlmann's 'Grossadmiral Dönitz' Battalion that had arrived. Mohnke did not consider either himself or his troops answerable to General Weidling. Seifert had troops of his own under command, such as the 'Nord-West' Regiment, and various *ad hoc* units of Volkssturm, military stragglers and sailors, but there was a constant, distrustful overlap with the Waffen-SS units in the city centre.[11]

The anticipated meeting between the 4th Guards Tank Army and the 47th Army also took place that morning, when elements of the 6th Guards Mechanized Corps met with troops of the 328th Rifle Division and the 65th Guards Tank Brigade near Ketzin, somewhat later than Krukenberg's account would have led us to expect, but again illustrating the extreme caution with which this operation was conducted by the troops on the ground.[12]

The 125th Rifle Corps continued with attacks on Spandau and Gatow Airfield. They succeeded in isolating the Spandau defence, which consisted mainly of *ad hoc* units, Volkssturm and Hitlerjugend under the command of SS Obergruppenführer (Police General) August Heissmeyer, cutting them off from the Havel and the rest of the Berlin garrison. The Gatow defence continued to hold their ground, and it would appear that overall the Soviet forces deployed west of the Havel were inadequate in numbers for their role, the various objectives being too diversified to enable effective strength to be brought to bear in response to the situation.[13]

Air Chief Marshal Novikov mounted a special operation on 25 and 26 April, massing aircraft to maintain heavy bombing of the city in what he called 'Operation Salute'. The first strike was by 100 heavy bombers of the 18th Air Army, followed by waves of bombers throughout the day from the 16th Air Army. In all 1,368 aircraft took part, including 569 dive-bombers (PE-2s), which were given specific targets to attack.[14]

The two armoured corps of the 2nd Guards Tank Army were involved in a hard struggle to clear the modern industrial suburb of Siemensstadt, in which the scarcity of supporting infantry led to allegedly severe losses. The attack into the built-up area was not launched until 1430 hours that day and it was to take them until 28 April to close up to the line of the Spree. Their opponents appear to have been mainly local Volkssturm backed by some *ad hoc* Wehrmacht units and a few tanks from the 11th SS 'Hermann von Salza'

1. Prime Minister Winston Churchill, President Franklin D. Roosevelt and Generalissimo Joseph Stalin at the Yalta Conference in February 1945. (*Chronos*)

2. The last pictures of Adolf Hitler were taken on the occasion of his 56th birthday when he emerged from the Führerbunker to meet and address a small parade of representatives of the Hitler jugend, Waffen-SS and Kurland Army. Reichsjugendführer Arthur Axmann is on the left with SS Lieutenant-General Hermann Fegelein behind between Axmann and Hitler. (*Chronos*)

3. Marshal Georgi Konstantinovitch
Zhukov. C-in-C 1st Byelorussian Front.
Deputy Supreme C-in-C Red Army.

4. Marshal Ivan Stepanovitch
Koniev. C-in-C 1st Ukrainian Front.

5. Colonel-General Nikolai Berzarin
GOC 5th Shock Army
First Soviet Commandant of Berlin.

6. Colonel-General Vassili Chuikov
GOC 8th Guards Army.

6a. Soviet Commanders conferring over the bonnet of a jeep during the street fighting.
(plates 3-6a, Chronos)

7. Armaments Minister Albert Sheer discussing the situation on the Oder Front with Colonel-General Gotthardt Heinrici. *(Hartmut Heinrici)*

8. Dr Joseph Goebels, Reichs Defence Commissar and Gauleiter of Berlin, addressing troops in Lauban. General Theodor Busse, wearing a field cap, is on the right. (*Chronos)*

9. General of Panzertroops Walter Wenck, GOC 12th Army. (*author's collection*)

10. Field Marshal Ferdinand Schörner, C-in-C Army Group 'Mitte'. (*author's collection*)

11. SS-General Felix Steiner, GOC IIIrd SS 'Germanic' Panzer Corps. (*author's collection*)

12. General Helmuth Weidling GOC LVIth Panzer Corps. Last Commander Berlin Defence Area. (*Chronos*)

13. SS-Major General Dr Gustav Krukenberg, GOC 32nd SS 'Nordland' Panzergrenadier Division. (*author's collection*)

14. Luftwaffe Colonel Harry Herrmann. Last Commander 9th Parachute Division. (*Wegner*)

15. Colonel Hans-Oskar Wöhlermann, Commander Artillery LVIth Panzer Corps. (*Chronos*)

16. Women digging trenches for the defence of the city. *(Bildarchiv Preussische Kulturbesitz)*

17. Men digging antitank ditches. *(Chronos)*

18. The Zoo flak-tower from the north. Crowned with eight 128mm guns and twelve multi-barrelled 20mm or 37mm 'pom-poms', this bunker formed the core of the defence south of the Landwehr Canal. *(Chronos)*

19. The barricades on Schloss Bridge, looking down Unter den Linden with the Zeughaus on the right and the boxed-in equestrian figure of Frederick the Great in the distance. *(Chronos)*

20. Barricades at the Knie end of Bismarckstrasse. *(Landesbildstelle Berlin)*

21. A Soviet soldier surveys one of the many water obstacles confronting the Red Army in Berlin. *(Jacques de Launay)*

22. The dreaded 'Stalin-Organs' come into the city. *(Chronos)*

23. A tracked, self-propelled 203 mm Soviet field gun in action. *(Chronos)*

24. Divisional artillery firing down a street. *(Chronos)*

25. Horse-drawn artillery moving up. *(Chronos)*

26. A Soviet howitzer battery in action in the city. *(Chronos)*

27. Soviet heavy mortar battery firing on Kaiser-Wilhelm-Platz in Schöneberg. *(Chronos)*

28. An American-made 'Sherman' tank of the 2nd Guards Tank Army flying the Red flag. *(Chronos)*

29. An obsolete T34–76 taking part in the battle. *(Chronos)*

30. Wrecked Soviet armour on the Charlottenburger Chausse where the Polish
infantry crossed in their attack on the Technical High School. *(Chronos)*

31. Soviet infantry and armour cooperating closely on the Berlin streets. *(Chronos)*

32. Soviet infantry crossing a street under fire. The gun positioned next to the lamppost demonstrates how closely the various arms had to work in the combat teams. The air is thick with smoke and dust. *(Landesbildstelle Berlin)*

33. Soviet SU–76 assault gun firing at point-blank range. *(Landesbildstelle Berlin)*

34. Soviet wounded being evacuated under fire by dog sledge. *(Chronos)*

35. A Soviet casualty. *(Chronos)*

36. Aftermath of the 9th Army's break-out from the Halbe pocket, in which some 40,000 soldiers and civilians were killed. *(Chronos)*

37. A destroyed gun team in the Halbe woods. *(Chronos)*

38. Stalin II tanks under fire at the Moltke Bridge, turrets closed. The demolition hole is indicated by the missing parapet. Two SU-100s and a T-34/85 have their guns trained on the far bank, and a dog sledge for evacuating wounded can be seen on the centre left. *(Bildarchiv Preussische Kulturbesitz)*

39. Looking down Moltkestrasse during the battle for the Reichstag with the Ministry of the Interior building burning on the right and the Reichstag in the distance. *(Chronos)*

40. The Reichstag after the battle, seen across the flooded obstacle with wrecked Soviet tanks on Moltkestrasse. *(Chronos)*

41. Captain V.N. Makov re-enacting the planting of the first Red Flag to be raised on the roof of the Reichstag with one of his gunners. *(Chronos)*

42. The staged hoisting of the official 'Red Banner No. 5' of the 150th Rifle Division by Sergeants M.A. Yegorov and M.V. Kantaria on the rear parapet of the Reichstag. *(Chronos)*

43. A wrecked armoured personnel carrier of the 3rd (Swedish) Company of the 11th Armoured Reconnaissance Battalion, 11th SS 'Nordland' Panzergrenadier Division after the abortive break-out over the Weidendamm Bridge. *(Westberg)*

44. German soldiers surrendering from a U-Bahn station. *(Chronos)*

45. General Weidling with senior staff officers after the surrender. From the left is retired General Schmid-Dankward, a police medical officer of general rank, Weidling, retired General Woytasch and Colonel Refior. *(Chronos)*

46. Colonel Theodor von Dufving, General Weidling's Chief of Staff and negotiator of his surrender, being interrogated afterwards. *(Chronos)*

47. Red Army soldiers celebrating their victory in the Lustgarten in front of the Altes Museum. *(Chronos)*

48. German youths being led away into the frightening uncertainty of Soviet captivity. *(Olle Björnfjell)*

49. German wounded being cleared from the Hotel Adlon under the eyes of a young Soviet soldier (left background). *(Chronos)*

50. German wounded awaiting collection from the centre of the Unter-den-Linden, after the surrender. *(Chronos)*

51. The Brandenburg Gate from Pariser Platz, showing a Soviet tank, officers in a jeep and a Panjewagen. *(Chronos)*

52. The Brandenburg Gate from Hindenburg Platz with Soviet armour and a captured German Kubelwagen. *(Chronos)*

53. Field Marshal Wilhem Keitel, accompanied by Luftwaffe-General Hans-Jürgen Stumpf and Admiral Hans-Georg von Friedeburg, at Karlshorst on 8 May 1945 for the signing of the capitulation of the German Armed Forces. *(Chronos)*

54. The Soviet War Memorial unveiled on the edge of the Reichstag battlefield on 11 November 1945, and incorporating the 2,200 Red Army soldiers killed there. *(Chronos)*

Panzer Battalion. The night of 25 April they were assigned the 2nd Polish Heavy Artillery Brigade and the 6th Polish Pontoon-Bridging Battalion in recognition of their difficult role.[15]

The 3rd Shock Army's 79th Rifle Corps crossed the Hohenzollern Canal at the Plötzensee Locks at dawn on 25 April under cover of a heavy artillery barrage. They took the prison and cleared the north bank of the Westhafen Canal but found that they could get no further. The canal extended right across their front, and the Königsdamm Bridge, which provided the only practical route forward to Moabit 'island', had been blown. The wreckage had been mined and obstructed so that it could only take five men at a time. The northern bank of the canal was fully exposed to crossfire from the enemy defences, which had been prepared to a depth of 200 yards from the canal to the parallel line of the S-Bahn. The S-Bahn stations had been developed as strongpoints, and the burnt-out warehouses around the quays provided further vantage points for the defence. After some suicidal attempts to force the bridge had failed, the Soviets were obliged to wait until darkness provided some degree of cover for the engineers to start clearing the way. During the night artillery and heavy machine-guns were brought up to the edge of the canal in preparation for further attempts the following day.[16]

Meanwhile the 12th Guards Rifle Corps crossed into Moabit by the Fenn Bridge at the Nordhafen, securing the bridge against possible counterattacks from that direction, but not going any further toward outflanking the Westhafen position. Hampered by the Humboldthain flak-tower position in the centre of their lines, they were to spend the next few days caught up in costly street-fighting among the factories and densely packed tenement blocks north of Invalidenstrasse. Reinforced by the remnants of the 9th Parachute Division, the defence in this area proved both tenacious and aggressive.

The 7th Rifle Corps fought their way right up to the edge of Alexanderplatz on 25 April, thereby coming up against the eastern bastion of 'Zitadelle', where the defences were based on the massively constructed Police Presidium, Hertie's department store, the S-Bahn station and the two-storey-deep U-Bahn station. Initially the defence had proved so weak in the southeastern approaches to this area that General Weidling had been obliged to commit some of his precious tanks and a battalion of the SS 'Anhalt' Regiment, to bolster the local resources, and SS Colonel Günther Anhalt was killed by shellfire while visiting the Police Presidium that day. However, this probe by the 7th Rifle Corps appears to have run into difficulties, for Alexanderplatz was eventually to be taken by the 5th Shock Army, while most of the area between there and the S-Bahn ring to the north remained in German hands until the end of the battle.[17]

The 5th Shock Army continued to make slow progress toward the city centre against determined resistance. On the right flank the 26th Guards Rifle Corps slowly worked its way through the dense housing either side of Frankfurter Allee toward the Friedrichshain flak-tower position.

One of the German units opposing this move, the 3/115th Siemensstadt Volkssturm Battalion was obliged to evacuate its overnight positions on Samariterstrasse by 0800 hours, having come under attack from both the south and east. Now down to only 50 rifles and two LMGs, the battalion joined the remains of other Volkssturm, Wehrmacht and police units in the defence of the west side of Richthofenstrasse (Auerstrasse) with their backs to the St Georg Cemetery and the flak-tower beyond. Despite the firing that went on day and night, neutral ground was found at the well on Richthofenstrasse on the junction with Friedenstrasse and Pallisadenstrasse, where both sides drew water under cover of darkness without disturbing each other.[18]

In the centre the 32nd Rifle Corps came up against a hard core of defence based on the Schlesischer Railway Station (Hauptbahnhof), whose broad tracks and sidings provided ample fields of fire for the defenders and enabled them to keep the attacking armour and infantry at bay for several days. The fight for this station was regarded by Marshal Zhukov as one of the 5th Shock Army's two most difficult tasks in this operation (the other being the forth-coming crossing of the Spree in the city centre). Soviet accounts of the attack on the Schlesicher Railway Station give the defence as being about 1,000–1,400 strong and using two bunkers several stories high, but the latter were in fact passive air raid shelters and totally unsuited for defensive positions. As the Soviet troops took the buildings around the station, they signalled their presence by hoisting red flags on the roofs, only to have them shot down again by the defence. The 89th and 266th Rifle Divisions of the 26th Guards Rifle Corps, and the 60th Guards Rifle Division of the 32nd Rifle Corps were involved in this action.

In Marshal Zhukov's Order No. 69 issued that day, the 5th Shock Army's left-hand boundary with the 8th Guards Army was defined as following the line of the Britzer-Zweig and Landwehr Canals to Potsdamer Railway Station.[19]

The Schlesicher Station was in fact defended by SS Captain Mrugalla's 1st Battalion of the SS 'Anhalt' Regiment, which had been detached in support of this Defence Sector and had made an advance to contact in this direction the previous day, supported by two 'Panther' tanks of the 'Müncheberg'

Panzer Division. They were now joined by the mortar platoon under SS Sergeant-Major Willi Rogmann, who placed his six 80mm mortars on the elevated S-Bahn tracks east of the Jannowitzbrücke S-Bahn Station, where the structure below provided a strong protective casement for his men. The 50 or so Hitlerjugend, who had insisted on supporting him, he placed in a suitable covering location nearby. Meanwhile his supporting Volkssturm company delivered about 500 bombs and went back for more. Soon afterward his deputy, whom he had sent forward as the mortar observer, reported a mass of Soviet infantry approaching, escorted by tanks, a prime target for the mortars. The ensuing barrage ripped the Soviet infantry apart as the bombs splintered on the roadway, but once his supply of bombs had been used up, retaliation was not long in coming. Rogmann and one of his NCOs were still above ground among the mortars when they heard the incoming salvo. They grabbed a mortar each and dived down into the casemate, where the other members of the platoon were sheltering. These were the only mortars to survive the Soviet bombardment, which also eliminated all the Hitlerjugend except for the four that had escorted the observer and returned safely with him.

Rogmann then withdrew some distance back toward Alexanderplatz to redeploy. While looking around his new location, he found a large cellar full of rockets, even larger than 'Stalin-Organs', stored in their wooden cases that also doubled as launchers. They looked so dangerous that he moved his platoon again, but then encountered a lone ordnance officer, who seemed to know all about the rockets and, under pressure, showed Rogmann how to use them. Rogmann then tried one out – it took eight men to move it – firing it in the direction of the Schlesischer Railway Station. The test proving apparently satisfactory, Rogmann then set up several against a barricade of sandstone blocks that had been built across Holzmarktstrasse, the main road leading from the station past the Jannowitzbrücke S-Bahn Station to Alexanderplatz. At dusk about a dozen Soviet tanks were seen approaching along Holzmarkt-strasse, and Rogmann fired his rockets at what he guessed was the right moment. The effect was devastating, with some tanks collapsing as if they had been made of cardboard, others brushed aside as scrap, and one even falling in the river. This time there was no retaliation, for the Soviet observers had failed to spot the discharge.[20]

On the other side of the river the 9th Rifle Corps forced the Landwehr Canal from Treptow and then became involved in heavy fighting around Görlitzer Railway Station, which dominated the centre of its front.[21]

At dawn on 25 April, under cover of a tremendous artillery barrage,

Chuikov threw his 8th Guards and 1st Guards Tank Armies (a total of three infantry and two armoured corps) across the Teltow Canal with the seizure of Tempelhof Airport as his main objective. The airfield was roughly one mile square, with a massive arc of hangars and administrative buildings in the northwest corner covering a complex of underground hangars and cellars where aircraft were known to be on stand-by to fly out the remaining Nazi leaders. The airfield defence included a strong Luftwaffe Flak unit with its guns readily convertible to the anti-tank role, the normal base personnel organized as infantry, Major Baechle's Hitlerjugend tank-hunting unit mounted in jeeps and equipped with Panzerfausts, and the bulk of the 'Müncheberg' Panzer Division. The southern edge of the airfield was skirted by the S-Bahn ring, thus forming part of the Inner Defence Ring, and had some of the garrison's fuelless tanks dug in along the southern and eastern edges of the perimeter. The Inner Defence Ring and the banks of the canal, which constituted the fallback position for the defenders of the Outer Defence Ring, were held by the usual miscellany of local defence units, including the 'Skorning' Combat Group. The banks of the canal were lined with industrial premises, and the focus of the local defence here appears to have been astride the Stubenrauch Bridge on the main Mariendorf–Tempelhof road, where the Ullstein printing works on the south bank and the Lorenz factory bunker on the north bank had been turned into strongpoints. The Mussehl Bridge in the centre had been blown up the previous night. The charges on the Neukölln–Mittenwalde railway bridge failed to function but, fortunately for the defence, the bridge was too narrow for tanks to cross.[22]

The attack on the airfield itself was conducted by the 28th Guards Rifle Corps, supported by two of the 1st Guards Tank Army's brigades, with the 39th Guards Rifle Division on the left, the 79th Guards Rifle Division on the right, and the 88th Guards Rifle Division mopping up the centre. Artillery fire was used to keep the runways clear, and as the Soviets did not know the exact location of the underground hangars and their exits, some combat groups with tanks were given the specific task of ensuring that no aircraft should escape. During the course of the first day the Soviets overran the two local defence lines and managed to get on to the airfield, but the main defence held. Second-Lieutenant Kroemer of the 'Müncheberg' Panzer Division recorded:

> Early morning. We are at Tempelhof Airport. Russian artillery is firing without respite. We need infantry reinforcements, and we get motley emergency units. Behind the lines the civilians are still trying to get away right under the Russian artillery fire, dragging along some wretched bundle containing all they have left in the world.

The Russians burn their way into the buildings with flame-throwers. The screams of the women and children are terrible.

1500 hours. We have barely a dozen tanks and 30 armoured personnel carriers. These are all the armoured vehicles left in the Government Sector. The chain of command seems all mixed up. We consistently get orders from the Chancellery to send tanks to some danger spot or other, and they never come back. So far only General Mummert's determination has kept us from being expended. We have hardly any vehicles left for carrying the wounded.

Afternoon. Our artillery withdraws to new positions. They have little ammunition left. The howling and explosions of the 'Stalin-Organs', the screaming of the wounded, the roar of engines and the rattle of machine-guns. Dead women in the streets, killed while trying to get water. But also, here and there, women with Panzerfausts, Silesian girls thirsting for revenge.[23]

To the left of the main action the 29th Guards Rifle Corps, supported by the 8th Guards Mechanized Corps, crossed the Teltow Canal in the sector between the Tempelhofer Dam and the railway line marking the interfront boundary. On the right flank the 4th Guards Rifle Corps, supported by the 11th Guards Tank Corps, crossed into Neukölln. It seems that both these flank attacks met only local defence resistance, and that the 4th Guards Rifle Corps did not come up against the 11th SS 'Nordland' Panzergrenadier Division until the following day. Nevertheless, the sheer size of the terrain meant that all points could not be covered by the Soviet advance, for Lieutenant-Colonel Skorning reports that he was with the remains of his battalion on the Neukölln sportsfields on 25 April and was able to communicate with his Defence Sector Headquarters, which were located in an air raid shelter opposite Tempelhof town hall. He was also able to inform the Flak divisional headquarters in the Tiergarten of a deserted but intact 88 mm flak battery position on the adjacent southeastern corner of the airfield, as a result of which a Flak officer and 20 men appeared to man the guns that night, but disappeared again by morning.[24]

Having first reported to General Krebs, who sent him on to General Weidling at his Hohenzollerndamm headquarters, SS Major-General Krukenberg was instructed to take over the 11th SS 'Nordland' Panzergrenadier Division from SS Major-General Ziegler, whom Weidling wanted replaced, for although Ziegler had been an outstanding commander, highly respected by his men, it seems that Weidling now regarded him as spent. The division had started the battle reduced to brigade size with its component regiments, the 23rd 'Norge' and the 24th 'Danmark' Panzergrenadier Regiments, down to between 600 and 700 men each. Krukenberg's 300 French volunteers from the former 33rd SS 'Charlemagne' Panzergrenadier Division therefore made a most welcome addition.[25]

According to Krukenberg, his arrival was expected by Ziegler, who warned him that the defensive situation was untenable and that Krukenberg would be unlikely to retain the command for another 24 hours. Krukenberg's arrival with a strong French SS escort, which promptly sealed off the area, gave rise to the suspicion that Ziegler was being arrested, but this was not the case. The handover of command having taken place, Ziegler drove off to the Reichs Chancellery with his driver and Adjutant, SS Major Alfred Bergfeld, where he was retained in 'Führer-Reserve' for the remainder of the battle.

Shortly after Ziegler's departure, two or three APCs arrived from the front filled with wounded, looking for a hospital. The French tried to stop them and when they failed to stop, one of the Frenchmen fired at the first APC. The co-driver in the APC, presumably taking the Frenchmen to be 'Seydlitz Troops', returned the fire with his machine-gun, wounding three or four of them.[26]

Again according to Krukenberg, when he arrived he was horrified to learn that Ziegler had only 70 men on duty in the line, the remainder being exhausted and resting. He then sent for the rest of his Frenchmen from the Olympic Stadium, and went on to call on the local Volkssturm commander, whom he found in an observation post in the towering Karstadt department store on Hermannplatz, from where he could see Soviet tanks approaching. Krukenberg then ordered half his French anti-tank team to assist the Volkssturm, and by the next morning they had accounted for 14 Soviet tanks between them.[27]

There was a hospital for French prisoners-of-war in Neukölln not far from the Landwehr Canal, and one of their doctors recalled the events of that day:

> I spent long periods at the window of my observation post. In the street there were several women with shopping bags, some files of soldiers keeping close to the walls and armoured vehicles passing to and fro. The 88mm gun on Weichselstrasse continued firing ceaselessly. Russian squadrons flew in a sky clear of German aircraft, but toward Tempelhof Airport the light flak was still in evidence. On the right the smoke of an enormous fire hid the two 80-metre-high towers of the large Karstadt department store that dominated the quarter.
>
> The battle was now very close for, particularly on the left, one could hear the rattle of automatic weapons. The Russian attack seemed to be following

two almost perpendicular axes; along the canal toward Tempelhof and along the Ring toward Hermannplatz. In the latter direction the signs of a German collapse were evident, numerous small detachments passing the hospital leading toward the city centre.

We hoped that the decision would not be long delayed, as our problems were mounting by the hour. We already had 300 sick prisoners to feed and care for.

The water supplies were running out and we did not know what to do about making the soup. We moved in the cellar with difficulty in almost total darkness. The situation of the seriously ill was particularly bad; they were lying on stretchers or even thin mattresses ranked side by side on the floor. The execution of medical attention or even simple hygiene became extremely difficult. The congestion was made even worse by the many German wounded being too ill to move after the initial bandaging.

The operating theatre had had to be moved long before because of the shelling, and we had improvised one in the former cloakroom, where amputations were carried out on an old wooden table covered with a mattress. The surgeons operated without gloves, practically without antiseptics, and with instruments hardly boiled. Everything was defective or exhausted. It was impossible to change one's overalls and even washing one's hands became a problem. The oil lamps were dead and the last candles consumed. Fortunately we had found two bicycles equipped with electric lights, and the pedals turned by hand provided sufficient illumination for the operating table. The Germans were grouped in some rooms under the meagre care of some local women who had offered their assistance.

A young French conscript appeared with a broken arm. He had failed in an attempt to escape with two comrades from Tempelhof Airport in a Fieseler 'Storch'. Having a pilot's licence and working for Lufthansa, he had long planned his escape but some security measures unknown to him had caused it to crash on take-off. He had been imprisoned at Alexander-platz (Police Presidium) awaiting trial, when the Russian advance resulted in the Germans throwing open the prison doors!

The hospital staff faced up to the situation with courage, volunteers from the sick replacing those few defaulters paralysed with fear who dared not leave the corners where they had gone to ground.[28]

At dusk more tanks rolled on to the airfield carrying infantry to sustain the attack, but the defence held and the hangars and administrative buildings remained in German hands.

This was a hard but successful day for the 3rd Guards Tank Army as they learned to adjust to street-fighting in the extensive garden suburbs of southwest Berlin. All night the troops, tanks and guns poured across the main bridgehead and deployed to their respective sectors. There had been no time to train or prepare for this phase. The infantry and armour had to learn to work closely together under novel conditions, the lessons proving expensive in both men and material. Later they would have to adapt to fighting under the more exacting conditions imposed by the densely built-up areas of the central districts. Gradually, as with the 1st Byelorussian Front, combat teams combining all arms were evolved. However, sheer weight of numbers told, and by the end of the day the 3rd Guards Tank Army with elements of the 28th Army's 20th and 128th Rifle Corps was well advanced toward the S-Bahn ring. The 9th Mechanized Corps, supported by the 61st Rifle Division, was through Steglitz and almost into Schöneberg on the right; the 6th Guards Tank Corps, supported by the 48th Guards Rifle Division, having quickly disposed of the heavy flak battery that opposed it in Königin-Luise-Platz opposite the Botanical Gardens, was almost into Schmargendorf in the centre; and on the left the 7th Guards Tank Corps, supported by the 20th Rifle Division, having secured the southern belt of suburbs as far west as Nikolassee, was heading up through Dahlem and had taken the Luftwaffe's Luftgau-kommando III complex on the way.[29] The fighting in this sector was very uneven, some areas having no form of defence whatsoever. Consequently various areas survived virtually unscathed while others suffered serious damage, for the Soviets reacted strongly whenever resistance was encountered.[30]

The task of covering the left flank of the main force and clearing first Zehlendorf and then the Grunewald forests was given to Colonel David Dragunsky's 55th Guards Tank Brigade, which was only 1,500 strong and having to use as infantry tank crews that had lost their tanks. It was later augmented by two companies from the 23rd Guards Motorized Rifle Brigade.[31] It is clear that the 3rd Guards Tank Army was being concentrated in a northeasterly thrust aimed directly at the Reichstag, for Koniev was determined to beat Zhukov to the prize. The rivalry between the two front commanders was reflected in their adjacent army commanders, between whom there was simply no communication of any kind, leading to some extraordinary and absurd situations. Stalin, having made his point to Marshal Zhukov with the introduction of Koniev's troops to the scene, now saw to it that Koniev's ambitions would be thwarted in turn, but neither yet knew of this, and the rivalry was to continue along these lines almost to the very end of the fighting.

The difficulties of aircraft co-ordination over such a congested battlefield soon became apparent with some embarrassing 'own goals'. An appeal was made to GHQ over the interfront boundary, which was then changed to run along the line Mittenwalde/Tempelhof (Goods Station)/Potsdamer Railway Station, all points being inclusive to the 1st Ukrainian Front, but by the time this came through part of the 9th Mechanized Corps was already east of this line and had to be recalled. It seems that GHQ was content to play the role of arbitrator in these interfront matters, rather than act as a co-ordinator.[32]

The 4th Guards Tank Army continued fighting at the approaches to Potsdam and Brandenburg, and made its long-awaited meeting with the 47th Army, as previously related. The 5th Guards Mechanized Corps and the 13th Army maintained pressure on Wenck's extended lines with the aid of the 2nd Air Army's 1st Air Attack Corps.[33]

During this period the energy of the defence varied considerably, despite Goebbels' efforts with whip and carrot. However, as the lines contracted the relative strength of the defenders, despite casualties, was gradually increasing, together with the proportion of experienced personnel. One of the officers at the Reichs Chancellery reported on 25 April that desertion continued to be rife among the Volkssturm but that the Hitlerjugend gave repeated proof of their courage and devotion, and that the regular units were fighting with calm resolution. It was noticed that the Soviets seemed to be deliberately picking on positions manned by the Volkssturm, which they then took fairly easily as a preliminary to attacking neighbouring positions from the flank and rear. They were also suspected of using German deserters as spies and guides.[34]

On 25 April Colonel-General Ritter von Greim visited General Koller at Berchtesgaden and discussed the situation with him. He did not share Koller's view on Göring's innocence in the affair of 23 April but promised to deliver Koller's plea of mitigation on Göring's behalf to the Führer in person. He then flew back to Munich, where he recruited a willing companion for his hazardous trip to Berlin, the famous female test pilot, Hanna Reitsch.[35] Hanna, a devotee of Hitler's, flew von Greim to Rechlin that night, hoping to find a helicopter there that could take them on to Berlin and land them somewhere near the Reichs Chancellery. However, the only remaining machine had been damaged and they were obliged to wait until daylight for an aircraft and escort to be arranged for them.[36]

The ammunition situation was now desperate for the few guns and tanks remaining. With both Gatow and Tempelhof Airfields under fire, it was decided to clear an airstrip on the East–West Axis in the Tiergarten between the Brandenburg Gate and the Siegessäule (Victory Column), and this was done on the afternoon of 24 April. At dawn on 26 April a squadron of Me 109s dropped over 100 ammunition containers in the Tiergarten, but barely one-fifth were recovered and the risks involved in getting through the Soviet air defences hardly justified this method of delivery, so transport aircraft were ordered to try to land on the airstrip instead. The many craters were hastily filled in and at 1030 hours two Ju 52s landed safely with their cargoes of tank ammunition. They took off again within half an hour, laden with seriously wounded from the Charité Hospital, but one hit an obstruction on take-off and crashed killing all aboard, so this method of supply was also abandoned.[37]

At 2330 hours on 25 April Jodl received Hitler's detailed instructions supplementing the OKW order of the previous evening. Hitler demanded the fastest possible execution of all the planned relief operations as part of an incredibly optimistic scheme for the restoration of a firm Eastern Front. In the north the 3rd Panzer Army was to contain the 2nd Byelorussian Front while Steiner attacked southeast toward Spandau, cutting off the Soviet forces west of the Havel, which the XXXXI Panzer Corps would then mop up; the 9th Army was to maintain a firm front to the east, with which Army Group 'Mitte' would then connect in its drive from the south, and at the same time link up with the 12th Army's drive south of Potsdam, so that the two armies could advance on Berlin together on a broad front. This plan, as usual, completely ignored the state of their own forces and the strength of the opposition.[38]

Jodl reported back that all relief operations had either already begun or were about to begin. He also informed Hitler of the Soviet build-up south of Prenzlau and of a build-up by the British 21st Army Group southeast of Hamburg threatening a drive on Lübeck, which could cut off the northern province of Schleswig-Holstein and the German forces in Denmark. Hitler then authorized the formation of the 21st Army under General Kurt von Tippelskirch from units drawn from the North Sea coast in order to counter the British threat to the 3rd Panzer Army's rear. However, the 21st Army could muster only two infantry regiments and would take at least one or two days to get into position for its role.

Jodl's misleading report on the relief operations caused 26 April to be a day of optimism in the Führerbunker, but outside in the bright spring sunshine the true situation was nothing less than desperate. Heinrici and his army commanders were wide awake to the realities, unlike Hitler and his blind disciples in the OKW, and were all covertly working at the problem of getting the maximum number of their troops back across the Elbe, which meant fending off the Soviets and deceiving the OKW about their intentions for as long as possible.

During the night the 25th Panzergrenadier Division had moved into Steiner's bridgehead south of the Ruppiner Canal at Kremmen from where the roads led southwest to Nauen and southeast to Spandau. However, two-thirds of his striking force had still to arrive, the 3rd Naval Division being stuck on the railways and the 7th Panzer Division in its assembly area near Neubrandenburg, and his troops were under strong Soviet pressure.[39]

General von Manteuffel had already used up all his available reserves trying to stem the Soviet flood in front of Prenzlau and was now forced to withdraw troops from his flanks to fill the centre of his line. With this contraction of his front, troops were evacuating the Schorfheide in the south, thereby exposing the rear of Steiner's forces. Under these circumstances Steiner's attack would be suicidal and therefore, sometime before noon on 26 April, Heinrici telephoned Jodl requesting the reinforcement of the 3rd Panzer Army by the three divisions assigned to Steiner. Jodl regarded any deviation from Hitler's orders as heresy, and refused. Heinrici decided to ignore this rejection and, without Jodl's knowledge, placed an embargo on the 7th Panzer Division. That night the 3rd Panzer Army withdrew from the north–south line of the Uecker River running through Prenzlau that had provided them with the last opportunity of making a concerted stand.[40]

That same night the survivors of SS General Heissmeyer's Spandau defenders managed to withdraw unnoticed from their encirclement and make their way back through the ruins of the old town to cross the Havel by the Charlotten Bridge. The Gatow defence continued to hold out on the west bank, and Weidling sent Luftwaffe Major-General Aribert Müller to take charge.[41]

At dawn on 26 April Wenck launched his relief attack with the XX Corps from the line Brandenburg/Belzig, not heading toward Jüterbog as the OKW expected, but toward Potsdam where the Soviet forces did not appear to be quite so strong. The roads were blocked with refugees, so the troops had to move across country. At first all went well, the angle of attack avoiding the prepared line held by the 5th Guards Mechanized Corps and the 13th Army, and caught the 6th Guards Mechanized Corps on an exposed flank. A whole number of Soviet units were captured intact, including tank workshops and supply columns. The young trainees of the 'Scharnhorst' and 'Theodor Körner' Infantry and 'Clausewitz' Panzer Divisions, reinforced by the brand new 'Ferdinand von Schill' Infantry Division, fought with all the elan of the German army during the first years of the war. They covered 11 miles that afternoon and by evening had reached Heilstätten Beelitz, a health resort only 15 miles from Berlin. There they recaptured a German field hospital complete with its doctors, staff, valuable medical supplies and 3,000 wounded and many civilian patients who had been in Soviet hands for the past three days. Their transport resources, including a commandeered train, were used to establish

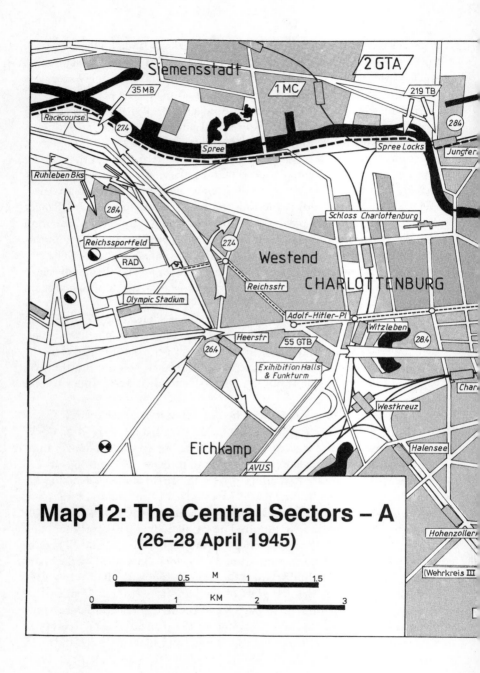

Map 12: The Central Sectors – A
(26–28 April 1945)

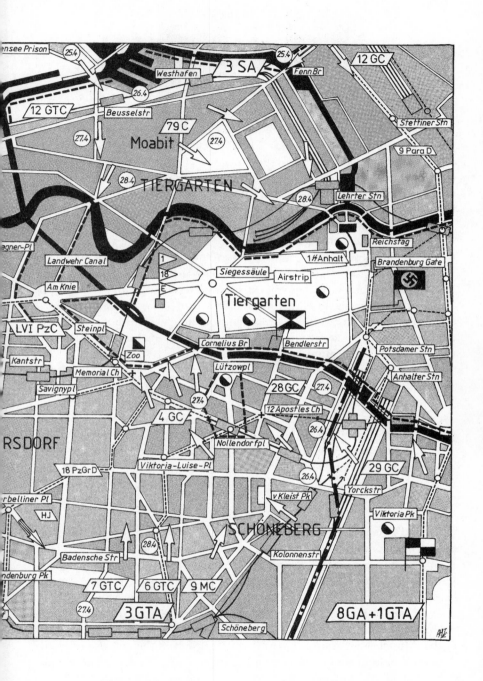

a shuttle service to evacuate the wounded, sick and refugees the 50 miles back to the Elbe.[42]

That morning Air Chief Marshal Novikov resumed 'Operation Salute' with a raid on the city centre by 563 heavy bombers of the 18th Air Army.[43]

At dawn the 79th Rifle Corps renewed its efforts to get across the Westhafen Canal. The 3rd Battalion of the 756th Rifle Regiment tried to cross the ruined Königsdamm Bridge under cover of a massive artillery concentration from corps and divisional artillery, including direct fire from the divisional artillery massed on the northern embankment. However, this attempt also failed with heavy losses, and the few men who managed to reached the southern bank were soon routed by a counterattack.

The Soviets then tried again with the same artillery support, but sending forward a chemical warfare company instead of infantry, and this time they managed to get enough men and equipment across to lay a dense smoke-screen to mask the operation. By these means a second wave of infantry managed to establish a small bridgehead that was rapidly expanded. Some close-support artillery was brought across with the infantry, although all the horses drawing the guns were killed in the vicious crossfire on the bridge and the guns had to be dragged into position by hand.

The strongpoint at Beusselstrasse S-Bahn Station was to hold out for a while longer, but this was bypassed and the Soviets were well into Moabit by the evening. Although losses had been extremely heavy, they had captured over 100 enemy and released 1,200 Soviet prisoners-of-war, who were promptly armed, fed and sent back into the line as replacements.[44]

The confused close-fighting in the remainder of the area north of the Spree continued from the previous day without any identifiable changes. The guns roared, the debris was churned over yet again, and casualties continued to mount on both sides.

On 26 April Weidling was suddenly informed that his immediate predecessor as Defence Commandant, Lieutenant-Colonel Erich Bärenfänger, who had been assigned to General Mummert's command, had been reinstated by Hitler as a Major-General and was to take over command of Defence Sectors 'A' and 'B' forthwith. Bärenfänger's successful wire-pulling with the hierarchy, where he was a favourite of Goebbels, ridiculous as it may seem, was in fact beneficial to the defence, for it enabled Mummert to resume command of the 'Müncheberg' Panzer Division at Tempelhof. It thereby also released Colonel Wöhlermann to return to his command of the defence artillery, and, as we shall see, Bärenfänger was to acquit himself well in the new role.[45]

The 'Nord-West' Regiment fighting at Alexanderplatz was now down to below half-strength, so Lieutenant-Colonel Seifert ordered its disbandment and transferred the survivors to Bärenfänger's command.[46]

That morning Krukenberg's SS 'Nordland' Panzergrenadier Division launched counterattacks in Neukölln and the area of the Görlitzer Railway Station against the 4th Guards and 9th Rifle Corps respectively. A Frenchman with the SS 'Charlemagne' Battalion, as it was now styled, described his experiences there:

> Our men advanced as if on exercise, jumping from doorway to doorway, over walls and rubble, and fell on the Russian infantry, who were spread out on the various floors. The following tanks spurted fire and flames, hardly giving the infantry a chance to fire back. Our attack made progress, and it was then that we received a blow. A reserve section coming from Neukölln townhall and thinking themselves safe were still in order of march when suddenly a series of Russian tank shells fell on the street corner. Broken-hearted, I counted about fifteen bodies of young soldiers lying on the roadway, which was running with blood.
>
> To our right and left the situation was even more confused. Whilst clearing the area into which we had penetrated we kept coming across the flanks of friendly units as well as Russians on every side. A strange order then reached us from Division: 'If the attack has not already begun, stop and await further orders; if it has, then do your best!'
>
> Three hours after our successful attack had begun we had to pull back. In fact there was no longer any front either alongside or behind us. 'What shall I do?' I asked myself: 'Surely we should hold on here. In the meantime let us make sure that we have not been surrounded.
>
> The townhall was then occupied by a group of Hitlerjugend who had been sent as reinforcements.[47]

Fires were spreading unchecked all over the central districts of Berlin on 26 April, as the firemen could not carry out their tasks under the heavy shellfire that was falling everywhere. Second Lieutenant Kroemer of the 'Müncheberg' Panzer Division recorded:

> 0530 hours. New, massive tank attacks. We are forced to withdraw. Orders from the Chancellery: our division is to move immediately to Alexander-platz.
> 0900 hours. Order cancelled.
> 1000 hours. Russian drive on the airport becomes irresistible. New defence

line Rathaus Schöneberg/Hallesches Tor/Belle-Alliance-Platz. Heavy street-fighting, many civilian casualties, dying animals, women fleeing from cellar to cellar. We are pushed northwest. New orders to go to Alexander-platz as before. General Bärenfänger has taken over Defence Sectors 'A' and 'B' from General Mummert. The Führerbunker must have false information; the positions we are supposed to be taking over are already in Russian hands. We withdraw again under heavy Russian air attacks. Inscriptions on the walls of the buildings: 'The hour before sunrise is the darkest' and 'We withdraw but we are winning!' Deserters hanged or shot. What we see on the march is unforgettable.

Evening. Announcement of a new organization, Freikorps 'Mohnke'. 'Bring your own weapons, equipment, rations. Every German is needed!' Heavy fighting in Dirckenstrasse, Königstrasse, the Central Market and inside the Stock Exchange. First skirmishes in the S-Bahn tunnels, through which the Russians are trying to get behind our lines. The tunnels are packed with civilians.[48]

This was the first indication of Soviet use of the underground railway tunnels to assist their advance and was probably the work of the 7th Rifle Corps, which was nearest to Alexanderplatz and finding it difficult to make progress after its initially rapid advance from Hohenschönhausen.

That day General Weidling went to visit Major-General Bärenfänger, now commanding what amounted to the eastern bastion of 'Zitadelle', and later commented:

Potsdamer Platz and Leipziger Strasse were under heavy artillery fire. The dust from the rubble hung in the air like a thick fog. Shells burst all around us. We were covered with bits of broken stone. The roads were riddled with shell craters and piles of brick rubble. Streets and squares lay deserted. Dodging Russian mortars, we made our way to the U-Bahn station by bounds. The roomy U-Bahn station, two storeys deep, was crowded with terrified civilians. It was a shattering sight.

From Platform 'E' we walked through the tunnel as far as Schillingstrasse station (the next east along Frankfurter Strasse) to General Bärenfänger's HQ. Bärenfänger reported strong Russian attacks near Frankfurter Strasse. This former Hitlerjugend leader and fanatical follower of Hitler's was full of praise for the valor of his soldiers and their heroic deeds. A considerable number of enemy tanks had been destroyed in his sector. He now pressed me for more men and ammunition, but I could promise him neither. Most of Bärenfänger's men were Volkssturm troopers that had been sent into the

fighting with captured weapons, French, Italian, etc. No ammunition for these could be found anywhere in Berlin.
> On my way back I visited one of the hospitals. It was terribly overcrowded. The doctors simply could not cope with the numbers of wounded. There was hardly any light or water.[49]

Heavy fighting continued in the 5th Shock Army's sector, where progress was slow and dominated by the pounding of the guns. The railway bridges at Küstin having been repaired, the captured siege artillery previously mentioned arrived and, together with the artillery of the Stavka Reserve used for the attack on the Seelow Heights now reallocated to Zhukov, the Soviet advance westward along Frankfurter Allee brought a swathe of destruction.

In the 9th Rifle Corps' sector, the 1050th Rifle Regiment cleared the Görlitzer Railway Station by 0700 hours, and the troops continued to push forward into Kreuzberg.[50]

The remnants of the 3/115th Siemensstadt Volkssturm Battalion and the other units on Richthofenstrasse, now under the command of a Captain Sobotta, held out until late afternoon on 26 April, repelling Soviet attacks, until orders were received to withdraw toward the Friedrichshain flak-tower at dusk. They managed to reach the Löwen-Bömisch Brewery on the corner of Landsberger Allee and Friedenstrasse undetected, but so exhausted that orders received next morning to return to their former positions on Richthofenstrasse were regarded as absolutely impossible of execution.[51]

That evening Chuikov's troops reached Kreuzberg and took the French prisoner-of-war hospital there. The following account by the doctor already quoted describes how the Soviets advanced in an area that had not previously been devastated by artillery fire:

> That morning I greeted daylight again with pleasure. A surprise awaited me. The Karstadt department store towers had vanished and the vast building itself was now on fire.
> Several spent bullets whistled up the street. The sound of automatic weapons now came from the right as well as the left and was mixed with drier, more regular rattlings presumably coming from Russian submachine-guns. The 88mm on Weichselstrasse was no longer firing, having been either silenced or removed.
> The inhabitants were now staying indoors. The withdrawal toward the

city centre was marked by a detachment of police and firemen following the lines of the walls with packs on their backs, rifles across their chests, and suitcases in either hand. And still the wounded were coming into the yard.

At about 1600 hours the retreat was still on but the Russians were already at the end of the street and more and more bullets were whistling past. A light tank went by, covering its withdrawal with bursts of machine-gun fire.

In the cellar, which had been permanently occupied for the past few days, the atmosphere was stifling. Civilians were packed against the other side of the partition separating our side of the cellar from theirs. The rumor ran round that Tempelhof had been outflanked from both east and west. Surgical patients were stretched out on mattresses wherever there was space; soldiers, old men, women, children, French, Russian, Serb and Italian workers, mixed up side by side and asking for water. There were already a dozen corpses stacked in an old shelter-trench nearby.

The ground trembled at length from the weight of the tanks passing in front of the yard only 15 metres away. The fire of automatic weapons increased little by little. Short cries were mixed with it and gradually as they approached we distinguished the sound of 'Stalin, hurrah!' Anxiety reigned in the cellar. The sick lying on the first landing of one of the staircases had seen Russian tanks pass. Then a soldier stuck his head through one of the holes in the metal plates reinforcing the porch grill and, no doubt perturbed by this apparently abandoned large building, sent a burst of submachine-gun fire into the windows.

It was necessary to act quickly if an irreparable error was to be avoided. A delegation composed of three Frenchmen, the senior doctor, a man we trusted and our youngest comrade, Medical Lieutenant 'T' who spoke Russian fluently, left the cellar to report to the Russians. We awaited the results of the encounter with impatience. The order had been given for everyone to remain below until the situation had been clarified. Faces were grave. Information was passed round from the men nearest to the exits.

Contact was established without incident, and the Russians visited our building, for they thought some shots had come from the south wing. The problem was finally resolved by two tank shells fired at the suspect windows.[52]

Chuikov's troops, having taken Tempelhof airport by noon, began to wheel left into Schöneberg with their right flank edging up to the Landwehr Canal. Viktoria Park was taken, giving them an elevation on which to mount their artillery, and next day an eyewitness saw 205mm guns being fired there over open sights at the Anhalter Railway Station less than a mile away.[53] During the afternoon, according to Chuikov's account, his troops were amazed to see a column of about 400 Hitlerjugend carrying Panzerfausts marching toward them down Kolonnenstrasse as if on parade. After some initial hesitation, the Soviets opened fire, killing their leaders and putting the rest to flight.[54]

By the end of 26 April the 8th Guards and 1st Guards Tank Armies were up to the line of Potsdamer Strasse on their left, and the 28th Guards Rifle Corps were engaged against a strongpoint at the southeast corner of the Heinrich-von-Kleist Park. Leading elements of the 34th Heavy Tank Regiment had penetrated even further and were fighting outside the Twelve Apostles Church in Kurfürstenstrasse, having already traversed the Yorck-strasse complex of tracks and marshalling yards serving the Anhalter and Potsdamer Railway Stations.[55]

Behind them the remains of Lieutenant-Colonel Skorning's battalion were able to follow the railway tracks of the S-Bahn ring westward, pursued all the way, to Tempelhof Goods Station, where they held out until the following day. Skorning handed over the remaining dozen men to a strange lieutenant who had joined up with them while he went off to seek his regimental headquarters. The regiment had meanwhile lost contact with the Defence Sector Headquarters and were considering surrender. He then returned to his unit location to find that the men had vanished, and so withdrew via Schöneberg S-Bahn Station, which was still manned by Volkssturm troops.[56]

This penetration westward by Chuikov's forces put the 1st Byelorussian Front well beyond the Tempelhof/Potsdamer Station boundary established by GHQ the night before, but either this order had not been transmitted to Chuikov, or it had been decided to ignore it with a view to establishing a firm base for the attack on the central enemy stronghold across the Landwehr Canal. In any case, the 3rd Guards Tank Army remained totally unaware that Chuikov's troops were working across their front.

On the morning of 26 April, the 18th Panzergrenadier Division sent the 30th Panzergrenadier Regiment, supported by six 'Tigers' and about 15 APCs from the 118th Panzer Regiment, south down the Avus to try and restore links with the 20th Panzergrenadier Division at Wannsee, but this armoured group met strong Soviet resistance near the Schlachtensee and, with the Soviet thrust through Dahlem threatening to outflank it, at 1000 hours it withdrew via the Jagdschloss Grunewald to Elsterplatz, where at 1200 hours it was engaged once more against Soviet armour. A new front line was established along Hagenstrasse to Roseneck on the Hohenzollerndamm. Meanwhile the 51st

Panzergrenadier Regiment was forced back to the line of Schildhornstrasse between Breitenscheidplatz and the Schlossstrasse in Steglitz.[57]

Confronted by this determined opposition, the 3rd Guards Tank Army continued to advance cautiously as it adapted to the fighting conditions in the more densely built-up areas of Grunewald, Schmargendorf and Steglitz immediately south of the S-Bahn ring. The 55th Guards Tank Brigade, after a 15-minute bombardment of German positions in the outskirts of Nikolassee and on the Havelberg, avoided the open expanse of the Avus and advanced up the east bank of the Havel through the Grunewald Forest. On its way the brigade came across a flak battery firing across the Havel in support of the defence of Gatow Airfield and called on its air support to destroy it. Eventually the brigade emerged from the woods at the bend in the Heerstrasse (East–West Axis) not far from the Olympic Stadium. Here it turned right toward Charlottenburg and started fighting its way slowly through the residential areas on either side of that broad thoroughfare against increasing opposition as the defence reacted to its unexpected presence. Colonel Dragunsky describes the advance with the tanks in column about 100 metres apart, scouts out on the flanks and submachine-gunners across their front, engineers, artillery and assault groups following the tanks, and his own command group on foot between two tank battalions so that they could see what was going on. All resistance was smothered with heavy concentrations of fire, while long-range artillery shelled the areas yet to be penetrated. By nightfall they had overrun the ammunition dump in the unfinished War Academy near the Teufelsee and occupied the Eichkamp area. Brigade Headquarters remained on the edge of the woods under heavy guard, as nothing was known of what enemy forces remained behind them or ahead.[58]

Although Koniev badly wanted the 4th Guards Tank Army's 10th Guards Tank Corps to meet the threat posed by the advance of the German 12th Army on Berlin, it remained fully committed in bottling up General Reymann's Army Detachment 'Spree' on Wannsee and Potsdam 'islands'.[59]

During the course of 26 April, General Weidling moved his headquarters from the Hohenzollerndamm to the cellars of the OKH buildings in Bendlerstrasse (Stauffenbergstrasse), following a rocket attack from 'Stalin-Organs' showing that Koniev's troops were getting uncomfortably close from the south. He and his staff first tried the flak-control tower in the Tiergarten, but found it too crowded, so he went on to the OKW building known as the Bendlerblock in the Bendlerstrasse (Stauffenbergstrasse). Shortly afterward he had to move again, this time to the cramped Army Signals bunker outside, when a shell smashed through the floors above, causing a heavy safe to smash down into the cellars below, killing a young BDM (Bund-Deutscher-Mädel) girl working there as a voluntary nurse. Axmann was also prompted to move his Hitlerjugend Headquarters from No. 86 on the Kaiserdamm to No. 64 Wilhelmstrasse, where he could be closer to the Führer.[60]

At the evening conference at the Führerbunker, General Weidling introduced his breakout plan but, after some consultation with Goebbels, Hitler rejected it, saying; 'Your proposal is fine, but what does it imply? I do not want to wander about in the woods to be attacked. I am staying here and will fall at the head of my troops. You carry on with the defence!' Despite this instruction, Weidling and his staff kept their breakout plan under constant revision, hoping that the opportunity would arise, being fully aware that although most of the Wehrmacht commanders would take part, the Waffen-SS might well hinder their purpose.[61]

The lack of proper communications facilities continued to bedevil the conduct of the defence and General Krebs' staff were reduced to picking out numbers at random in the civilian telephone directory to try to discover what was going on. Sometimes they were answered by Russian voices, and one Soviet officer claimed to have been connected with Goebbels from Siemens-stadt and to have conversed cheekily with him in German.[62]

That day the pilot who had previously flown Speer to Berlin and back from Rechlin, flew Colonel-General von Greim to Gatow in a Focke-Wulf 190, which had only one passenger seat, so the diminutive but determined Hanna Reitsch was stuffed into a storage compartment in the tail of the aircraft in order to accompany him on his visit to the Führer. They were escorted by 20 other aircraft and arrived safely with only a few holes in the wings but at a cost of seven of their number. Von Greim then tried to telephone Hitler from Gatow but without success. He therefore attempted to fly on to the Branden-burg Gate in a Fieseler 'Storch' with Hanna behind him in the passenger seat. Their fighter escort held off the attacking Soviet aircraft as von Greim took off and vanished into the murk shrouding the city. While flying over the Grunewald residential area the aircraft was hit and von Greim injured in the foot. Although they were only at rooftop height, Hanna managed to reach the controls over his shoulders and flew on to land the aircraft safely on the airstrip. They then commandeered a passing vehicle and were taken to the Chancellery bunker, where von Greim had his injuries attended to before they went on to report to Hitler. It then transpired that Hitler had summoned von Greim merely to confer upon him the command of the Luftwaffe in the rank of Field Marshal, something which could just as easily have been done by signal. Hitler wanted them to leave again immediately but von Greim's injuries were both painful and serious, and it proved impossible to fly in any more aircraft for this purpose. Six Fieseler 'Storch' aircraft flown in from Rechlin under fighter escort were all shot down, as were 12 Ju 52 transports bringing in SS reinforcements.[63]

During the course of 26 April Berlin's last telephone links with the outside world, which had been operating only intermittently over the previous two days, were finally severed.[64]

8

NO RELIEF

In Kreuzberg the pressure of Chuikov's forces caused the German defences to withdraw over the Landwehr Canal during the night of 26/27 April. SS Major-General Krukenberg's 11th SS 'Nordland' Panzergrenadier Division took up new defensive positions on the line Spittelmarkt/Belle-Alliance-Platz (Mehringplatz), and the divisional command post was set up in the cellars of the State Opera on the Unter-den-Linden, from where Krukenberg now reported direct to SS Major-General Mohnke in the Reichs Chancellery. This arrangement ignored the local Defence Sector Commandant, Lieutenant-Colonel Seifert, who had his command post in the Air Ministry, and further promoted the already existing atmosphere of distrust and misunderstanding between the Waffen-SS and Wehrmacht in this area.

The 'Norge' and 'Danmark' Panzergrenadier Regiments, now down to about 600 men each, were deployed on the left and right flanks respectively. A third of each regiment was kept in the line, another third at the regimental command post in immediate reserve and a third on Leipziger Strasse in divisional reserve with some of the division's tanks and some 'Charlemagne' tank-hunters. The armoured reconnaissance battalion and some of the 'Charlemagne' took up positions around the Anhalter Railway Station.[1]

Operating behind them as far out as Alexanderplatz were elements of the 'Müncheberg' Panzer Division, as Second Lieutenant Kroemer recorded:

> The night is fiery red. Heavy shelling. Otherwise a terrible silence. We are sniped at from many buildings, probably by foreign labourers. About 0530 hours another grinding barrage. The Russians attack with tanks and flame-throwers. We withdraw to the Anhalter Station. Defence of Askanischer Platz, Saarlandstrasse (Stresemannstrasse) and Wilhelmstrasse. Three times during the morning we enquire: 'Where is Wenck?' Wenck's spearheads are said to be at Werder. Incomprehensible! A reliable release from

the Propaganda Ministry that all the troops from the Elbe Front are marching on Berlin.

About 100 hours 'L' comes from the Propaganda Ministry, his eyes shining, with an even more reliable release straight from Secretary of State Werner Naumann. There have been negotiations with the Western Allies. We shall have to make sacrifices but the Western Allies will not stand by and let the Russians take Berlin. Our morale goes up enormously. 'L' says it is absolutely certain that we will not have to go on fighting for more than 24 hours – 48 at the very most.[2]

On 27 April the situation on the 3rd Panzer Army's front deteriorated rapidly when the Soviets broke through just north of Prenzlau during the morning. Eventually, late that afternoon, Keitel was reluctantly forced to concede to Heinrici's request that the 7th Panzer and 25th Panzergrenadier Divisions be assigned to relieve the pressure on his front instead of participating in Steiner's attack as originally intended. (By this time, the 3rd Naval Division appears to have ceased to exist as a formation, having been caught up piecemeal in the 3rd Panzer Army's withdrawal.) However, Keitel insisted that these two divisions be used specifically in an attack on the 2nd Byelorussian Front's southern flank, laying down the assembly area, line of attack and objectives, and that they revert to their original task immediately thereafter. Heinrici had no intention of adopting such an impractical course of action, and instead gave them orders to dig in on the line Neubrandemburg–Neustrelitz to cover the main line of retreat.[3]

Further south the remains of General Busse's 9th Army continued to try to break out of their encirclement on the evening and night of 27 April, but these attempts coincided with Soviet thrusts that tightened the noose around the trap, and casualties were heavy, the Soviets claiming 6,000 prisoners taken in one sector alone.[4]

That day, Gatow finally fell and the Soviets were able to finish clearing the west bank of the Havel opposite the city. On the way to the Elbe the leading elements of the 47th Army reached the towns of Rathenow and Fehrbellin but then paused. They were up against strong opposition from General Holste's XXXXI Panzer Corps and it was no longer feasible to continue the advance without flanking support. Until more formations could be withdrawn from the city fighting, further progress westward would have to be delayed.[5]

The 1st Mechanized Corps and the 12th Guards Tank Corps finished clearing the Siemensstadt area and closed up to the banks of the Spree from its junction with the Havel in the west to the Westhafen Canal in the east. All the bridges across their front had been destroyed. However, part of the 35th Mechanized Brigade managed to cross over to the area of the Ruhleben racecourse (now waterworks) and this happened to coincide (there was no question of co-ordination) with a thrust northward along the Reichsstrasse by the 55th Guards Tank Brigade of the 3rd Guards Tank Army. The latter had just been reinforced by the 7th Guards Tank Corps' reserves of a battalion of motorized infantry, a rocket-launcher battalion, ten heavy tanks and a company of self-propelled guns, plus two artillery brigades. Their instructions were to seal off the defence by reaching the banks of the Spree at Ruhleben, locating the troops of the 1st Byelorussian Front and linking up with them. According to Colonel Dragunsky, progress was down to 50 yards an hour, with frequent detours due to blocked streets. Map-reading proved extremely difficult in these circumstances, their compasses would not function properly with the amount of metal about, and their internal radio communications were also not working. Eventually elements of the two brigades met near the Charlottenburger Chaussee about noon, after which the 35th Mechanized Brigade appears to have been withdrawn again over the Spree, leaving Dragunsky's troops mopping up and securing the Westend residential area for the rest of the day and night in furtherance of their orders. However, they were under increasing pressure, as General Weidling could not afford to lose this potential escape route to the west and so sent part of the 18th Panzer-grenadier Division to assist the local defence. It is clear that Dragunsky had insufficient numbers for his task, as German units were able to infiltrate through his lines time and time again, and even his rear echelon of supply vehicles was obliged to seek shelter with the main body that morning after having been forced out of their base at the Reichssportfeld (Olympic Stadium) U-Bahn station.[6]

The 79th Rifle Corps had a difficult time fighting its way through Moabit. The defence was the usual mixed bag of units, and some of the individual strongpoints could be bypassed and eliminated later, but the heavily built-up nature of the district made progress slow and costly. Once isolated, with the lack of water and provisions now being experienced, and the unnerving screams of women being raped at night, the defenders of these strong points rarely held out for long. However, among them were some of General Andrei Vlassov's White Russian units, and these invariably fought with true desperation until the bitter end. Losses continued to be heavy but the prisons in this area yielded large numbers of Soviet prisoners-of-war, who were immediately used to replenish depleted units. It can be seen that the 79th Rifle Corps was deliberately heading southeast through Moabit for the big prize, the Reichstag building, leaving the 2nd Guards Tank Army to clear the

Beusselstrasse area behind them down to the Knie (Ernst-Reuter-Platz).[7] As for the rest of the 3rd Shock Army, the position is far from clear. The 9th Parachute Division was fighting well and the Humboldthain flak-tower, Stettiner Railway Station (Nordbahnhof) and other positions in the area were holding out, with street-fighting going on all around them. Wolfgang Karow, the infantry NCO with an *ad hoc* combat team based on the flak-tower, reported:

> The next order was to retake Wedding S-Bahn station, which had been lost. We only got as far as Schönwalder Strasse on the night of the 27 April for it was impossible to establish who was in front of us, or to the left and right. The command post was in No. 27. Suddenly we heard 'Urrah! Urrah!' and the Russians attacked over the railway embankment. 'Come on, let's get out of here!' The men fired and then we rushed up the cellar steps. Up above the Stalin-Organs met us with a rocket salvo and we could hardly see the yard through the smoke. We reached the street in short bounds and ran down Kunkelstrasse to Schönwalder Strasse. In Schönwalder Strasse we had to cross the bridge over the Panke. It was about four in the morning and all we could see were some shadowy figures. I ran over to ask them where they came from, thinking they were a couple of our chaps, but discovered straight away that they were Russians. The accompanying Volkssturm and myself immediately took cover in the nearest building and opened fire on the Soviet stormtroops.[8]

Marshal Zhukov wrote:

> Our advance did not stop by day or by night. Our every effort was aimed at giving the enemy no chance to organize a defence or new strongpoints. The basic formations of the armies were well organized in depth. By day the first wave would advance and by night the second wave would take over.
> Each army taking part in the assault had been assigned zones of action. The units and smaller elements were assigned specific street, squares and other objectives. Behind the seeming chaos of street-to-street fighting was a logical and well-thought-out system. Its main objectives became targets for devastating fire.[9]

This may have been what was required by the Stavka manuals, but in reality to try and continue the advance at night proved highly impractical for the combat teams. It was a noted characteristic of this battle that most Soviet troops used the nights as opportunities for rest, drunken orgies, looting and rape, leaving the higher-echelon artillery to harass the enemy. In the area assigned to the 12th Guards and 7th Rifle Corps the apparent chaos became real, and the situation so confused that the command was unable to exercise proper control, as becomes evident later.

The street-fighting techniques used by the 1st Byelorussian Front were based on the principle that each street should be tackled by a complete rifle regiment, one battalion working down either side of the street and the third battalion in reserve and bringing up the rear. The frontage of a rifle regiment was thus as little as 200–250 yards, while that of higher formations varied according to the terrain. Individual units were each day assigned immediate tasks, subsequent tasks and an axis for further advance, the depth of penetration expected of them varying according to the circumstances. Usually the troops did not advance down the streets themselves but mouseholed their way through the buildings at different levels, while the supporting artillery pushed their way through the backyards and alleys with engineer assistance. The light infantry guns and dismantled rocket-launchers were manhandled up into buildings and used with great flexibility. In attacking a heavily defended building the assault group would usually split into two, one part concentrating on quickly bottling up the enemy in the cellars, where they would normally have taken shelter during the preliminary bombardment, and the other clearing the upper storeys.[10]

Throughout the 5th Shock Army's area irregular fighting continued on 27 April. The front was now greatly fragmented with isolated pockets of resistance all over the combat zone, such as the Löwen-Böhmisch Brewery position, which held out to the very end. The whole area between Alexanderplatz and the Spree was in uproar, and there were still fighting around the Friedrichshain flak-tower and Schlesischer Railway Station. On the other side of the river the 9th Rifle Corps continued to advance through Kreuzberg and reached Moritzplatz.[11]

During 27 April the bulk of Chuikov's forces closed up to the line of the Landwehr Canal along their northern front and consolidated their positions. In the centre the 28th Guards Rifle Corps with its strong armoured support continued to clear a firm base for the launching of the forthcoming operation, and appear to have secured the area roughly from the Heinrich-von-Kleist Park through Nollendorfplatz to Lützowplatz, although the last two squares remained in German hands and were to hold out until the very end of the battle. These positions were bypassed but heavy fighting took place around the Cornelius Bridge on Budapester Strasse, and some Soviet tanks broke through the Zoo boundary wall and started firing at the flak-towers.[12]

Chuikov established his command post in a house at No. 2 Schulenburgring near the Viktoria Park and started planning the next and final phase of his operation for the crossing of the Landwehr Canal. He decided to use the next day for resting his troops and making his preparations, leaving the artillery and mortars to keep the enemy occupied. In conjunction with the 79th Rifle Corps' attack on the Reichstag building and the 5th Shock Army's push westward through the city centre, Chuikov was responsible for clearing the southern part of the Tiergarten as far as the East–West Axis, and especially for the area including the Potsdamer and Anhalter Railway Stations leading to the Reichs Chancellery.[13]

The Soviets sent forward reconnaissance parties to probe the German defences, and three of these parties seem to have been in sufficient strength to have caused some concern. Fighting was reported near the Potsdamer Railway Station and two Soviet tanks were knocked out on the Hallesches Tor Bridge. SS Major-General Mohnke reported that a group of Soviet tanks accompanying two Czech tanks bearing German insignia had managed to penetrate as far as Wilhelmstrasse before being destroyed.

With the pressure increasing, Mohnke deployed some 105mm howitzers in the Gendarmenmarkt to cover Belle-Alliance-Platz, in Pariser Platz to cover the Unter-den-Linden and in Leipziger Strasse to cover the Spittelmarkt area, but there were only 12 rounds per gun and once they had been fired the gunners were ordered to fight on as infantry.[14]

On 27 April elements of the 3rd Guards Tank Army attacked up both sides of the Hohenzollerndamm and up the Avus motorway, but were blocked by the 30th Panzergrenadier Regiment with the assistance of the 118th Panzer Regiment, and together these German units then mounted a counterattack as far as the Platz-am-Wilden-Eber, while the 51st Panzergrenadier Regiment fought a stubborn delaying action further east in Schöneberg. However, by evening these elements of the 18th Panzergrenadier Division were obliged to withdraw to the line of the Inner Defence Ring along the S-Bahn between the Westend and Schmargendorf stations, which provided them with a firm base and good fields of fire. The divisional artillery was now down to 40 rounds for its remaining guns.[15]

Meanwhile the elements of the 55th Guards Tank Brigade in the Heerstrasse area launched a two-pronged attack on Ruhleben to keep the defence occupied. A mainly infantry group cut cross-country between the Hitlerjugend Regiment guarding the Havel bridges and the Reichsarbeitsdienst troops covering the Olympic Stadium. They overran a mixed flak and field artillery position in the grounds of the Reichs Sport Academy[16] sharing the

134

same hilltop as the Olympic Stadium, and pushed on down the back of the hill over the Ruhleben ranges toward the Charlottenburger Chaussee. The defence had about 1,000 troops in this area, survivors of the fighting in Spandau and Siemensstadt, who concentrated on the line of the Ruhleben U-Bahn Station on its high embankment and Alexander Barracks, where Colonel Anton Eder had his Defence Sector 'F' command post. Then, reinforced by about 2,000 local Hitlerjugend boys taken from their homes, most of whom were unarmed and relying upon picking up weapons from the battlefield, the bulk of the defending forces counterattacked and drove the Soviets all the way back over the hill to the Heerstrasse. On their way they suffered heavy casualties when caught in enfilade fire from other Soviet troops ensconced in the Academy buildings before the latter could be evicted by another group of the defence attacking them from the rear. The other part of the Soviet attack, in which tanks emerging from Reichsstrasse tried to force their way down the Charlottenburger Chaussee to the barrack gates, was also defeated by the defence and several tanks destroyed. However, this action had successfully served its purpose of distracting and tying down the defence in this area.[17]

In 'Zitadelle' conditions were gradually deteriorating, as observed by Second Lieutenant Kroemer:

> The new command post [is] in the S-Bahn tunnels under Anhalter Railway Station. The station looks like an armed camp. Women and children huddle in niches, some sitting on folding chairs, listening to the sounds of battle. Shells hit the roof, cement crumbles from the ceiling. S-Bahn hospital trains trundle slowly by.
>
> Suddenly a surprise. Water splashes into our command post. Shrieks, cries and curses. People are struggling around the ladders reaching up the ventilation shafts to the street above. Gurgling water floods through the tunnels. The crowds are panicky, pushing through the rising water, leaving children and wounded behind. People are being trampled underfoot, the water covering them. It rises a meter or more then slowly runs away. The panic lasts for hours. Many drowned. Reason: on somebody's orders engineers have blown up the safety bulkhead control chamber on the Landwehr Canal between the Schöneberger and Möckern Bridges to flood the tunnels against the Russians. The whole time heavy fighting continues above ground.
>
> Late afternoon command post moved to Potsdamer Platz station first level, the lower tunnels still being flooded. Direct hit through the roof. Heavy losses among wounded and civilians. Smoke drifts through the hole.

Outside stocks of Panzerfausts explode under heavy Russian fire. Terrible sight at the station entrance, one flight of stairs down where a heavy shell has penetrated and people, soldiers, women and children are literally stuck to the walls. At dusk a short pause in the firing.[18]

The flooding, according to Captain Boldt, had been ordered by Hitler as a result of reports of the Soviets using the tunnels to infiltrate the German lines. However, when Reichsleiter Martin Bormann had enquired of the Berlin Transport Authority (BVG) on 24 April as to the feasibility of such a measure he had been advised that the water would not rise above one metre or so in the affected section. Whether this flooding on 27 April was deliberate, despite the fact that the tunnels were of considerable value to the defence, providing shelter to thousands, stores and command posts, as well as accommodating the hospital trains that were parked in the S-Bahn section near the Brandenburg Gate, or whether it was a result of external damage to the tunnel structure, remains uncertain.[19]

SS Major-General Krukenberg moved his SS 'Nordland' Panzergrenadier Division into the city centre and was allocated a derelict railway carriage as his command post in the Stadtmitte U-Bahn station beneath the junction of Mohrenstrasse and Friedrichstrasse. There was no electric light or telephone but food supplies were readily available from commandeered grocery shops in the Gendarmenmarkt nearby.[20]

There was an unusual development at the evening conference on 27 April when Hitler suddenly noticed the absence of SS Lieutenant-General Hermann Fegelein, Himmler's liaison officer and Eva Braun's brother-in-law, who had not been seen for the past three days. Hitler immediately issued orders for him to be found, suspecting desertion. Eventually Fegelein was traced to an apartment in Bleibtreustrasse off the Kurfürstendamm. Telephoned instructions failed to bring him back and so an escort was sent to fetch him, although technically they could not arrest him as there were no officers of senior enough rank available for the task. They found him drunk and unshaven, and returned with his promise to follow as soon as he had cleaned himself up. When he still failed to appear, a second escort was sent, and found him clean-shaven and properly dressed but no more sober than before. There was a young woman present, and they appeared to have been packing a suitcase together. On the pretext of getting fresh glasses, the woman left the room and was later discovered to have fled through a kitchen window. Fegelein and the suitcase were brought back to the Chancellery, where he was stripped of his rank and handed over to SS Major-General Mohnke for trial. However, he was found to be too drunk to stand trial at that time.[21]

In the meantime the SS colonel in charge of the escort had reported to Bormann, who, from the circumstances of the incident and contents of the suitcase (which included passports, valuables and money suitable for an escape attempt), immediately deduced that they had at last uncovered the source of the leak of information from the Führer's headquarters that had been a cause of deep concern for the past few months. It was assumed that the missing woman was a British agent and that Fegelein had been about to flee the city with her.

Bormann had Fegelein handed over for interrogation to the Gestapo chief, Heinrich Müller, who was in charge of the security investigation, and Fegelein was eventually shot in the Innenhof of the Reichs Chancellery at dawn on 29 April. The fate and identity of the woman remain a mystery.[22]

In the early hours of 28 April, Lieutenant-Colonel Hans Rudel, the Luftwaffe's ace tank-busting 'Stuka' pilot, flew to Berlin in a Heinkel 111 in response to Hitler's radioed instructions, with the intention of landing on the East–West Axis airstrip. He reported:

> Upon arriving near Berlin we were picked up by the Russian detectors and the anti-aircraft artillery opened up on us. It was very difficult to recognize the features of the capital because of enormous clouds of smoke and a thin layer of mist. The fires were so fierce in some places that we were dazzled by them and prevented from seeing anything. I had to concentrate on the shadows in order to see anything and was unable to pick out the East–West Axis. There were flames and cannon-fire everywhere. The spectacle was fantastic.
>
> We then received a message saying that landing was impossible as the East–West Axis was under heavy artillery fire and the Russians had already taken Potsdamer Platz.[23]

When Keitel visited Steiner at 0400 hours on 28 April, he was unaware of the latest developments on the 3rd Panzer Army's front, and Steiner could give him no information on the 7th Panzer Division. Steiner assured him that, despite the diversion of his expected reinforcements, he was still preparing his remaining forces for an attack that night.

Keitel promised to give him the 'Schlageter' RAD Infantry Division to make up his numbers. However, this division, part of the 12th Army's ill-fated XXXIX Panzer Corps, had been virtually wiped out in operations west of the Elbe a week previously. In any case, Steiner was bluffing, having no intention of committing his men to an attack with such little chance of success. Meanwhile, unknown to either of them, Hitler had already despaired of

Steiner's procrastination and issued orders the previous evening for his replacement by Lieutenant-General Holste of the XXXXI Panzer Corps. Holste had promptly asked for 48 hours in which to prepare his attack, as his troops were some distance from the bridgehead and would need time to get into position; he also had the 47th Army to contend with.[24]

It was on his way back to Jodl's headquarters that Keitel discovered what had happened to the 7th Panzer and 25th Panzergrenadier Divisions, and that the 3rd Panzer Army was actually in full retreat, not only without the permission of the OKW but in direct contravention of Hitler's orders. Mad with anger, he hastened to inform Jodl and then summoned Heinrici and von Manteuffel to a rendezvous at a crossroads west of Neubrandenburg that afternoon. Von Manteuffel's Chief-of-Staff, General Müller-Hillebrand, was suspicious of Keitel's intentions toward his chief, and organized his staff officers to lay a precautionary ambush at the rendezvous. It was a bitter encounter, a show-down among the military hierarchy, with Keitel accusing the generals of cowardice and treason, and Heinrici countering that he could not obey orders issued by the OKW when it was so obviously out of touch with events. Keitel shouted that if they had had the guts to shoot a few thousand deserters as an example there would have been no retreat, whereupon Heinrici invited Keitel to start the executions with the exhausted columns staggering past them. Stared down, Keitel left without another word.[25]

The only realistic hope for the city's defenders now lay in Wenck's 12th Army opening an escape corridor to the west. Wenck's attack continued to make progress on 27 April and by the evening of that day his leading elements had reached the village of Ferch at the southern tip of the Schwielowsee, some six miles south of Potsdam.[26]

The Soviets rallied, but they were in a predicament. General Wenck's attack had isolated the 6th Guards Mechanized Corps from the rest of the 4th Guards Tank Army at a time when this corps was extended over a distance of some 18 miles. The 5th Guards Mechanized Corps and the 13th Army were having to form a double front, expecting General Busse's 9th Army to try and break out to the west at any moment from behind them, while the rest of the 4th Guards Tank Army was still heavily engaged in the containment of the Potsdam and Wannsee 'islands'. Koniev had located the 13th Army's reserve corps at Jüterbog, but it would appear that it had already been deployed to form screens across the German 9th Army's anticipated route.[27]

By the evening of 28 April General Busse was all set to break the 9th Army out of its 'pocket'. Now incorporating the survivors of the Frankfurt-an-der-

Oder Garrison, his formations were all concentrated ready for the move in a small area roughly between Halbe and Märkische Buchholz west of the Dahme River.[28]

Busse's intention was to save as many people as he could from the Soviets' clutches. Although he had lately received approval for his move from Hitler in the guise of the order instructing the 9th and 12th Armies to link up near Jüterbog to strike jointly toward Berlin, Busse, in his own words, 'neither acknowledged, nor answered'. He was in direct radio contact with General Wenck, who advised him of his secret line of march toward Beelitz, where the Soviet lines were considered weakest (in fact the 5th Guards Mechanized Corps' lines ended there), and, as far as both generals were concerned, this was strictly a salvage operation.

The point of breakout suggested by reconnaissance was at Halbe, roughly on the Soviet interfront boundary, where co-ordination would be the least effective, particularly once the 9th Army had crossed the territory of one front, thus automatically checking the fire of the other. From there the proposed escape route ran some 37 miles through a wide belt of woodland running westward past Luckenwalde. They would have to move day and night to keep ahead of the inevitable countermeasures, but the trees would serve to hamper the effectiveness of the Soviet tanks and aircraft.

The 9th Army's preparations were both thorough and drastic. Anything not essential for the breakout was destroyed or discarded. The last remaining motor vehicles were wrecked and their tanks drained to provide fuel for the fighting vehicles. Artillery pieces lacking ammunition were rendered unserviceable and every soldier with a firearm, whatever his trade or employment, was organized into a combat unit.

It was planned to move in a tight wedge, for which the formations had been deployed as follows:

XI SS Panzer Corps
Facing the breakout line near and north of Halbe with all the available armoured vehicles, and tasked with effecting the initial breach and then taking over the northern flank of the breakthrough.

V Corps
Covering the southern flank of the breakout position, then responsible for following the XI Panzer Corps through the breach and taking over the point for the breakthrough while also covering the southern flank.

V SS Mountain Corps
Covering the breakout from the east and northeast, thereafter covering the rear of the breakthrough.

21st Panzer Division
Covering the breakout from the northwest with orders to fall back on Halbe as soon as the V SS Mountain Corps were through the breach and to follow on as rearguard under command of that corps.

The remaining artillery were massed near Halbe with the few rounds that were left for them.

Between the military units swarmed tens of thousands of refugees opting to break out with the troops, although they must have realized how slim their chances of survival were. Having spotted some of the preliminary moves from the air, the Soviets knew where to concentrate their artillery and air efforts, including bombing the crossings over the Dahme River, and inevitably the toll exacted from these wretched refugees was high. Nevertheless, for most of them the conditions and prospects were now so bad that the breakout, however slender a chance it offered of getting safely across the Elbe, presented a worthwhile gamble, and this time Busse did not try to stop them.

As soon as dusk started falling, the operation began with a brief artillery barrage on the area selected for the breach and the XI SS Panzer Corps started a night-long battle to clear the way.

Directly opposing them was the extreme left wing of the 3rd Guards Army, with the 21st Rifle Corps deployed in the woods between the front boundary on the Halbe-Teupitz road and the village of Teurow, where the Dahme River became the front line as far as Märkische Buchholz and was manned by the 120nd Rifle Corps of the same army. The Dahme valley south of Teurow, where the forest had been cleared for cultivation, was crammed with Soviet artillery. In addition to their integral artillery support, the whole of the 1st Guards Artillery Division was assigned to this operation with the sole object of eliminating the 9th Army. The Soviet deployment was facilitated by the proximity of the Breslau–Berlin autobahn, which also served as their main supply route.[29]

After a night of desperate fighting a breach was opened by first light. Before it was full light the commanders had to get their people flooding through this breach. It was a hectic scramble, but the XI SS Panzer Corps and the V Corps managed to get through and away. For the rearguard it was not so easy. It seems that the Soviets managed to close the breach before the V SS Mountain Corps could get through, and they then had to bear the brunt of the Soviet artillery fire in their own struggle to break through an area already strewn with the casualties of the preceding corps. Meanwhile the main body worked its way westward through the woods, reaching the Soviet cordon on the

Zossen–Baruth road by midday, and by evening they had succeeded in breaking through this barrier.[30]

On the morning of 28 April, with Gatow Airfield now secured, the 175th Rifle Division of the 47th Army's 125th Rifle Corps attacked Potsdam from the north with the assistance of the 50th Guards Tank and 33rd Guards Mechanized Brigades. General Reymann's 20,000-strong garrison, which had meanwhile established contact with the 12th Army on the far side of the Schwielowsee, pulled back before them, abandoning the town. The same night they made good their escape along the lake side or across the water in inflatable boats.[31]

The 28 April was an important day for the 2nd Guards Tank Army. Having abandoned the Ruhleben scene to the 1st Ukrainian Front, General Bogdanov redeployed his forces during the night for the three attacks commencing at dawn. The 1st Mechanized Corps concentrated on the bend in the Spree due north of the Schloss Charlottenburg gardens, where the Spree Locks provided a potential crossing point for their infantry, its 219th Tank Brigade conducting an assault on the adjacent Jungfernheide S-Bahn station strongpoint, where the overpasses provided the only gaps in the railway embankment screening the western part of Moabit. Despite all their efforts, the Soviet troops were unable to break through here that day. Meanwhile the 12th Guards Tank Corps crossed by the 79th Rifle Corps' route over the Westhafen into Moabit, and began fighting its way down the tongue of land between the Spree and the mouth of the Landwehr Canal.[32]

On the afternoon of 28 April, the leading elements of the 79th Rifle Corps advancing down the street known as Alt Moabit first caught sight of the Reichstag building through the swirling clouds of smoke and dust that obscured the central districts of the city. The fixation of the Soviets on the Reichstag as their goal was to highlight this particular part of the battle to heroic proportions. Heroic as it undoubtedly was in its execution, this episode also emphasizes the ruthless exploitation of the troops involved and the fundamental military errors made by the commanders in their haste to meet a politically dictated deadline. The pressure from Stalin downward to get the Red Flag flying from the top of the Reichstag in time for the May Day celebrations was such that no one in the chain of command wanted to be in a position where he could be accused of sabotaging the project. The cost was of no consequence.[33]

The news created great excitement and the Corps Commander, Major-General S.N. Perevertkin, hastened forward to see for himself. He decided to set up his command post in the tall Customs building at the end of the

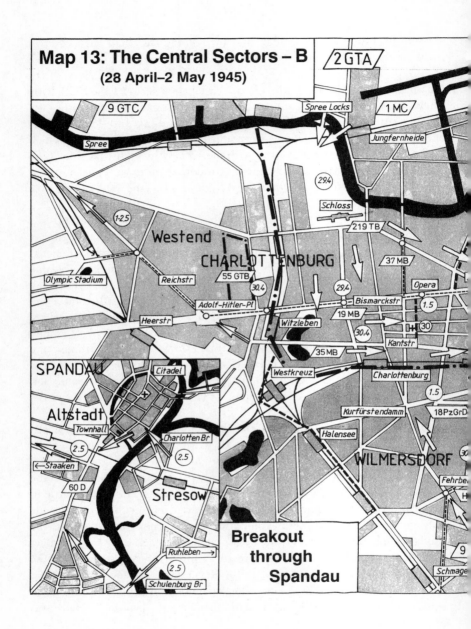

Map 13: The Central Sectors – B
(28 April–2 May 1945)

2 GTA

9 GTC

Spree Locks

1 MC

Spree

Jungfernheide

29.4

Schloss

219 TB

Westend

CHARLOTTENBURG

37 MB

1-2.5

Olympic Stadium

Reichstr

55 GTB

30.4

Opera

Adolf-Hitler-Pl

29.4

Bismarckstr

1.5

19 MB

Heerstr

Witzleben

30

30.4

Kantstr

35 MB

SPANDAU

Citadel

Westkreuz

Charlottenburg

Altstadt

1.5

Townhall

Kurfürstendamm

18 PzGrD

2.5

Charlotten Br

2.5

Halensee

←Staaken

WILMERSDORF

30

60 D

Fehrbe

Stresow

H

**Breakout
through
Spandau**

Ruhleben→

9

2.5

Schmage

Schulenburg Br

1	Reichstag	11	Potsdamer Platz	21	Friedrichstrasse
2	Brandenburg Gate	12	Potsdamer Station	22	Gendarmenmarkt
3	Pariser Platz	13	RHSA and Gestapo HQ	23	Schloss Berlin
4	Adlon Hotel	14	Saarlandstrasse	24	Reichsbank
5	Propaganda Ministry	15	Anhalter Station	25	Spittelmarkt
6	Reichs Chancellery	16	Möckern Bridge Station	26	Reichs Patent Office
7	Kaiserhof Hotel	17	Weidendammer Bridge	27	Natural History Museum
8	Keipziger Strasse	18	Friedrichstrasse Station	28	Jebenstrasse
9	Post Office Ministry	19	Unter-den-Linden	29	Steinplatz
10	Air Ministry	20	Stadtmitte Station	30	Karl-August-Platz

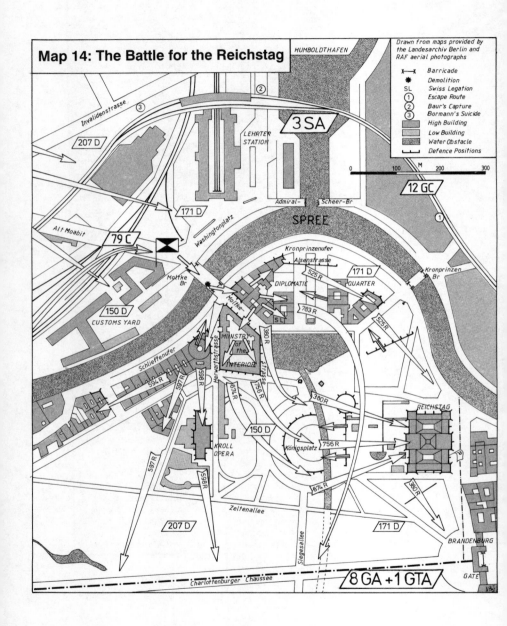

Map 14: The Battle for the Reichstag

HUMBOLDTHAFEN

Drawn from maps provided by
the Landesarchiv Berlin and
RAF aerial photographs

×—× Barricade
✴ Demolition
SL Swiss Legation
① Escape Route
② Baur's Capture
③ Bormann's Suicide
High Building
Low Building
Water Obstacle
Defence Positions

0   100   M   200   300

Invalidenstrasse ③

207 D

3 SA

LEHRTER STATION

12 GC

Admiral-   Scheer-Br

171 D

SPREE

Alt Moabit

79 C

Washingtonplatz

Kronprinzenufer

Alsenstrasse

525 R

171 D

QUARTER

Kronprinzen-
Br

Moltke
Br

Moltke-

DIPLOMATIC

150 D

CUSTOMS YARD

783 R

S.L

525 R

Schlieffenufer

MINSTRY
of
the
INTERIOR

380 R

594 R   597 R   598 R

674 R

756 R

380 R

REICHSTAG

KROLL
OPERA

150 D

Königsplatz

756 R

597 R

598 R

Zeltenallee

207 D

Siegesallee

674 R

380 R

171 D

BRANDENBURG

GATE

Charlottenburger Chaussee

8 GA + 1 GTA

street overlooking the Moltke Bridge and the approaches to the Reichstag. The 150th Rifle Division were already beginning to assemble in the vicinity of the Customs building and he called forward the 171st Rifle Division to assemble in the ruins of the Lehrter Railway Station on the other side of the street.

Immediately to the left was the Schiffahrts Canal denoting the corps boundary, behind which the Germans were still holding out as far north as Invalidenstrasse against the 12th Guards Rifle Corps. There were also German troops north of the Spree on his right in Lehrter Goods Station, which had not been on his corps' line of advance and so remained uncleared. Across his front the river was some 50 yards wide, the stone quay of the Customs Yard dropping ten feet to water level in full view of the enemy opposite. The only ready means available for crossing the river was the massive stone-built Moltke Bridge, which was strongly barricaded at either end, ready mined for demolition, strewn with barbed wire and other obstacles, and swept by artillery and machine-gun fire from positions concealed in the buildings on the far bank. Across the bridge on either side of Moltkestrasse were the badly damaged but still standing and heavily fortified buildings of the Diplomatic Quarter and the Ministry of the Interior. Behind them aerial reconnaissance had revealed the presence of a large flooded pit from which an anti-tank ditch extended right across Königsplatz (Platz der Republik) in front of a series of trenches and gun emplacements connecting with the Reichstag itself. Further artillery and mortars were entrenched in the Tiergarten and the whole area was expected to be mined, as indeed it was. Like the other buildings in the area, the Reichstag had its doors and windows bricked up except for small gunports, and was to prove virtually impervious to shelling. All these buildings had street-level cellar windows providing ready-made gun embrasures, and high in the burnt-out frame of the Reichstag dome were hidden further machine-guns.

The large water obstacle, which would influence the line of attack, was in fact part of the cutting intended for the diversion of the Spree to enable the construction of Albert Speer's Great Hall on the north side of the square, the anti-tank ditch being a cutting for a U–Bahn tunnel leading to Moltkestrasse. The tunnel, running parallel to Siegesallee, had been completed as far north as Königsplatz before work had been abruptly abandoned two or three years previously, leaving the construction site littered with temporary buildings, all of which had been incorporated into the defence system.[34]

The Red Air Force's attacks had to be called off due to the narrowness of the battlefield, but ground-attack aircraft continued to simulate attacks as a deterrent in support of the ground forces, and the massed Soviet heavy artillery were now concentrating their efforts on this area between the Spree and the Landwehr Canal, which Chuikov's troops were preparing to cross from the south, and there was no shortage of ammunition.[35]

It was decided to attempt a surprise infantry attack across the Moltke Bridge with a view to establishing a foothold in the near corner building of the Diplomatic Quarter on the left, using one battalion from each of the two leading divisions. This could then be expanded into a bridgehead to enable the 150th Rifle Division to launch an attack across the Moltkestrasse into the Ministry of the Interior building dominating the crossing point, while the 171st Rifle Division cleared the remainder of the Diplomatic Quarter. Once secured, these buildings would provide a firm base for the attack on the Reichstag itself.

Casualties sustained in the fierce fighting through Moabit had been replaced by released prisoners-of-war, and the leading Soviet battalions were now back up to full strength. A battalion had an establishment of 500 men and consisted of three rifle companies, a support weapons company and a battery of 45mm field guns, but for this operation the battalions were split into two assault groups each, to which were added detachments of armoured self-propelled artillery. Also under the command of the 79th Rifle Corps were the 10th Independent Flame-Thrower Battalion and the 23rd Tank Brigade.

Soviet estimates of the opposition are later quoted as being some 5,000 German troops of various kinds. However, SS Sergeant-Major Willi Rogmann, who in addition to commanding the 'Anhalt' Regiment's mortar platoon was also responsible for taking forward groups of rounded-up stragglers to reinforce the regiment's various companies throughout this stage of the battle, reports that an unknown number of Allgemeine-SS under a police colonel were defending their offices in the Ministry of Interior, and that only SS Lieutenant Babick's company of some 100 potential NCOs was deployed between the bridge, the Reichstag and the Brandenburg Gate. As reinforcements, Babick belatedly received about 250 sailors from the 'Grossadmiral Dönitz' Battalion and about 100 Volkssturm. There were also some tanks of the 11th SS 'Hermann von Salza' Tank Battalion in the Tiergarten.

During the early evening of 28 April, Rogmann went forward to reconnoitre the Moltke Bridge area with Sergeant-Major Kurt Abicht of a battery commanded by a one-armed artillery lieutenant who, having lost his own unit, had attached himself to Rogmann's platoon with two guns, for which the officer had managed to scrounge some rounds from the Reichs Chancellery. The police colonel refused to allow them to set up an observation post in the

Ministry of the Interior building, so they went across the road into the Diplomatic Quarter. Rogmann first tried out some of his rockets on the Customs Yard and Washingtonplatz, causing havoc among the Soviet artillery massing there. Rogmann and Abicht then set up their last two mortars and the guns to cover the bridge.[36]

Throughout the 5th Shock Army's sector on 28 April the fighting remained extremely confused, although steady progress was being maintained. On the right flank in the 26th Guards Rifle Corps' sector, the 94th Guards Rifle Division came to the aid of the 89th Guards Rifle Division, attacking Alexanderplatz from the east and northeast, while the 266th Rifle Division stormed the solidly built Police Presidium with the support of Lieutenant-Colonel Doroshkin's 322nd Independent Heavy Artillery Battalion, but it took until 1500 hours the next day until the building was finally secured. Behind them around the Friedrichshain flak-tower, Landsberger Chaussee and Frankfurter Allee area German pockets of resistance continued to hold out. The flak-tower held out until 0500 hours on 1 May, the civilians sheltering there having been evicted on the night of 23 April.[37]

The 32nd Rifle Corps was still engaged with the reduction of the Schlesische Railway Station and other positions holding out in their rear. The 416th Rifle Division on the right flank, where it had been making its way along the north bank of the Spree, was checked by a German position at the elevated Jannowitzbrücke S-Bahn Station.

The 9th Rifle Corps on the west bank of the river seized the Spittelmarkt area, which had been completely pulverized by artillery fire beforehand and its defenders obliterated in the ruins. On the left flank, the 1050th and 1052nd Rifle Regiments of the 301st Rifle Division took the Reichs Patent Office on the Landwehr Canal embankment, claiming to have killed 80 and taken 146 prisoners in this strongpoint. Thus the end of the day saw the leading elements of the 5th Shock Army at the eastern end of the broad expanse of Leipziger Strasse and less than 1,500 yards from their goal: the Reichs Chancellery.[38]

That evening Captain Albert Lieselang was ordered by Lieutenant-Colonel Ernst Seifert to take an assault group to the Spittelmarkt area, where the Soviets were threatening to outflank some SS 'Nordland' troops. The assault group consisted mainly of Volkssturm, some of Commander Kuhlmann's sailors and a few military stragglers. His first concern was to ensure that there was suitable ammunition for the variety of weapons with which this group was armed. However, this counter-probe foundered when the group was caught in an artillery barrage and Lieselang wounded.

Persistent attacks by Soviet tanks trying to force their way up Friedrichstrasse, Wilhelmstrasse and Saarlandstrasse (Stresemannstrasse), supported by heavy artillery fire, were effectively countered by the French tank-hunters of the SS 'Charlemagne' Battalion with their Panzerfausts.[39]

Chuikov's preparations for his assault across the Landwehr Canal provided for the maximum possible deployment of heavy artillery and rocket-launchers in the direct-fire support role. These were brought up and positioned during the day under cover of smoke-screens. Ammunition was plentiful and orders went out not to spare it. However, the artillery and mortar fire plans had to be carefully co-ordinated with those of the other converging armies in order to avoid overshooting and inflicting casualties on their own troops, for now only 2,000 yards separated them on a north–south line through the Tiergarten.[40]

The area of assault extended between a point opposite the OKW in Bendlerstrasse in the west to Belle-Alliance-Platz in the east, an area about 2,000 yards long, and it was decided that individual units should determine their own means of getting across in small groups as the circumstances varied so considerably. The humpbacked Potsdamer Bridge was the only bridge still intact along this stretch of the canal, and Chuikov reserved for himself direct control of the operation there. Two large aerial mines were suspended from the structure ready for detonation, and the whole area was swept by heavy enfilade fire from artillery, tanks and Panzerfausts, but it offered the only means of getting armour across during the initial assault, and was therefore vital for the operation. From there the Potsdamer Strasse led toward the Reichs Chancellery only 1,500 yards away.[41]

Reconnaissance activity continued throughout the day, and the scouts investigating the tunnels leading under the canal (that is, the S-Bahn tunnel leading from the Yorckstrasse marshalling yards and the U-Bahn leading from Belle-Alliance-Strasse (Mehringplatz) into Friedrichstrasse) reported that they were impracticable as a means of approach, being blocked by manned barricades at regular intervals and very narrow. However, reinforced reconnaissance patrols were sent by these routes to try to harass the Germans from the rear.[42]

In his preparations for this final battle Chuikov paid particular attention to the political reinforcement of his units. In the confined and confusing conditions of street-fighting it was impossible for higher field commanders to see exactly what was going on. It was therefore important to have reliable cadres of Communist Party and Komsomol members throughout the deployed units to ensure that orders passed down from above were duly executed, especially in these closing phases of the war when everyone was so reluctant to take risks.[43]

On the morning of 28 April, in accordance with orders issued the night before after the Inner Defence Ring had been breached in Schöneberg, the 3rd Guards Tank Army launched a concerted attack on the extreme right wing of their area of operations, their startline being Badensche Strasse between Kaiserallee (Bundesallee) and Potsdamer Strasse, with their objective the crossing of the Landwehr Canal by nightfall.[44] In support of this operation the 55th Guards Tank Brigade was taken from its blockading role in the Westend and thrust down the axis of Kantstrasse for Charlottenburg Station, Savignyplatz and the Zoo.[45]

The main attack got under way as planned and it was not until sometime later during the morning that it was suddenly realized that virtually the whole of the eastern half of their proposed line of advance was already occupied by Chuikov's troops, on whom the weight of Koniev's artillery preparations could hardly have been welcome. As a result of this discovery, the 9th Mechanized Corps and its supporting 61st Guards Rifle Division had to be switched from the right to the left flank and the whole army redirected northwestward with the new right flank heading for Savignyplatz. The emotions that this event raised can well be imagined!

However, this change of plan came as a welcome relief to the 56th Guards Tank Brigade on the exposed left flank of the 7th Guards Tank Corps' two-brigade front, which had been attracting the full attention of the German tank-hunting units based on Fehrbelliner Platz and suffering accordingly. The 51st Panzergrenadier Regiment of the 18th Panzergrenadier Division still held on grimly to its positions, especially at Schmargendorf S-Bahn station and in the adjacent Hindenburg Park (Volkspark), where it had good fields of fire. However, the incessant hammering from the massed Soviet artillery eventually forced the defence to give ground. There followed some bitter fighting around Fehrbelliner Platz where it was to take the Soviets another day to break through. After a German battery had been eliminated there, Major Baechle's Hitlerjugend tank-hunting unit, using Panzerfausts mounted on staff cars, carried out a series of raids in the Wilmersdorf District. Soviet casualties continued to be high.[46]

With his Berlin ambitions thus thwarted, Koniev left Colonel-General Rybalko to complete the 1st Ukrainian Front's role in the city as best he might. Koniev had taken a tremendous gamble in concentrating all his available resources in a single powerful thrust on the Reichstag, leaving only one reinforced brigade to cope with all the enemy forces between the Havel and Schöneberg, but he had in fact been defeated by factors arising out of the rivalry between himself and Zhukov, which had been skilfully exploited by Stalin without regard for the military implications. At midnight Moscow time (2200 hours in Berlin) GHQ issued orders for a new interfront boundary, which was to run along the line Mariendorf/Tempelhof Goods Station/Viktoria-Luise-Platz/Savignyplatz S-Bahn Station and thence along the S-Bahn line via Charlottenburg, Westkreuz and Witzleben Stations.[47]

Meanwhile Colonel Anton Eder of Defence Sector 'F' sent a strong patrol from Ruhleben Barracks to re-establish contact with Defence Area Headquarters. Passing through the Westend with all its evidence of the 55th Guards Tank Brigade's passage, the patrol split into two groups on Adolf-Hitler-Platz (Theodor-Heuss-Platz) to follow the U-Bahn tunnels in the direction of the Zoo above and below ground. The group groping its way forward in the dark tunnels came under attack when passing the junction to Richard-Wagner-Platz, but eventually reached as far as Wittenbergplatz before returning above ground to the Zoo flak-tower. The patrol returned by the same route during the early hours of 29 April.[48]

Second Lieutenant Kroemer of the 'Müncheberg' Panzer Division wrote of 28 April:

> Continuous attacks throughout the night. The Russians are trying to break through in Leipziger Strasse. Prinz-Albrecht-Strasse (Niederkirschener Strasse) has been retaken, as has Köthener Strasse.
>
> Increasing signs of disintegration and despair, but it makes no sense surrendering at the last moment and then spending the rest of your life regretting not having held on to the end.
>
> 'K' brings news that American armoured divisions are on the way to Berlin, which makes them in the Reichs Chancellery more certain of ultimate victory than ever before.
>
> Hardly any communications among the combat groups, in as much as none of the active battalions have radio communications any more. Telephone cables are shot through in no time at all. Physical conditions are indescribable. No relief or respite, no regular food and hardly any bread. Nervous breakdowns from the continuous artillery fire. Water has to be obtained from the tunnels and the Spree and then filtered. The not too seriously wounded are hardly taken in anywhere, the civilians being too afraid to accept wounded soldiers and officers into their cellars when so many are hanged as real or presumed deserters and the occupants of the cellars concerned being ruthlessly turfed out as accomplices by the members of the flying courts martial.

These flying courts martial are particularly active in our sector today. Most of them are very young SS officers with hardly a decoration between them, blind and fanatical. Hope of relief and fear of these courts martial keep our men going. General Mummert has requested that no further courts martial visit our sector. A division that contains the most highly decorated personnel does not deserve to be prosecuted by such youngsters. He has made up his mind to shoot any court martial team that he comes across in person.

Potsdamer Platz is a ruined waste. Masses of wrecked vehicles and shot-up ambulances with the wounded still inside them. Dead everywhere, many of them frightfully mangled by tanks and trucks.

In the evening we try and get news from the Propaganda Ministry of Wenck and the American divisions. There are rumors that the 9th Army is also on its way to Berlin and that peace treaties are being signed in the west.

Violent shelling of the city centre at dusk with simultaneous attacks on our positions. We cannot hold on to Potsdamer Platz any longer and at about 0400 hours make for Nollendorfplatz (south of the Landwehr Canal) as Russians heading for Potsdamer Platz pass us in the parallel tunnel.[49]

At about 2100 hours on 28 April, news of Himmler's peace talks with Count Bernadotte of Sweden was intercepted by the Propaganda Ministry from a Reuter news broadcast in German on Radio Stockholm. This news profoundly shocked Hitler; that *der treue Heinrich* could do this to him was absolutely unthinkable; it was treachery of the worst kind and must be avenged at all costs.[50]

The intrepid warrant officer that had flown Speer to Berlin and back, and then von Greim and Hanna Reitsch to Gatow, had managed to fly in an Arado 96 that night to take them out again. Hitler instructed von Greim to use all the remaining Luftwaffe resources in assisting the defence of Berlin and, above all, to find Himmler and bring him to justice. Von Greim was in pain and on crutches but he was helped out of the bunker into an armoured vehicle that took them up Hermann-Göring-Strasse (Ebertstrasse) to the airstrip. Dodging small-arms fire, flak and searchlights, the warrant officer pilot took off and found safety in a cloudbank at 4,500 feet above the city and then followed a trail of burning villages marking the extent of the Soviet advance back to Rechlin Airbase.[51]

At this stage one sees that Hitler's personal influence on the conduct of the battle as a commander had ceased to have any direct effect. He could of course have brought about an immediate end to the conflict but that was not his intention. Direction was now effectively in the hands of the field commanders who, although still bound by oaths of loyalty to the Führer, saw these as less important than the loyalty they owed to their troops in this predicament.

Weidling's forces were now confined in a sausage-shaped area extending from the Alexanderplatz in the east some eight and a half miles to the banks of the Havel in the west, and barely a mile wide in places. He still had about 30,000 combatants and a handful of tanks and guns, but food and ammunition were running out fast, and he estimated that they could not hold out longer than another 48 hours.[52]

General Weidling himself could have little influence on events. He had been given command of the defence too late to inject any idea of his own and, although he had substituted proper military commanders for the Defence Sectors, each had to fight his own battle with the existing resources, for Weidling had nothing extra to give them. SS Major-General Krukenberg later complained that he did not receive any orders or instructions from Weidling during the battle, but there were none to give, and, in any case, once Krukenberg had withdrawn to 'Zitadelle' he had subordinated himself and his division to Mohnke, who did not consider himself answerable to Weidling. Weidling was not even in a position to take unilateral action as Wenck, Busse, Heinrici and von Manteuffel were doing, for his forces contained too many hard-core Nazis like these to permit either a breakout or a surrender without Hitler's sanction. Indeed, there are many recorded instances of these fanatics shooting down their fellow countrymen when they did attempt to surrender.[53]

At about 2230 hours von Manteuffel telephoned Heinrici to report that half his divisions and all his supporting flak were in full retreat. He said that he had not seen anything like it since 1918: 100,000 trekking westward; it would take hundreds of officers to stop them. He suggested that Jodl be invited to see the situation for himself. Shortly afterwards, Heinrici passed on the news of the debacle to Keitel and asked permission to abandon Swinemünde where the garrison of naval cadets was in immediate danger of being cut off. The scandalized Keitel accused him of flagrant disobedience of the Führer's orders. Heinrici rejoined that he could not accept the responsibility for continuing to command troops under the impossible conditions expected of him by the OKW, whereupon Keitel promptly relieved him of his command and would have had him court-martialled if he had had the chance.[54]

There was a surprise in the Führerbunker that night when Hitler announced his intention of marrying his mistress, Eva Braun. Goebbels sent out for a suitably qualified official to perform the ceremony and at about 0130 hours a bewildered man wearing a Volkssturm armband, Gauamtsleiter Walter Wagner, was brought in briefly from the street-fighting to legalize their union.

Shortly afterward Hitler began dictating his personal and political testaments to one of his secretaries, naming Grand Admiral Dönitz as his successor in the role of President and Goebbels as Chancellor. Clearly he was preparing himself for the end, having lost all hope in the future.[55]

During the course of the night of 28 April, commencing at 2100 hours, the 10th Guards Tank Corps, supported by the 350th Rifle Division, launched an attack across the Teltow Canal on the southwestern tip of Wannsee 'island'. Within an hour they had established a bridgehead and begun connecting a pontoon bridge to it. The few survivors of the 20th Panzergrenadier Division, now down to 75 all ranks, and other remnants of Lieutenant-General Reymann's Army Detachment 'Spree' resisted fiercely and seem to have been able to contain this incursion for the time being, blowing up the Glienicker Bridge in the process. From Koniev's account it is clear that he did not approve of this operation, which to him must have appeared as an unnecessary distraction from his more pressing issues with the German 9th and 12th Armies.[56]

General Reymann radioed General Weidling for the last time that evening with the information that he had established contact with Wenck's 12th Army at Ferch, south of Potsdam.[57] The 47th Army and the 9th Guards Tank Corps had invaded Potsdam 'island' earlier that day from the north.

That same night the 9th Guards Tank Corps reverted to the command of the 2nd Guards Tank Army, which was now heavily engaged in the Charlottenburg and Moabit districts of Berlin, taking over the reserve position in the Siemensstadt area from the 1st Mechanized Corps.[58]

9

THE LAST ROUND

Throughout 29 April General Wenck's troops held on to their extended positions against increasing Soviet pressure all along the line as they awaited the arrival of the 9th Army. It was clear that they would not be able to advance any further and Wenck signalled General Weidling in Berlin:

> Counterattacks by 12th Army stalled south of Potsdam. Troops engaged in very heavy defensive fighting. Suggest you break out to us.

This signal was not acknowledged and it is doubtful that Weidling even received it.[1]

That same evening Wenck's position was further imperilled by a sudden attack northward toward Wittenberg by American troops bursting out of their bridgeheads in his rear. Fortunately, this attack was not pursued, presumably because of the policy imposed from above of not intervening in the Soviet area of operations.[2]

As already mentioned, General Busse's spearhead broke through the Soviet lines on the Zossen–Baruth road that day, and the survivors then rested in the woods west of the road prior to undertaking the next desperate stage of their breakout. The number of refugees managing to keep up with the wedge was diminishing rapidly. Contact had been lost with the V SS Mountain Corps, and one assumes that the whole of the rearguard with the majority of the refugees had been caught in the Soviet trap and were in the course of being liquidated. In the obscurity of the woods the Soviets may well have been misled, at least temporarily, into thinking that they had caught the bulk of the 9th Army and later, having realized their error, were happy to prolong the myth.[3]

The V SS Mountain Corps and the 21st Panzer Division fought desperately to break out of the reinforced Soviet cordon: in doing so they not only inflicted heavy casualties on the enemy but also served to distract attention from the remainder of the 9th Army. Although they managed to break out of the Halbe position, they were unable to break through the Soviet cordon and remained under a hail of shell and mortar fire. This bitter struggle continued for two days. The Soviets then claimed to have killed 60,000 and captured 120,000 prisoners, 300 tanks and self-propelled guns and 1,500 pieces of artillery. Shortly afterwards, a Soviet writer driving north along the autobahn found it littered for miles with wrecked vehicles and equipment, mingled with dead and wounded German soldiers, whom the Soviets had not yet had time to remove.[4]

However, the state of the troops in the breakout party was now such that General Busse signalled General Wenck:

> The physical state and morale of the officers and men, as well as the states of ammunition and supplies, permit neither a new attack nor long resistance. The misery of the civilians that fled out of the pocket is particularly bad. Only the measures taken by all the generals have enabled the troops to stick together. The fighting capacity of the 9th Army is obviously at an end.[5]

Wenck immediately passed this discouraging information on to the OKW, who in the meantime had themselves put an end to any chances of relief from this direction by disclosing the 12th Army's disposition and intentions in their afternoon radio communiqué. This made it even more difficult for the 12th Army to hold on to their positions in a situation already precarious enough with the 5th Guards Mechanized Corps and the 13th Army trying to cut off their line of retreat to the Elbe.

Wenck signalled the OKW again that evening:

> The Army, and in particular the XX Corps which has temporarily succeeded in establishing contact with the Potsdam Garrison, is obliged to turn to the defensive along the whole front. This means that an attack on Berlin is now impossible, having ascertained that we can no longer rely on the fighting capacity of the 9th Army.[6]

During the night Wenck received the following reluctant acknowledgement of the situation by signal from Field Marshal Keitel:

> If the Commanding General 12th Army, in full knowledge of the current situation at the XX Corps, and despite the high historical and moral responsibility that he carries, considers continuing the attack toward Berlin impossible ...

Wenck now had a free hand to pursue his own plans.[7]

General von Manteuffel was ordered to take over the Army Group 'Weichsel' but, loyal to his own troops and Heinrici, he refused with the words: 'Beg not at this time of crisis to be charged with the mission that the present Commanding General, who has the full confidence of all Commanders, is alleged not to have fulfilled.' Keitel and Jodl then decided to fly back Colonel-General Kurt Student, the famous paratroop commander, from Holland to take over the Army Group. In the interim General von Tippelskirch of the new 21st Army was to stand in. He too refused the appointment, but Keitel and Jodl went to see him and persuaded him to accept the post on the grounds that it was imperative for the Army Group to hold on to as much territory as possible, not with the intention of relieving Berlin, but in order to give the politicians something to bargain with.[8]

However, the 2nd Byelorussian Front was pressing hard and that day overran Anklam in the north, Neubrandenburg and Neustrelitz in the centre, and crossed the Havel in the Zehdenick–Liebenwalde sector on the southern flank. From the other side of the Elbe the British 21st Army Group established a bridgehead at Lauenburg, where Field Marshal Ernst Busch was struggling to keep open the Elbe–Lübeck gap as an escape route to the northwest.[9]

Rain during the night caused the balloon supporting the OKW radio-telephone aerial to sink, but the weather was bright and warm on the morning of 29 April, and communications were soon re-established with the Führer-bunker. Unfortunately the weather also brought the Soviet aircraft out in swarms and in the middle of a conversation between Hitler and Jodl the balloon was shot down. This being the last one available, communications from then on were reduced to normal radio transmissions. The Soviet ground forces were now very close to their location and at midday the OKW started moving out. Keitel and Jodl waited for dusk before taking the road to Waren, barely an hour before the camp was overrun.[10]

With the 3rd Panzer Army in full retreat there was no longer any question of relieving Berlin from the north, or indeed of providing any further support for the city from that quarter.

It was decided that two copies of Hitler's personal and political testaments should be sent to Grand Admiral Dönitz by separate couriers to ensure delivery. Bormann selected his personal adviser, SS Standartenführer (Colonel) Wilhelm Zander, and Heinz Lorenz of the Propaganda Ministry for this task. A third set of copies was to go to Field Marshal Schörner in the care of Hitler's army aide-de-camp, Major Willi Johannmeier, who, with his orderly, would escort the others through the Soviet lines. They set off at noon on 29 April, making their way slowly through the Tiergarten to the Zoo position and then along Kantstrasse to Adolf-Hitler-Platz (Theodor-Heuss-Platz), up Reichsstrasse to the Olympic Stadium and then down to the Hitlerjugend Regiment's position on the Heerstrasse, where they rested until midnight before setting off in two boats down the Havel.[11]

Inspired by this departure, three young and now redundant aides, Lieutenant-Colonel Weiss, Major von Loringhoven and Captain Gerhard Boldt, obtained permission to try to join up with Wenck's army. They left between 1400 and 1500 hours, taking the same route through the fighting and shellfire. Boldt later recorded that they had passed a position of 12–15 artillery pieces in the Tiergarten, all abandoned for lack of ammunition.[12]

Then at midnight Colonel von Below and his aide, escorted by their orderlies, also left the Führerbunker, taking with them a letter from Hitler to Field Marshal Keitel concerning the appointment of Grand Admiral Dönitz as his successor. This letter contained praise for the work of the Navy and the Luftwaffe, and also praised the common soldiers, but denounced the generals for betraying his trust in them. Just before dawn this group caught up with Lieutenant-Colonel Weiss' party at the Olympic Stadium, from where they continued their journey with a Hitlerjugend patrol to the Hitlerjugend Regiment's position on the Havel. There they had to wait until the following night before they could continue downriver by boat.[13]

In the meantime Johannmeier's party had reached the Wannsee 'island' before dawn on 30 April. There they found the remains of the 20th Panzer-grenadier Division, with whose assistance they managed to radio a request to Grand Admiral Dönitz to send an aircraft to collect them. They then moved to Pfaueninsel (Peacock Island) to await its arrival and were joined by Weiss' party early next morning. However, von Below landed on the other side of the Havel near Gatow Airfield and struck off due west for the Elbe, later burning the papers he was carrying when he realized the futility of his mission.[14]

The morning of 29 April saw a breakthrough in the 2nd Guards Tanks Army's sector. The 1st Mechanized Corps' motorized infantry crossed the Spree at the locks and fought their way through the gardens of Schloss Charlottenburg and into the ruins of the building, while the 219th Tank Brigade broke through the Jungfernheide S-Bahn Station position. Sappers of the 6th Polish Pontoon-Bridging Battalion built a pontoon bridge under fire for the Soviet infantry, then repaired the damaged railway bridge to enable the tanks to join them. Meanwhile the 12th Guards Tank Corps, using massive artillery support, continued to make steady progress through western Moabit heading for the tongue of land between the Spree and the western end of the Landwehr Canal. However, the 2nd Guards Tank Army was now desperately short of infantry and appealed to Marshal Zhukov for reinforcements. The latter then arranged for the 1st Polish Infantry Division to come to its aid, for he had no Soviet reinforcements available, but it was to take all the following day for the Polish troops to be ferried by truck down from the Oranienburg area.[15]

The 79th Rifle Corps' attack across the Moltke Bridge was a daring and bloody affair. During the evening of 28 April both sides made their preparations. The Soviets used heavy tanks to push aside the northern barricade on the bridge, while the Germans reinforced the two 'Anhalt' companies, one on either side of the Ministry of the Interior, with 250 of the sailors that Dönitz had had flown in, and sent forward observers to control mortar, rocket and artillery fire, all of which weapons were then zeroed in on their targets. The rockets caused much confusion among the exposed Soviet artillery massed on Washingtonplatz, but no fire was returned.

Then at midnight, the two leading battalions launched their surprise attack across the bridge, unheralded by any artillery barrage, but immediately supported by their artillery firing across the Spree either side of the bridge at point-blank range. However, the 'Anhalt' was ready for them; the attackers were caught on the wire of the southern barricade in a hail of fire from enfiladed machine-guns and blasted by the guns and mortars directed at the bridge. At the same time, the supporting Soviet artillery was brought under rocket attack from a battery located at Potsdamer Platz, causing considerable disruption.

General Perevertkin then resumed his attack by sending in heavy tanks to push aside the southern barricade. To counter this, the Germans used the fire of anti-tank guns and some tanks of the 11th SS 'Hermann von Salza' Panzer Battalion located in the Tiergarten, but were then joined by the heavy guns on the Zoo flak-tower, the impact of whose shells hurled the tanks aside in an orgy of destruction that blocked the bridge with wreckage.

The Soviet infantry then came forward once more and with the cover provided by this wreckage were able to secure a small bridgehead in the near corner of the Diplomatic Quarter. By daybreak the remaining troops of the 150th and 171st Rifle Divisions are said to have got across the bridge into this building, from where they began expanding their bridgehead by the usual method of mouseholing their way through the line of buildings fronting Moltkestrasse, while the 171st Rifle Division cleared the remainder of the block, with the 525th Rifle Regiment working the Kronprinzenufer side on the left and the 380th Rifle Regiment in the middle. That so many units were able to cram into such a small space is indicative of the number of casualties that must have been sustained in crossing the bridge and the determination of the Soviet command.

The SS officials in the Ministry of the Interior building also joined in the fight, firing machine-guns across Moltkestrasse. Then, as dawn broke, Soviet SPGs and field artillery pieces could be seen firing openly from the Customs Yard. These were engaged with devastating effect by the Zoo flak-tower's heavy guns, but the Soviets simply brought in more SPGs and tanks to replace them.

The 'Anhalt' then mounted a counterattack, which unexpectedly combined with another on the northern bank, where a unit of the 9th Parachute Division that had been defending the Lehrter Railway Station and had meanwhile withdrawn to the goods station, suddenly broke through the Soviet lines to cross the bridge, creating havoc on its way and bringing a welcome reinforcement of 100 men to the defence. The effect on the Soviet bridgehead appears to have been to pin it down temporarily. Further advantage was taken of the ensuing confusion to send forward a demolition team to blow the bridge. Unfortunately the charges proved inadequate for the massive structure, and only half of the southern of the three central spans fell into the river, still leaving sufficient room for vehicles to pass.[16]

At 0700 hours the next stage of the operation began with a ten-minute barrage as the 150th Rifle Division prepared to cross Moltkestrasse into the main entrance of the Ministry of the Interior, or 'Himmler's House' as they dubbed it. The two middle buildings on the Soviet side of the street had their carriage entrances directly opposite, so one can assume that this was the route taken. The Soviets dashed across the street and flattened themselves against the walls of the Ministry, threw grenades into the doorway and then charged through into the hall beyond. Fighting rapidly spread up the main staircase and along the various floors, and was to last all day amid the choking smoke of fires started among the carpets and furniture littered about. The SS defenders resisted fiercely and eventually the 150th Rifle Division had to call in their second echelon, the 674th Rifle Regiment, to clear the southwest corner of the building.

Between 0830 and 1000 hours there was a massive artillery bombardment of the Reichstag position in an attempt to weaken the defences there for the forthcoming attack, but there was no follow-up, for the attacking divisions were still busy clearing the buildings in their path, as they would be for the rest of the day.[17]

Fighting in the northeastern arc, in the sectors of the 12th Guards and 7th Rifle Corps of the 3rd Shock Army, continued in the same manner as before with little outward progress made in the confusion. Strong resistance was encountered at the Stettiner Railway Station strongpoint where the northern end of the S-Bahn tunnel emerged above ground.

For the 5th Shock Army 29 April was a particularly difficult day as it gradually closed in on the city centre against strong resistance from predominantly Waffen-SS troops. On the right flank in the 26th Guards Rifle Corps' sector, the 94th Guards Rifle Division headed toward the Börse (Stock Exchange) S-Bahn Station through the narrow streets of the old city centre, while the 89th Guards Rifle Division mopped up around Alexanderplatz. The 266th Rifle Division remained fully engaged within the Police Presidium building until 1500 hours, as previously mentioned, then closed up to the Rotes Rathaus, the massive red-brick city hall, which was defended by elements of the 11th SS 'Nordland' Panzergrenadier Division, who had some BDM girls with them who had volunteered to act as runners. The Soviet attack was supported by tanks and self-propelled artillery, but no headway was made until holes had been blown through the walls from an adjacent building to enable access. The Soviets were then obliged to fight for every room in turn through the clouds of dense smoke that filled the burning building, and it was not until early morning the following day that they could claim full possession.[18]

The 32nd Rifle Corps' 416th Rifle Division took the Jannowitzbrücke S-Bahn Station that day and closed up to the Spree as far as the remains of the Kurfürsten (Rathaus) Bridge and began making preparations to cross.

The 9th Rifle Corps' troops, supported by the 92nd Guards Tank Regiment, headed up Saarlandstrasse (Stresemannstrasse) for the Anhalter Railway Station, but German strongpoints were also encountered in the Christus Church on that street and in the Post Office building on Möckernstrasse. A German counterattack, supported by tanks, emerging from Bernburger Strasse was beaten back with difficulty. Meanwhile the 301st Rifle Division began attacking the Gestapo and SS Main Security Offices on Prinz-Albrecht-Strasse (Niederkirchnerstrasse), buildings desperately defended by those officials remaining.[19]

An hour before Colonel-General Chuikov's artillery preparation was due to begin, the infantry took up their positions for the assault across the Landwehr Canal in an arc extending from opposite the Bendlerblock on the left flank to the Hallesche Tor (Halle Gate) on the right, making their way forward either singly or in small groups. Some would be swimming or using improvised rafts and floating devices to get across the canal, and others were to try to rush the bridge under cover of a smoke-screen. Among the latter was the standard-bearer of the 220th Guards Rifle Regiment, Guards Sergeant

Nikolai Masalov, with his standard and two assistants, who were in the 79th Guards Rifle Division's sector opposite the Potsdamer Bridge. In the intense quiet that preceded the storm they suddenly heard the sound of a young child crying for its mother coming from the other side of the bridge. Masalov then handed over the standard to one of his assistants and approached his commanding officer for permission to attempt to rescue the child before the barrage started. He managed to crawl across under covering fire from his comrades and found a three-year-old German girl lying in the rubble next to her dead mother. As soon as the artillery fire opened up he dashed back with the child in his arms.[20]

By this stage of the battle the Soviet armour had developed some ingenious methods of countering the prolific German anti-tank weapons. Their tanks were now festooned with sandbags, bedsprings, sheet metal and other devices to cause the projectiles to explode harmlessly outside the hull, and it was an inspired adaptation of one of these devices that finally enabled them to get their tanks across the Potsdamer Bridge. Sappers had first to remove the mines planted on the bridge as well as neutralize the two large landmines suspended beneath the structure, all the while working under heavy machine-gun fire. Initial attempts to rush the infantry across the bridge met with costly failure and the Soviet tanks found themselves helpless against the fire of a dug-in 'Tiger' tank covering the crossing from an enfilade position. More artillery fire and smoke were called for, and eventually some infantry managed to get safely across, but the tanks were still being knocked out one by one as they approached. Then someone had the idea of steeping the protective covering of one of the tanks in inflammable oil and adding some smoke canisters. This tank then led the next armoured assault, bursting into flames as if it had been hit as it reached the bridge. Thinking the tank was merely careering forward out of control, the Germans ignored it until it was too late and the Soviets were across the bridge and firing into their flanks at point-blank range.[21]

Meanwhile other attempts to cross the canal along the assault line had met with varying degrees of success. In the 39th Guards Rifle Division's area toward the right flank one successful unit used the sewers to provide it with concealed approach and exit routes for swimming across, emerging in the middle of the German defences. Another unit of the same division, a company of the 120th Guards Rifle Regiment, used similar covered approaches to reach the wrecked footbridge leading across the canal to the elevated Möckern-brücke U-Bahn station on the northern bank and were able to get across the wreckage and seize the station, establishing a route for the rest of the battalion to follow. Further east at the Hallesche Tor, the engineers managed to get pontoons into the water so that tanks could reach Belle-Alliance-Platz, thereby giving Chuikov some powerful leverage on his right flank.[22]

Although several bridgeheads were established one way and another, the cost was appallingly high. The defence's artillery and machine-guns had been cleverly concealed in enfilade positions behind the buildings and the rubble on the northern bank. They could fire on these intrusions while remaining impervious to direct fire from Soviet guns on the other side of the canal. Chuikov eventually decided to bring his artillery right up to the edge of the canal from where they themselves could fire in enfilade across the convex curves of the waterway, thus using 'a wedge to knock out a wedge', as he puts it. The artillery also had to cover the enemy rear areas as the lines were now too close for air support.[23]

However, the scale of Chuikov's assault is somewhat reduced and its purpose becomes questionable when one examines Lieutenant-General F.E. Bokov's account of the 5th Shock Army's activities, for, as mentioned above, Bokov claims that the Anhalter Railway Station had already been cleared by 28 April, which is confirmed by the German report that, by nightfall on 29 April, the whole of Saarlandstrasse was in Soviet hands. Bokov further gives the boundary between the 5th Shock and 8th Guards Armies as the line between the goods and main railway stations there, i.e. barely 400 yards from the canal at that point. It therefore seems that Chuikov's assault across the canal was going into a very narrow defensive strip that had already been decisively outflanked by his neighbours. Then, once this strip had been cleared, Chuikov appears to have directed the bulk of his troops northwest into the Tiergarten area, his 74th Guards Rifle Division taking the Potsdamer Railway Station on the way.[24]

Colonel-General Rybalko now redistributed his 3rd Guards Tank Army more evenly for the reduction of Wilmersdorf. Its progress along the streets leading to the Kurfürstendamm was marked by the pounding of the guns. One consequence of the previous night's change of interfront boundary was that the 55th Guards Tank Brigade fighting its way down Kantstrasse had to be withdrawn from what had become the 2nd Guards Tank Army's sector. However, the orders did not reach the brigade until after daylight, by which time fighting had resumed to such an extent that many of the units could not be extricated. Subsequently the arrival of some tanks from the 2nd Guards Tank Army, and even some infantry from the 55th Guards Rifle Division, all added to the confusion in this sector, and it was not until after nightfall that the brigade could effect its withdrawal and return to its blockading role in Westend. Those elements of the 55th Guards Tank Brigade that had been driven off the Olympic Stadium the previous day resumed their attacks on that position and regained some ground, but the Westend district remained no man's land all day.[25]

At Fehrbelliner Platz some 'Tiger' tanks of the 503rd SS Heavy Panzer Battalion, which had come from SS General Steiner's III SS 'Germanic' Panzer Corps with the 11th SS 'Nordland' Panzergrenadier Division, made a strong counterattack during the day, but the defence was being slowly driven back, albeit only some 300–500 yards that day. The line of the Inner Defence Ring from Westkreuz to the Hohenzollerndamm was still held by the 18th Panzergrenadier Division together with the territory astride the Kurfürsten-damm behind it as far as the Zoo position, but minds were concentrating on the possibility of a breakout, and Major-General Rauch ordered his engineers to ensure that the Pichelsdorf Bridges (Stössensee and Frey) were up to the 30-ton capacity needed for his tanks.[26]

The Hitlerjugend Regiment's position on the Heerstrasse also stood firm, although under sporadic fire from across the Havel. Captain Boldt described their situation as follows:

> The Hitlerjugend lay alone or in pairs with their Panzerfausts at irregular intervals in the trenches on either side of the Heerstrasse in front of the Pichelsdorf bridges. The dawn was sufficiently advanced to be able to distinguish the dark shapes of heavy Russian tanks against the even darker background, their guns pointing at the bridge. We found the leader of the combat group, who told us what had happened to his people: 'When the fighting started here five days ago there were about 5,000 Hitlerjugend and a few soldiers available to take on this desperate struggle against over-whelming odds. Inadequately equipped with only rifles and Panzerfausts, the boys have suffered terribly from the effects of Russian shelling. Of the original 5,000 only 500 are still fit for combat.'[27]

At 2200 hours it was reported that the Soviets had occupied all of Saarland-strasse and the southern part of Wilhelmstrasse almost as far as the Air Ministry. From the north they had overrun Bismarckstrasse and were approaching Kantstrasse. General Weidling wrote of 29 April:

> Catastrophe was inevitable if the Führer did not reverse his decision to defend Berlin to the last man, and if he sacrificed all who were still alive and fighting in this city for the sake of a crazy ideal. We wracked our brains to see how we could avert this fate. Surely the Führer must realise that even the bravest soldier cannot fight without ammunition. The struggle was

devoid of sense or purpose. The German soldier could see no way out of the situation. I set out for the next briefing with a heavy heart.

Once again I mentioned the possibility of a breakout and drew attention to the general situation. Like a man fully resigned to his fate, the Führer answered me, pointing to his map. Sarcastically he commented that the positions of own troops had been sketched in from reports on the foreign radio as our own headquarters were no longer reporting them. Since his orders were not being carried out, it was pointless to expect anything – for example from the 7th Panzer Division, which according to instructions should have been approaching the Nauen area.

As a gesture permitting me to leave, this completely broken man got up from his chair with a great effort, but I urged him to decide what should be done when the ammunition ran out, which would be by the evening of the next day at the latest. After a brief consultation with General Krebs, the Führer replied that in that case the only thing to do would be to break out of Berlin in small groups, since he refused to surrender Berlin. I could go ...[28]

On the evening of 29 April, in response to Hitler's query, SS Major-General Mohnke reported that the Soviets had almost reached the Weidendammer Bridge from the north, were in the Lustgarten in the east, in Potsdamer Strasse to the south and at the Air Ministry. In the west they were only 300–400 yards away in the Tiergarten. Hitler then asked how much longer they could hold out, and was told no more than 24 hours.[29]

Even Hitler could now see that the situation was truly desperate and shortly before midnight he sent the following message to the OKW:

I am to be informed immediately:
1. Where are Wenck's spearheads?
2. When will they resume the attack?
3. Where is the 9th Army?
4. Where is it breaking through?
5. Where are Holste's XXXXI Panzer Corps' spearheads?[30]

Field Marshal Keitel's surprisingly honest reply was received at 0100 hours on 30 April and read as follows:

1. Wenck's point is stopped south of the Schwielowsee. Strong Soviet attacks along the whole east flank.
2. Consequently the 12th Army cannot continue its attack toward Berlin.

3. & 4. The 9th Army is surrounded. An armoured group has broken out
to the west; location unknown.

5. Corps Holste is forced on the defensive from Brandenburg via
Rathenow to Kremmen.

The attack toward Berlin has not developed at any point since
Army Group 'Weichsel' was also forced on the defensive on the
whole front north of Oranienburg via Neubrandenburg to
Anklam.[31]

There was nothing further to be done; suicide was the only solution. Hitler
spent a restless night, eventually summoning Mohnke at about 0600 hours
on 30 April for a chat. Mohnke reported that the Soviets were now in the
famous Adlon Hotel at the junction of Wilhelmstrasse and the Unter-den-
Linden. They were also in the U–Bahn tunnels in Friedrichstrasse and just
outside the Chancellery beneath Vossstrasse.[32] His own troops were exhausted
and could not possibly hold out much longer. In any event he expected a
massive frontal attack on the Chancellery at dawn next day, being May Day.
At the end of their talk Hitler gave Mohnke typed copies of his testament for
delivery to Grand Admiral Dönitz.[33]

Early on 30 April a young SS Lieutenant delivered to General Weidling at
his headquarters in Bendlerstrasse a letter from Hitler that read:

> In the event that there should be a shortage of ammunition or supplies in
> the Reichs capital, I hereby give my permission for our troops to attempt
> a breakout. This operation should be organized in combat teams as small
> as possible. Every effort should be made to link up with German units still
> carrying on the fight outside the city of Berlin. If such cannot be located,
> then the Berlin forces must take to the woods and continue resistance from
> there.

Mid-morning, General Weidling convened a conference of Defence Sector
commanders at which he told them of the Führer-Order authorizing a
breakout attempt. Weidling instructed them to plan to break out at 2200 hours
that night and that, if necessary, it would take place on his own authority.
Neither SS Major-General Mohnke, who was not under Weilding's command, nor SS Major-General Krukenberg, who had unilaterally placed
himself and his division under Mohnke, attended, and the attitude of the
Waffen-SS to such a breakout was a matter of concern to Weidling and his
staff. Major-General Bärenfänger's sentiments were: 'We fought under this
flag in the good times and won. Why should we be ashamed to show it now
when things are foul?'[34]

At the morning briefing in the Führerbunker General Krebs reported that the Soviets now controlled both sides of Leipziger Strasse and that the Anhalter Railway Station had just fallen. Everywhere the Soviets were closing in.[35]

Of the vicious fighting that was taking place in the streets near the Zoo, a civilian witness reported:

> The barricades built by the Volkssturm under the supervision of Party members were defended by the remnants of Volkssturm units and some youngsters [Hitlerjugend]. The Russians had mounted some light guns outside our building to fire at these obstacles.
>
> The Russians pushed any men and women that appeared capable of work out of the cellars at gunpoint and made them clear the streets of rubble, scrap metal and steel plates used as anti-tank obstacles, and that without any tools. Many were killed by the fire of German soldiers still holding out.[36]

By 0400 hours on the morning of 30 April, the 150th Rifle Division had eliminated the German defenders of the Ministry of the Interior and the 171st Rifle Division had finished clearing the western half of the Diplomatic Quarter. The latter's 525th Rifle Regiment were lining Alsenstrasse and there was to be no respite.

The frantic urgency imposed from above can be seen in the way the Soviets launched the next stage of the operation only half an hour later. The decision to push the exhausted soldiers forward without a break, involving a complete change in tactics as they emerged into the open from the building they had just taken and without time for proper reconnaissance or preparation, was to prove a costly error. The constant long-range bombardment had not silenced the defence, and the exposed infantry immediately came under a hail of fire, not only from the front and flank, as expected, from the Reichstag and Tiergarten, but also from the rear as they wheeled to face their objective, for the Germans had established a formidable strongpoint in the ruins of the Kroll Opera House with machine-guns and artillery mounted high in the bombed-out structure. Under the circumstances the attack quickly fizzled out.

It was now obvious that the Kroll Opera would have to be tackled before the attack on the main objective could be developed further, and the 597th and 598th Rifle Regiments of the 207th Rifle Division were brought forward for this purpose. However, in order to get to the Kroll Opera they first had to clear the buildings standing on the Schlieffenufer, and this would take time.

Meanwhile more support weapons were being brought across the bridge to assist the main attack, all having to run a gauntlet of fire coming from the same Schlieffenufer buildings and the Tiergarten beyond. Tanks, guns and rocket-launchers were brought up, some 90 barrels in all. Some of the guns of the 420th Anti-Tank Artillery Division were placed on the upper floors of the Ministry of the Interior building, and ten rocket-launchers set up in the courtyard.

The attack was resumed at 1130 hours with the usual heavy preliminary bombardment, and this time the infantry got as far as the flooded anti-tank ditch. The Germans mounted some local counterattacks, including one of battalion size in Alsenstrasse that the 525th Rifle Regiment managed to beat back.

At 1300 hours the Soviets tried again with a massive barrage from their close-support artillery and tanks, plus many more guns lined up across the river, and even some of the infantry joined in with captured Panzerfausts. After some 30 minutes of this fire the infantry started forward once more but were promptly pinned down again with the assistance of the anti-aircraft batteries on the Zoo flak-tower. However, on the left flank the 171st Rifle Division managed to clear the eastern half of the Diplomatic Quarter and secured the southern end of the Kronprinzen Bridge against the possibility of a German counterattack from across the river. This progress also enabled the introduction of tanks and self-propelled guns forward of the line of the anti-tank ditch to assist the exposed infantry in front of the Reichstag.

The area which the infantry now had to cross was littered with the temporary structures and other debris of an abandoned works project, among which a series of trenches, barbed-wire, mines and a determined enemy presented formidable obstacles for the infantry to overcome, and it was now clear that they would need the cover of darkness for these last 200 yards.

Meanwhile at 1425 hours, Major-General V.M. Shatilov commanding the 150th Rifle Division, reported up the chain of command that he thought he had seen a red flag over the steps of the Reichstag near the right-hand column. As the leading battalions contained several dare-devils eager to have a go at planting a flag on the Reichstag, including a group of volunteers from Corps Headquarters under the Commander's aide, Major M.M. Bondar, with the 380th Rifle Regiment and some gunners under Captain V.N. Makov with the 756th, the possibility that someone had got forward with a flag was not totally unlikely. However, the wild enthusiasm with which this report was received resulted in Marshal G.K. Zhukov issuing his Operational Order No. 06 of that day in which he said: 'Units of the 3rd Shock Army ... having broken the resistance of the enemy, have captured the Reichstag and hoisted our

Soviet Flag on it today, April 30th, 1945, at 1425 hours.' This erroneous report was flashed on to Moscow and reported abroad, but when the war correspondents and photographers started converging on the Reichstag they found the Soviet troops still only half way across Königsplatz and pinned down by gunfire.

Clearly painfully aware of his error, according to Captain S.A Neustroev, Major-General Shatilov was now dementedly ordering his troops: 'Somehow you have to hoist a flag or pennant, even on the columns at the main entrance. Somehow!'

The first attempt is said to have been made sometime that day by two groups of pilots of the 115th Air Fighter Regiment, who dropped some six-metre-wide red silk panels inscribed with the word '*Podeba*' ('Victory') on the dome of the building while flying at minimum height and speed.

Eventually it was 1800 hours before the attack could be resumed, but this time, with the close support of their armour, some of the infantry were able to get right up the front steps of the Reichstag to the still-intact bricked-up doorways. Fortunately, they had two light mortars with them, and by aligning these weapons horizontally were able to blast a small hole in the brickwork and so make their way into the main entrance hall.

In these attacks across open ground the infantry had been led by their regimental and battalion standards, and the survivors of the leading battalion, which had in fact spearheaded the entire corps' operation through Berlin, took their standard in with them as they began to expand their position within the building. By the time they had established telephone communication with their regimental headquarters, their radios having failed to work indoors, they had already fought their standard up to the second floor. However, the Military Council of the 3rd Shock Army had previously issued special banners, distinguished by extra large hammer and sickle emblems, to each of its nine rifle divisions for such an eventuality, and so the 150th Rifle Division's 'Red Banner No. 5', which had a hand-picked escort of Party and Komsomol members, was hastily despatched with instructions to hoist it on the roof of the Reichstag without delay.

Meanwhile the vicious hand-to-hand fighting was spreading out on the various floors of the building as more and more Soviet troops broke their way in. The Germans put up a very stubborn resistance and the Soviets experienced great difficulty trying to find their way in almost total darkness in the unfamiliar surroundings. Eventually, by using small groups to distract attention from their main purpose, two sergeants of the special banner party managed to find their way to the rear of the building, from where a stairway led up to the roof, and there they found a mounted statue and wedged the staff of their banner into a convenient crevice high above the ground. This was officially recorded as having taken place some 70 minutes before midnight and the commencement of May Day in Moscow.

Next day, photographs were taken in daylight to commemorate the great event, but the flag was so high that the photographer had Sergeants M.A. Yegorov and M.V. Kantaria change places with him, thus producing the famous image of hoisting the flag against the background of the Brandenburg Gate instead of an unidentifiable piece of sky. Although Yegorov and Kantaria were both made 'Heroes of the Soviet Union' for their deed, they had in fact failed to meet the deadline, having been soundly trounced by the group of gunners under Captain V.N. Makov, who had voluntarily accompanied the infantry in their attack on the Reichstag, and secured their flag on the Goddess of Victory statue that stood high above the front of the building. Captain Makov was able to report their achievement by radio direct to the corps commander. They too had been followed about ten minutes later by members of Lieutenant Sergei E. Sorokin's reconnaissance platoon, who had also hoisted a flag on the roof, both parties achieving their aim before midnight and some two to three hours before the official party, but these initiatives were only rewarded by a lesser decoration, the Order of the Red Banner.[37]

In the 5th Shock Army's area on 30 April, the 26th Guards Rifle Corps was primarily engaged with the reduction of a strongpoint located in the elevated Börse (Stock Exchange) S-Bahn Station, which was eventually overcome when an underground passage was found that enabled the infantry to get behind the German position. Meanwhile Soviet sappers blasted a gap in the embankment for the supporting armour to get through. Leading elements then pushed forward up Oranienburger Strasse to contest the next strongpoint located in the Telegraph Office. By the end of the day the 94th Guards Rifle Division had reached as far as the Charité Hospital, while the 266th Rifle Division had crossed the Spree to take Museuminsel (Museum Island) with the Dom (cathedral).

Meanwhile, the 32nd Rifle Corps launched its attack across the Spree on Fischerinsel (Fishermen's Island), the southern part of the central island on which stood Schloss Berlin (the old royal palace) and the Cathedral. Elements of the 60th Guards and 416th Rifle Divisions on the right flank attacked the Schloss, while the 295th Rifle Division headed for the massive Reichsbank, but here the buildings on the far side of the Kupfergraben Canal formed the new German front line, even though the bridges across it were still intact, unlike those across the river. No details of the crossing are given, although Marshal Zhukov regarded it as one of the 5th Shock Army's most difficult tasks. With all the bridges blown, the sheer granite-lined banks must have presented considerable difficulties. However, both banks of the river upstream being in Soviet hands, it can be assumed that the Dnieper River Flotilla contingent took part and that some commercial barges would have been brought downstream from the Osthafen to assist with the crossing and the improvisation of pontoon bridges.[38]

At 1520 hours on 30 April Hitler and his bride committed suicide in their sitting-room in the Führerbunker. Their bodies were then taken up into the Chancellery garden and placed in a ditch. Petrol was poured over them and set alight. Sometime later the charred bodies were buried in a shell-hole nearby. The whole affair was kept a close secret among the very few in the know.[39]

This left Goebbels as Chancellor and anxious to establish the new government decreed by Hitler in his will with a view to opening negotiations with the Soviets and obtaining their recognition before the treacherous Himmler could do the same with the Western Allies. What neither Goebbels nor Himmler appreciated was that the Allies jointly regarded all the Nazi leaders as war criminals and had no intention of dealing with them in any other way. Their pretensions to continue in power were utterly ridiculous to all but themselves. Even Dönitz decided that he would have neither Goebbels nor Bormann in his cabinet.[40]

Bormann, who had achieved so much in his struggle for power during the past week, was still trying to dominate the scene. Instead of informing Dönitz of Hitler's death, as was his duty, he merely sent the following signal at 1835 hours:

> The Führer has appointed you, Admiral, as his successor in place of former Reichs Marshal Göring. Confirmation in writing follows. You are hereby authorized to take any measures the situation demands.

One wonders what Dönitz was meant to make of this message. Certainly he did not read from it that Hitler was dead and that he was now President of the Third Reich, for at 0122 hours that night he signalled back a further declaration of loyalty to Hitler.[41]

Meanwhile General Weidling, who had continued his preparations for the breakout on Hitler's authority, received a message from Krebs ordering him to report to the Führerbunker and cancelling permission for a breakout. Weidling received the message at about 1900 hours and later recorded:

> It took us nearly an hour to make our way to the Chancellery through the ruins of buildings and half-collapsed cellars. In the Chancellery I was taken

straight to the Führer's room where there were Reichsminister Goebbels, Reichsleiter Bormann and General Krebs. The latter informed us of the following:

– The Führer had committed suicide at about 1515 hours today, the 30th April.

– His body had already been cremated in a shell-crater in the Chancellery garden.

– The strictest silence must be maintained about the Führer's suicide. I was made personally responsible for keeping the secret pending subsequent developments.

– Of the outside world only Marshal Stalin had been informed of the Führer's suicide by radio.

– The Sector Commander, Lieutenant-Colonel Seifert, had received orders to make contact with the local Russian commanders to request safe passage for General Krebs to the Soviet High Command.

– General Krebs was to give the Soviet High Command the following information: the Führer's suicide, the contents of his will, a request for an armistice, and the government's wish to open negotiations with the Russians for the surrender of Germany.

I was deeply shocked. So this was the end.[42]

Thus the breakout was cancelled and General Krebs was to attempt to negotiate with the Soviets. The troops would have to hang on and the population continue to suffer with them while Goebbels and Bormann played out their futile power game.[43]

General Bokov recorded that at 1700 hours on 30 April, a Colonel Heinersdorf, escorted by Lieutenant-Colonel Seifert, an interpreter by the name of Second Lieutenant Seger and a corporal carrying a white flag, approached the lines of the 150th Rifle Regiment. The route taken was Möckernstrasse. They had a pass signed by Goebbels authorizing them in German and Russian to negotiate the safe passage of General Krebs to speak to the Soviet High Command. Colonel Heinersdorf told Colonel V.S. Antonov, the commander of the 301st Rifle Division, that Hitler was dead and in his testament had named Goebbels as to succeed him as Reichs Chancellor, adding that Antonov was the first Russian to be informed of Hitler's death. When informed of this by telephone, General Berzarin ordered that the German parliamentarians be sent back with the information that General Krebs would be received only when properly authorized to negotiate a surrender and that no ceasefire would be given until that occurred.[44]

Lieutenant-Colonel Seifert had been briefed by Goebbels, in the presence of Bormann and Generals Burgdorf, Krebs and Mohnke for this mission, but the units in the area through which they had to pass had not been informed, and Seifert was arrested on his return by members of the 11th SS 'Nordland' Panzergrenadier Division as a spy. Fortunately his pass had been counter-signed by Mohnke, for the Waffen-SS would only accept their own leader's authority, as another incident had already demonstrated. According to Captain Albert Lieselang, Seifert had already established a field-telephone connection with the Soviet troops opposite his command post in the cellars of the Air Ministry building, presumably on instructions from the Reichs Chancellery, and an officer was permanently on duty beside this telephone, although no communication by this means had yet been made. This was, however, without the knowledge of SS Major-General Krukenberg, and on the morning of 1 May, Lieselang entered Seifert's command post to find Krukenberg and some of his officers there, the duty officer, Seifert's chief-of-staff, just having been shot and mortally wounded, Krukenberg believing the installation to be an act of treachery. Only a call to General Weidling was able to clarify the situation and prevent further internecine bloodshed.[45]

The last day of April saw some particularly bitter fighting in the Charlotten-burg and Wilmersdorf Districts as the 2nd and 3rd Guards Tank Armies converged on the S-Bahn tracks denoting the interfront boundary and German troops struggled to maintain a passage through to the western parts of the city still in their hands. However, now back in the Westend area, following its probe down Kantstrasse in support of Koniev's abortive attack of 28 April, Colonel Dragunsky's 55th Guards Tank Brigade appears to have gone to ground in the tram sheds and barracks off Königin-Elisabeth-Strasse for the rest of the battle.[46]

The 2nd Guards Tank Army found itself in difficulties as it deployed in Charlottenburg, for its integral infantry had been greatly depleted in the previous fighting and the tanks found themselves increasingly vulnerable. The 1st Mechanized Corps sent the remains of the 19th and 35th Mechanized Brigades down Schlossstrasse to clear the areas north and south of Kantstrasse respectively, heading toward the Zoo. The 35th Mechanized Brigade encoun-tered German resistance on the line of Kaiser-Friedrich-Strasse and on the right flank near Charlottenburg Station, and so made slower progress than the 19th Mechanized Brigade, which was not held up until it reached the strongpoint on Karl-August-Platz that Dragunsky's troops had previously failed to overcome. Both flanks of the 19th Mechanized Brigade's were exposed, for contact had been lost with the 37th Mechanized Brigade on the

172

far side of Bismarckstrasse, where the latter was heavily engaged with the German defences between there and Berliner Strasse (Otto-Suhr-Allee), and was also separated from its northern neighbour, the 219th Tank Brigade, which was even further forward facing Marchstrasse, north of the Knie (Ernst-Reuter-Platz). Consequently the deployment of these brigades presented a series of steps on the map, all with exposed flanks and rear.

When the 12,000-strong 1st Polish 'Tadiuscz Kosciuszko' Infantry Division arrived that evening, the Poles were horrified to learn that some of the infantry units of the 2nd Guards Tank Army that they were replacing had suffered up to 95 per cent casualties. The 3rd Polish Infantry Regiment was then assigned to the 66th Guards Tank Brigade of the 12th Guards Tank Corps, which through lack of infantry support had already lost 82 tanks, mainly in Berlin. The 1st Polish Infantry Regiment was then split up into combat teams under the 19th and 35th Mechanized Brigades, and the 2nd Polish Infantry Regiment assigned to the 219th Tank Brigade, all of the 1st Mechanized Corps.[47]

The territory still held by the defence in the city centre was now reduced to an area roughly defined by the Reichstag, Friedrichstrasse Railway Station, the Gendarmenmarkt, the Air Ministry and the Reichs Chancellery. In this area alone were about 10,000 troops, police and Volkssturm, the SS 'Nordland' Panzergrenadier Division, the 15th SS 'Latvian' Fusilier Battalion and the 1st Battalion of the SS 'Anhalt' Regiment, the Waffen-SS units consisting mainly of foreign volunteers.[48]

Meanwhile the remains of General Busse's 9th Army, guided by General Wenck's radio, headed for the village of Wittbrietzen four miles south of Beelitz. During 30 April they reached the village of Kummersdorf by noon and then had a brief rest in the woods on the artillery ranges northwest of the village before going on to the next stage. This involved breaking through yet another Soviet cordon on the Berlin–Luckenwalde road and then fighting their way westward through the night. The whole time they were being harassed by Soviet aircraft, artillery and mortar fire, attacks by infantry and tanks, and deception attempts and attacks by German troops fighting for the Red Army, the so-called 'Seydlitz-Troops'. In the early-morning darkness they had to make several detours in order to avoid pockets of Soviet troops and at dawn they came up against the 5th Guards Mechanized Corps' positions. However, they managed to fight their way through this obstacle with the last serviceable 'Tiger' tank in the lead, breaking through utterly exhausted into the 12th Army's lines on the morning of 1 May.[49]

Busse later estimated that some 40,000 men and several thousand refugees reached Wenck's lines. Other estimates are lower. Koniev says that about 30,000 of the 200,000 that broke out of the Halbe 'pocket' reached the Beelitz area, but were then set upon again by his forces, and that at the most only 3–4,000 could have got through to the 12th Army. In any case, when one considers the odds ranged against them, the unification of the 9th and 12th Armies was a considerable feat, for which both generals deserve full credit.[50]

10

ULTIMATE VICTORY

At midnight on 30 April, the battle suddenly quietened down. It was May Day and with victory just round the corner the most joyous day in the history of the Soviet Union. The generals would have preferred to have completed their conquest of the city, and when Colonel-General Vassili D. Sokolovsky, Marshal Zhukov's Chief-of-Staff, visited Chuikov and asked him why his men were only crawling along when they had barely 300 yards to go and one last assault would finish the matter, Chuikov could only reply that his men were exhausted, they knew that the war was all but over and none of them wanted to die in Berlin. Fighting and shelling continued in a desultory fashion, sometimes building up briefly and then dying down again, as was to occur in the late afternoon of 1 May, and the Soviet advance remained cautious. Only in Charlottenburg, where the newly arrived Polish troops took a leading part, does there appear to have been much activity that day. The Germans seized the opportunity to rest and ponder their fate, while the Soviets celebrated as best they could.[1]

Shortly after midnight SS Major-General Mohnke led General Krebs' party to Lieutenant-Colonel Seifert's Sector Headquarters, from where the latter had arranged safe passage through to the Soviet lines near the Anhalter Station. With Krebs as his aide was Colonel von Dufving, Weidling's Chief-of-Staff, and as official interpreter, SS Lieutenant Neilands, commander of the 15th 'Latvian' Fusilier Battalion, although in fact Krebs spoke perfect Russian. Neilands had changed his uniform for that of an Army Sonderführer (specialist), aware that the Soviets were particularly hostile to the Waffen-SS. Krebs' party arrived safely at the command post of the 102nd Guards Rifle Regiment of the 35th Guards Rifle Division, 4th Guards Rifle Corps, and was sent on by jeep to Colonel-General Chuikov's headquarters in the Schulenburgring, where they arrived at 0350 hours.[2]

Chuikov received them accompanied by a bevy of officers, including what might loosely be described as war correspondents, such as the writer Vsevelod

175

Vishnevsky, the poet Jevgeny Dolmatovsky and the composer Blanter, but as all wore officer uniforms and no introductions were made it took Krebs quite a long time to discover even Chuikov's identity. Later Colonel-General Sokolovsky was also to join them.[3]

The discussion dragged on for hours. Krebs was out to obtain recognition of the new government and the opportunity to assemble it, but had no authority to negotiate unconditional surrender, which was all that the Soviets were interested in. The documents that Krebs had brought with him were immediately sent to Marshal Zhukov at Strausberg, who telephoned the contents through to Stalin in Moscow.

During the meeting it was agreed to establish telephone communications with Goebbels in the Führerbunker and so Colonel von Dufving was sent back with a Soviet signals major to lay the field cable. However, they were fired on by German troops and the major was severely wounded, the cable proved too short, and Colonel von Dufving was arrested by SS troops upon returning to the German lines, only to be released when he insisted that SS Major-General Mohnke be consulted. He went on to report to Goebbels and Bormann in the Führerbunker, noting that although Goebbels appeared calm and composed, Bormann was definitely scared. When Goebbels heard that Krebs was making no progress and that the Soviets were insisting upon unconditional surrender jointly to all the Allies, Goebbels said that he could never agree to this and sent von Dufving to bring Krebs back.

Von Dufving set off again at 1100 hours and telephoned Krebs from the regimental command post. Krebs said that they were still awaiting a call from Moscow and that in the meantime von Dufving should make another attempt at establishing telephone communications with the Führerbunker. Von Dufving took another field cable and attached it to the first, but almost immediately the latter was cut by shellfire. He telephoned Krebs again and was told that the call had come through from Moscow and that Krebs was on his way back. They returned through the lines together and Krebs then dismissed von Dufving, saying that the German reply to the Soviets would be sent in writing.[4]

This, however, was not Goebbels' only attempt at negotiations with the Soviets, for Colonel V.S. Antonov, commanding the 301st Rifle Division of the 9th Rifle Corps, 5th Shock Army, also received a delegation of four officers led by a colonel that morning. At this stage the 301st Rifle Division was on the right flank of the 9th Rifle Corps, approaching Wilhelmplatz from the east, with the 248th Rifle Division in the centre and the 230th Rifle Division on the left flank, advancing north and south of Leipziger Strasse respectively. When Colonel Antonov reported the arrival of the mission, he was told not to negotiate with them but to go ahead and storm the Chancellery instead. In the meantime the German colonel had contacted the Chancellery on the civilian telephone network and was instructed to return, since he was making no progress. Colonel Antonov allowed him to leave with one officer but detained the other two. The whole business had lasted three to four hours, during which time fighting had been suspended in this sector.[5]

Goebbels and Bormann signalled Dönitz the news of Hitler's death only that afternoon, 29 hours after the event, together with details of the government listed in Hitler's will, which Dönitz chose to ignore. However, now officially President of the Third Reich, he had the news of Hitler's death announced by Radio Hamburg that evening without disclosing the cause of death as suicide, and then spoke to the German people. This news did not percolate through to the troops in Berlin until very much later, although rumours abounded.[6]

Both missions having failed, Goebbels prepared himself and his family for suicide as they had previously arranged. General Krebs, General Burgdorf and SS Colonel Franz Schaedl of Hitler's honour guard also opted for suicide.[7] Between 1700 and 1800 hours that evening Frau Goebbels put her six children to bed with drugged chocolates and then killed them all by forcing cyanide capsules into their mouths. Later it was discovered that the eldest child had struggled in the process. Then, after a chat over old times with some of their familiars in the Führerbunker, Goebbels and his wife put on their outer garments and climbed the stairs to the Chancellery garden to commit suicide there. First Magda Goebbels bit into her cyanide capsule and slumped to the ground. Goebbels then shot her in the back of the head before simultaneously biting his own capsule and shooting himself in the head, as Hitler had done. Their bodies were then burnt in a ditch in a similar manner.[8]

Colonel Antonov was just about to launch an attack on the Chancellery at dusk when the German colonel reappeared with a white flag, announcing that Goebbels and his family had committed suicide and that Hitler's only successor was now Grand Admiral Dönitz. It is not clear what happened as a result of this second visit, but it seems that the Soviets used it as an excuse not to go ahead with their attack.[9]

On the morning of 1 May, Spandau Citadel, an ancient moated fortress dominating the even older town at the junction of the Spree and Havel Rivers, surrendered to the 47th Army. The small military garrison had already exacted a toll from the 2nd Guards Tank Army with Panzerfaust forays, as several wrecked tanks on the approaches from Siemensstadt testified, but the massive walls also sheltered several hundred civilians, a field hospital and some laboratories for testing military equipment under poison gas conditions.[10]

Fighting continued inside the Reichstag all day on 1 May. The German defence fought on desperately under the command of SS Lieutenant Babick of the SS 'Anhalt' Regiment, whose command post was located in a cellar across the street from the rear of the building and connected to it by a tunnel. The building caught fire, adding to the misery of the contestants, for whom there was no water to quench the thirst aroused by the dust and smoke that choked them. Gradually the upper storeys of the building were cleared, but the defence fought on from the cellars (which also accommodated a hospital), and it was not until General Weidling's order to surrender was received that the survivors laid down their arms at 1300 hours on 2 May.

It seems that both the 674th and 756th Rifle Regiments of the 150th Rifle Division actually fought inside the Reichstag, and that the 380th Rifle Regiment of the 171st Rifle Division, after they had assisted in the storming of the building, re-emerged to secure the Brandenburg Gate corner of the Tiergarten, from where they appear to have penetrated as far as Pariser Platz and the Adlon Hotel. The 171st Rifle Division's two other rifle regiments, the 525th and the 713th, secured the river bank and Siegesallee approaches respectively, and the two regiments of the 207th Rifle Division closed up to the Charlottenburger Chaussee (Strasse des 17. Juni) airstrip to await the arrival of the 8th Guards Army from the south.

In accomplishing this particular mission the 79th Rifle Corps claim to have taken some 2,600 prisoners and counted 2,500 enemy dead, but these numbers exceed the defenders known to have been fielded in this area about tenfold. Their own casualties were not published separately but, significantly, the Soviet War Memorial, which was erected across the top of the adjacent Siegesallee shortly afterward, has 2,200 of their dead buried in its grounds.[11]

The orders to the 5th Shock Army for 1 May read:

> The 26th Guards Rifle Corps is to send forward a division and establish contact with the troops of the 3rd Shock Army there; to clear the north bank of the Spree with one rifle division, and to secure the Army's northern flank with the remaining forces.
>
> The 32nd Rifle Corps is to maintain the attack on Berlin in conjunction with the 26th Guards Rifle Corps and to push forward as far as Pariser Platz by the end of 1 May.
>
> By the evening of 1 May, the 9th Rifle Corps is to take the Ministry for

Justice, the Foreign Office, the Air Ministry, the Reichs Main Security Office, the Reichs Chancellery and the Post Office Ministry.[12]

These aims proved wildly ambitious, for the massively constructed buildings in this area favoured the defence. Although the 94th Guards and 266th Rifle Divisions were able to take the Zeughaus (Armoury) and State Library on the north side of the Unter-den-Linden, and the 416th and 295th Rifle Divisions took the State Opera building across the road and the Reichsbank between them, while the 301st and 248th Rifle Divisions of the 9th Rifle Corps managed to capture the Gestapo and Reichs Main Security Office buildings on Prinz-Albrecht-Strasse (Niederkirschnerstrasse), the day's progress overall still left the area roughly demarcated by the Admirals Palast on the eastern side of Friedrichstrasse, the Gendarmenmarkt, Air Ministry and Potsdamer Platz, in German hands. The Soviets could safely claim interruption of progress by the 9th Rifle Corps in the south being attributable to the ceasefires accompanying German attempts to parley during the day, but any excuse would have been welcome to celebrate May Day and personal survival.[13]

General Krebs' attempts at negotiation having been refuted, Stalin called for a renewed offensive in the city, in which both fronts participated at 1630 hours. As usual Chuikov began with a heavy rocket and artillery bombardment. Soon the 29th Guards Rifle Corps were reporting that they had crossed Budapester Strasse and had knocked gaps in the perimeter wall of the Zoological Gardens, where their tanks and artillery were now exchanging fire with the defence. They had also taken the Kaiser-Wilhelm-Gedächtniskirche (Memorial Church) at the eastern end of the Kurfürstendamm, from where their artillery observers and snipers had an excellent view over the Zoo area. With the race-course on the west side of the railway embankment from the Zoo under attack from the 12th Guards Tank Corps, and the 28th Guards Rifle Corps' penetration of the Tiergarten residential area just north of the Landwehr Canal, the Zoo position was now almost completely surrounded as well as being cut off from Weidling's headquarters and the rest of 'Zitadelle'.

In the 8th Guards Army's sector, Soviet troops had crossed Bellevuestrasse into Siegesallee, and the 79th Guards Rifle Division of the 28th Guards Corps reported that they had taken Potsdamer Railway Station and were fighting for the Saarlandstrasse (Potsdamer Platz) U-Bahn station. The junction of Wilhelmstrasse and Leipziger Strasse was also reported to be in Soviet hands.[14]

With nightfall the fighting died down again and the Soviets resumed their festivities. In Pariser Platz a group of men roasted an ox where earlier the poet

Dolmatovsky, in naval uniform and standing on a tank, had recited some of his popular works to an enthusiastic audience.[15]

Boosted by the 1st Polish Infantry Division, the 2nd Guards Tank Army was able to make some progress that day. The 1st Polish Infantry Regiment, supported by the 1st Battery of the 1st Polish Field Artillery Regiment, assembled on the line of Fritschestrasse in support of the 19th and 35th Mechanized Brigades of the 1st Mechanized Corps. The first task for the 1st Battalion was to clear a defended barricade on Kaiser-Friedrich-Strasse that blocked the entrance to Pestalozzistrasse and had already cost three tanks. This was achieved with the aid of tank and artillery fire, while the infantry infiltrated the surrounding buildings, and the remaining tanks then advanced with them to join up with the 19th Mechanized Brigade and its assigned 2nd and 3rd Battalions fighting at Karl-August-Platz at 1600 hours. For this latter operation, in which the Trinitatis Church formed the main defensive position, three infantry assault groups had been formed, those of the 2nd and 3rd Battalions and one of the surviving Soviet infantry, each of which was supported by three tanks. The ensuing assault, conducted under cover of a dense smokescreen, succeeded, and by evening the church was in Polish hands. The Poles claimed 407 Germans were killed in the action, and two 'Ferdinand' assault guns and five artillery pieces taken, while the 1st Polish Infantry Regiment had lost only 20 men.[16]

The 2nd Polish Infantry Regiment, supported by the 2nd Battery, advanced through the 219th Tank Brigade's sector and occupied the wedge of ground bounded by the Landwehr Canal opposite the Technical High School (Technical University), which was the main objective, being part of the western bastion of 'Zitadelle'. Meanwhile the 219th Tank Brigade itself was tied up in fighting for some positions along the Landwehr Canal. This put the Poles in a predicament, for the street they now had to cross in order to assault the High School had been deliberately widened by Albert Speer before the war to accommodate the reviewing stands for Hitler's parades along the East–West Axis, and attempts to cross without armoured support at 0900, 1000 and 1430 hours were easily beaten back by machine-gun fire. Although some Soviet tanks did support the first two of these attacks with gunfire, they were not prepared to expose themselves to the Panzerfausts that the defence were using, and at 1500 hours they were ordered elsewhere. The regiment now had to rely on its artillery support alone, the guns being deployed at a range of only 500 yards, and two 76mm guns were dismantled and reassembled on the third floor of the surviving building next to the bridge. However, scouts were sent out to find alternative lines of approach, and eventually at 0140 hours next day a flanking attack was carried out across the narrower

Hardenbergstrasse that proved to be successful. The regiment had lost 26 men killed in this action.[17]

The 3rd Polish Infantry Regiment, supported by the 3rd Battery, came to the aid of the 66th Guards Tank Brigade of the 12th Guards Tank Corps north of the Landwehr Canal. The brigade was down to only 15 tanks, and stuck on the line of Franklinstrasse. The Poles broke through the German defences and fought their way through a dense industrial area, reaching the line of Englische Strasse, immediately north of the Charlottenburger Bridge, by 2100 hours. The tanks found themselves exceedingly vulnerable to Panzerfausts in these conditions, even 'Stalin IIs' being knocked out, and those crews that did succeed in pushing forward found it difficult to manage their vehicles with such limited visibility. The brigade was tasked with securing the bridge and taking the Tiergarten S-Bahn station. However, scouts reported the station complex strongly defended, and so it was decided to await daylight to enable a thorough reconnaissance. Meanwhile, attempts to cross the Charlottenburger Chaussee and secure the bridge proved futile until three 'Stalin IIs' came forward to form a wall of steel across the road for the Polish infantry. The following morning the Poles managed to take the station by storm, thus opening the way into the Tiergarten, where they hastened to raise their national flag on the Siegessäule (Victory Column).[18]

The 3rd Guards Tank Army were across the Kurfürstendamm by evening, where the 'Müncheberg' Panzer Division had held on to the Savignyplatz area all day, and closed up to the railway embankment denoting the interfront boundary. They then infiltrated sideways through the buildings lining the embankment, and at 0830 hours on 2 May the two tank armies met near Savignyplatz.[19]

Second Lieutenant Kroemer of the 'Müncheberg' Panzer Division recorded:

> Our anti-aircraft guns on the Zoo bunker fire without stopping. The division now has only five tanks and four guns left. One group is fighting in front of the Zoo bunker, where thousands of people are on the point of asphyxia. The Memorial Church has been taken by the Russians. Late afternoon there are rumors that Hitler is dead and that surrender talks are in progress. That is all. Civilians ask us if we are going to break out.
>
> At dusk a patrol managed to cross the Spandau bridges and discovered that the Russian forces in Spandau are quite weak. We are planning to break out to the west via Spandau.
>
> Russian pressure along Budapester Strasse cannot be contained much longer. We will have to withdraw again. Wounded are screaming in the

cellars. There is nothing to ease their pain. Here and there, despite the fire, women come up out of the half-demolished cellars with their hands over their ears, unable to bear the screaming any longer.[20]

These developments had created a vast difference in the situation since Hitler had given his approval for a breakout on the night of 29/30 April and now General Weidling saw no alternative to surrender. However, some of his commanders at the Zoo still thought it worth while attempting a breakout to the west, while SS Major-General Mohnke changed his original plan for a breakout in that direction to one which would first take him north to the Humboldthain flak-tower before swinging northwest out of the city. Thus a miscellany of breakout plans evolved, with Weidling holding back his surrender negotiations until after midnight in order to give the others a chance to get away under cover of darkness.[21]

In the meantime the main corridor to the west had been closed. That morning Wenck's 12th Army began withdrawing to the Elbe near Tangermünde, having held out as long as they dared. With them went the survivors of Busse's 9th Army and Reymann's Army Detachment 'Spree' with several hundred thousand refugees. Wenck sent Lieutenant-General Reichsfreiherr von Edelsheim to negotiate their surrender to the American 9th Army. Although the commander of the latter, General William L. Simpson, agreed to let as many soldiers as were able to make their way across the river, and offered assistance with the wounded, he absolutely refused to accept any of the civilian refugees. This extraordinary decision, which was presumably based on the problems of feeding, would have resulted in their involuntary abandonment to the vengeance of the pursuing Soviet forces on the east bank of the Elbe, had not the Soviets themselves intervened. Their air attacks on the German crossing points forced the Americans to withdraw sufficiently to enable the Germans to control their own crossings, which began on 4 May, using the XX Corps as a covering screen, and were not completed until midnight on 7 May, by which time General Wenck reckoned some 100,000 soldiers and 300,000 civilians had been successfully evacuated.[22]

Unfortunately for some of these evacuees, the Americans genuinely could not cope with the numbers thrust upon them and were obliged to give some of their prisoners away. The lucky ones went to the British in the north, but a large contingent had the bitter experience of being handed over to the Soviets.[23]

General Weidling called for all those officers, warrant officers and NCOs that were accessible to attend a meeting at the Bendlerblock at 2300 hours that evening. The field telephone had just been reconnected with the

Tiergarten flak-control tower, having been out of order most of the day, and Colonel Wöhlermann was thus summoned to attend. He set off with a small escort and, because of the progress made by the Soviets, his route took him via the Tiergarten S-Bahn station on the East–West Axis, which he followed as far as the Siegessäule (Victory Column), but then came under heavy shellfire and was obliged to crawl and sprint the rest of the way between the rows of badly damaged statuary in Neue-Siegesallee (Grosser Sternallee) to Bendlerstrasse.[24]

Weidling consulted with his two Chiefs-of-Staff, then recounted to the packed assembly the events of the past 48 hours. The news of Hitler's death and Weidling's conviction of the need to surrender came as a shock. In his speech, Weidling stressed the point that Hitler had betrayed his oath, thereby invalidating their own oath of allegiance to him, an important point of conscience with which many had had to wrestle of late. It was eventually agreed that there was no alternative to surrender and that they should attempt to enter into negotiations with the Soviets soon after midnight.[25]

After the conference, armed sentries were stationed outside the offices of General Weidling and Colonels Refior and von Dufving, to prevent any putsch by dissidents.[26]

When Colonel Wöhlermann returned to his command post, he found that a considerable number of his troops had already embarked on breakout bids, but that there were still some 2,000 combatants as well as thousands of civilians in his care.[27] As soon as it was light enough, Colonel Wöhlermann and his troops paraded outside the flak-towers in front of their Soviet captors. The scene was marred by a sudden burst of machine-gun fire from some recalcitrant Nazis, the bullets ricocheting off the concrete and killing several of his troops. When they marched off he was surprised to see the number of Soviet tanks lining the streets. At one point Soviet tankmen suddenly offered them cigarettes in a gesture of friendship, and Wöhlermann took advantage of the situation to obtain permission for the Hitlerjugend boys included among them to fall out and make their way home.[28]

On the night of 1/2 May, Luftwaffe Major-General Otto Sydow of the 1st Flak Division organized a breakout attempt from the Zoo. The remaining tanks and armoured personnel carriers of the 'Müncheberg' Panzer and 18th Panzergrenadier Divisions made their way up Kantstrasse to Adolf-Hitler-Platz and then by Reichsstrasse via the Olympic Stadium to Ruhleben, being joined on their way by survivors from the Kurfürstendamm area. Several hundred infantry with walking wounded and some hundreds of civilians followed the five miles of U-Bahn tunnels as far as the Olympia Bridge close to the Stadium, from where they still had another two-and-a-half miles to the

Spandau bridges. Miraculously, the plan worked. The trek through the tunnels had to be done in silence and without lights, for virtually the whole route lay under the Soviet lines and there were many holes in the tunnel roof to the streets above. Although the going was slow, they were out of the tunnels by midnight.

Those coming from the Kantstrasse and Kurfürstendamm areas assembled on Masurenallee, as Lothar Loewe describes:

> The big assembly point for the breakout from Berlin to the west was on the big square between the Haus des Rundfunks and the Exhibition Halls. It was the morning of the 2nd May. The last tanks, self-propelled guns, fire engines of the Berlin Fire Brigade from the Suarez and Ranke stations, military stragglers, BVG double-decker buses, three-wheeled delivery vans, all in a tangled muddle. Mothers with prams were hoisted on trucks, whose woodgas generators burned smokily. Elegant ladies slung rucksacks over fur coats. Paymasters, army veterinary surgeons, SA and Party leaders, 'Gold Pheasants' in brown uniforms, paratroopers and the remainders of still passably organized units, set off. The last German attack in Berlin, that was to cost thousands of lives in the course of the day, had begun.[29]

There were still two bridges available across the Havel, the Frey Bridge having blown up at 1800 hours that evening when a chance Soviet shell hit the prepared demolition chamber. The Schulenburg and Charlotten Bridges leading into Spandau had already changed hands three times and had to be taken yet again for this breakout, but fortunately the Soviet forces on the opposite bank were relatively weak. While the troops fought their way across, the refugees assembled in the pouring rain and were shelled by the Soviet artillery. Eventually the way was opened by Major Horst Zobel leading the remaining tanks of the 'Müncheberg' Panzer Division across the Charlotten Bridge in an armoured personnel carrier, and the crowds fought their way through, some being crushed by the armoured vehicles running the gauntlet of enemy fire. The troops then cut a path through the Soviet lines down Brunsbüttler Damm to Staaken Airfield, which was the dispersal point. Most units headed for Döberitz but as each unit tended to fend for itself in this *sauve qui peut* atmosphere, most of them were rounded up fairly quickly over the next few days.[30] Lothar Loewe relates:

> The Odysee of this last breakout from Berlin ended for about 5000 men, including 400 untended severely wounded, on the evening of the 3rd May in the village of Tremmen, about 45 kilometers west of the

Kurfürstendamm. There was no more ammunition, the fuel was all but finished, and the last German tank was securing the entrance to the village. Soviet troops had encircled the village. The commanding general, Major General Sydow of the 1st Flak Division and a Colonel Rossbach arranged the surrender through intermediaries for 22 hours. The wounded were to be taken immediately by truck to hospitals in Potsdam.[31]

Eventually, only a handful of survivors from the Spandau breakout actually managed to get through to and across the Elbe.

Another group of 300 soldiers from Jebenstrasse made their escape via the U-Bahn tunnels from the Zoo station to Adolf-Hitler-Platz (Theodor-Heuss-Platz), which took them two hours, and then headed straight down Heerstrasse. All went well until someone carelessly struck a match, attracting a burst of machine-gun fire. However, this was not followed up and so they turned off for Ruhleben, where they came across the remaining 15 'Tiger' tanks of the 503rd SS Heavy Tank Battalion and their Austrian crews, and went on with them to Stresowplatz, which was thronged with refugees waiting to cross the Charlotten Bridge into Spandau–Altstadt. Soviet machine-gunners suddenly opened fire on them from the rooftops, but the tanks fired back and the survivors scrambled across the bridge under this cover into the old town centre and headed for Döberitz. The Soviets pursued them and they were eventually obliged to surrender at 0500 hours in the morning of 2 May, having expended all their ammunition.[32]

Soon after dusk Colonel-General V.I. Kutznetsov of the 3rd Shock Army telephoned Marshal Zhukov to report that some 20 German tanks had broken through the lines of the 52nd Guards Rifle Division and had set off at a high speed for the northwest. Zhukov alerted the 47th, 61st and 1st Polish Armies with instructions to seal off all routes to the west and north, and the 2nd Guards Tank Army and 3rd Shock Armies were ordered to organize a pursuit. At dawn on the 2nd May the German tanks were found ten miles northwest of Berlin and destroyed.[33]

The story of this attempt was related in the *History of the Grossdeutschland Panzer Corps*, which gives the following account:

> Major Lehnhoff gave orders to his combat teams of the 'Grossdeutschland' Guard Regiment to assemble at 2300 hours on the 1st May in Kastanienallee to attempt a break-out to the west via Rathenow.
> The remaining vehicles were tanked up, millions of Reichsmark coins were shared out among the men, the last rations issued, and then away. The break through the Soviet lines was made at the Schönhauser Allee station,

where Stalin-Organs and tankfire inflicted heavy casualties. With five tanks and 68 men Major Lehnhoff broke out of the city toward Oranienburg, where unfortunately the tanks had to be blown up because of breakdowns. Divided into four groups the men then pushed on toward the Elbe and Schleswig-Holstein.[34]

However, this successful breakout had fully alerted the Soviets in this area, and a subsequent attempt at dawn along the same route up Schönhauser Allee by the various German units still surviving between Alexanderplatz and Friedrichshain was met by an impenetrable hail of fire. Major-General Bärenfänger, who was hoping to take this route with his young wife and brother-in-law, committed suicide with them in a side-street.[35]

SS Major-General Mohnke's breakout from the Reichs Chancellery had been delayed because of the cutting of the East–West Axis by the Soviets on 30 April. While he was planning a new route he advised his men to get some rest. As a courtesy he checked over his plans with Generals Krebs and Burgdorf, both of whom had already opted to commit suicide. He had also telephoned General Weidling to inform him of his intentions, obtaining the latter's agreement not to sign any surrender articles before daybreak on 2 May.[36]

The SS 'Anhalt' Regiment, now under the command of SS Major Wahl, had been informed of Hitler's death and the men relieved of their oath of loyalty. The surviving members of the regiment were then told to make their way to Friedrichstrasse Railway Station and await Mohnke's further orders. However, SS Major-General Krukenberg, although he was contemplating plans for his own troops' breakout, does not appear to have been briefed and so was extremely annoyed when Mohnke began while his division was still unprepared to act in concert.[37]

The breakout from the Reichs Chancellery started at 2300 hours on 1 May and was conducted in ten groups of irregular size, with Mohnke leading the first. His plan was for all groups, which would set off at ten-minute intervals, to follow the U- and S-Bahn tunnels as far as the Stettiner Railway Station, which would hopefully bring them behind the Soviet lines. From there they would march as far as the Gesundbrunnen Station next to the Humboldthain flak-tower before splitting up and each group making its own way via Neuruppin to find the main German forces. This plan took advantage of the Soviet troops' recognized reluctance to use the tunnels, but also showed Mohnke's ignorance of the situation north of the Spree.[38]

Mohnke's group sprinted the 120 yards across Wilhelmplatz to the Kaiserhof U-Bahn station, which was packed with sheltering civilians, and marched in complete darkness to the Stadtmitte Station, from where they took the northern line to Friedrichstrasse Station. While they were in this last section heavy shelling broke out overhead and lasted about an hour. They changed to the S-Bahn tunnel at Friedrichstrasse Station and when they came to pass under the Spree, they found their way blocked by a waterproof steel bulkhead guarded by two transport authority watchmen. The watchmen were acting in accordance with standing instructions, whereby the bulkhead was locked between the last train at night and the first in the morning and, although no trains had passed for a week, they were sticking to the rules. Mohnke's party returned to Friedrichstrasse Station to seek another route above ground. The Weidendammer Bridge was blocked by a German anti-tank barrier and was being shelled by the Soviets, but they found a narrow metal footbridge (the Schlütersteig), leading across the Spree from the station, and cut their way through the barbed wire blocking it.[39]

They then worked their way northward through a wilderness of rubble until they found themselves in the ruins of the Natural History Museum, by which they recognized that they had just crossed Invalidenstrasse. So far they had seen no Soviets but had been joined by a few German stragglers. The civilians they encountered told them that only the odd Soviet patrol had come through the area, although the Charité Hospital to their left was strongly occupied. The shelling, which had died down at 0130 hours, suddenly resumed at 0230 hours and, looking back, they saw that Friedrichstrasse and the Weidendammer Bridge were under heavy artillery and rocket fire from the Tiergarten, the whole area being illuminated by searchlights operated by the Soviets.[40]

This fire had been provoked by other groups from the Chancellery making their way above ground and thereby attracting enemy attention. The third group had lost their way at the Stadtmitte Station and had then decided to travel above ground. Another party led by Axmann went all the way to the bridge safely above ground only to suffer many casualties thereafter.[41] Meanwhile several hundred soldiers of all kinds, as well as male and female civilians, had gathered in the Friedrichstrasse Railway Station area. Now that the Soviets had been alerted, SS Major-General Krukenberg, whose foreign volunteers were holding this sector, was obliged to take the opportunity of breaking out with those troops immediately to hand, abandoning the others to their fate.

A 'Tiger II' with a damaged turret led the way, smashing through the barricade on the Weidendammer Bridge, followed by five armoured personnel carriers commanded by SS Major Tennede of the 23rd SS 'Norge' Panzer-grenadier Regiment, and these were followed by the horde of people waiting.

But the Soviet troops were also waiting in ambush on the northern extension of Friedrichstrasse, and Ziegelstrasse on the right was full of their tanks. In the ensuing fire all the armoured vehicles were destroyed, and the Germans suffered heavy casualties. Only a few survivors managed to get through with Krukenberg.[42]

Mohnke took advantage of this distraction to take his party up Chaussee-strasse, the northern continuation of Friedrichstrasse, but when they came to a barricade outside the gates of the old Maikäfer Barracks they found it guarded by a Soviet tank and were obliged to return to Invalidenstrasse. Just then a shell intended for the battle dropped short and killed SS Major-General Jürgen Ziegler, Krukenberg's predecessor. They moved on to take shelter in a disused goods yard by Stettiner Railway Station, where they were eventually joined by Krukenberg and the survivors of his group, together with other parties of German soldiers hiding in the vicinity.[43]

Meanwhile seven Chancellery survivors who had turned left after crossing the Weidendammer Bridge – Bormann, Axmann, Secretary of State Werner Naumann, SS Colonel Dr Ludwig Stumpfegger (Hitler's last physician), Major Weltzin (Axmann's aide), SS Captain Schwägermann (Goebbels' aide) and General Baur (Hitler's personal pilot), took shelter on the Schiffbauer-damm until the firing abated. They then followed the S-Bahn tracks leading into Moabit. Opposite the Reichstag they came under sniper fire and General Baur became separated from the rest and left behind. The six men crossed the Humboldthafen (another of Berlin's inland ports) by the railway bridge and dropped down into the roadway beneath Lehrter S-Bahn Station to find themselves in the middle of a bivouacking platoon of Soviet soldiers who took them to be Volkssturm making their way home. Bormann and Stumpfegger edged away from the group and started running, thereby arousing the Soviets' suspicions, but the others managed to get away unnoticed. However, when Baur appeared shortly afterward he was shot and seriously wounded by the same troops before being captured.[44]

Axmann and Weltzin went on into Moabit until they were turned back by tankfire. In crossing the road bridge over the main tracks leading into Lehrter Railway Station they came across the bodies of Bormann and Stumpfegger, who had apparently committed suicide. They decided to split up, Axmann taking shelter with an old girlfriend and later getting away safely to the west, as did Naumann, but Weltzin was caught that same morning.[45]

At 0700 hours Mohnke's party, now between 150 and 200 strong, marched through the deserted streets up Bernauer Strasse and Brunnenstrasse and at 0900 hours arrived at the Humboldthain flak-tower. While they were there, they heard the news of General Weidling's surrender, but Mohnke's group decided to break away and marched off to the Malzbrauerei Groterjan brewery nearby in Prinzenallee.[46]

At the brewery they found other groups of soldiers and civilians sheltering. While the men settled down to a final party with ample beer supplies and willing female partners, the officers went below into the cellars to decide what to do. Some people left to make their own escape attempts, including two of Hitler's secretaries and Bormann's secretary, all three women eventually getting safely through to the west. Finally Mohnke sent Colonel Claussen, who was not Waffen-SS and therefore more acceptable to the Soviets as a spokesman, to organize their surrender before the Soviets should decide to attack. The surrender was completed by 2000 hours but Ambassador Walter Hewel and a fanatical young SS lieutenant both committed suicide beforehand rather than give themselves up.[47]

During the lull in the fighting on the night of 1 May the 80 surviving men of SS Lieutenant Neilands' 15th SS 'Latvian' Fusilier Battalion had withdrawn to new positions in the vast, massively constructed Air Ministry. Somehow they had been overlooked in the breakout plans, and in the morning they found themselves abandoned. The streets were empty of both German and Soviet troops. Once they discovered what had happened they decided to make their way north through the ruins to escape from the Soviets, for they knew what to expect from the people that had annexed their country in 1940. Eventually, they reached a square in Pankow, where they found about 1,000 German soldiers waiting to be marched off into captivity, and there they split up, each man making his own bid for freedom.[48]

Some of the French Waffen-SS volunteers also found themselves in the same predicament at the Air Ministry but, after consulting with General Weidling's headquarters, opted for surrender.[49]

General Bokov devotes nearly an entire chapter to the storming of the Reichs Chancellery by elements of the 5th Shock Army's 9th Rifle Corps. He relates how it had been planned to conduct a massive air strike on the building between 0800 and 1030 hours on the morning of 2 May, for which the troops would first have to be pulled back as a safety precaution, but that during the night, as a result of reconnaissance reports, the air strike was cancelled and an earlier assault ordered, in which the building was simultaneously attacked from three sides while the fourth was kept under fire. The story ends with Major Anna Nikulina triumphantly hoisting her red flag on the roof. He even quotes Marshal Zhukov's comment: 'The last battle for the Reichs Chancellery, conducted by the 301st and 248th Rifle Divisions, was a hard one. At the entrances and inside the building there was some extremely heavy fighting. Major Anna Vladimirovna Nikulina, the Chief Instructor of the 9th Corps's Political Department displayed exceptional courage.'

However, as we know, the defence had withdrawn to Friedrichstrasse, so the only troops remaining would be those who either did not know of the breakout or had decided to stay and fight to the end. Certainly, there was no organized resistance, but the cellars contained some 1,500 wounded and 400 dead, all of whose weapons had been taken over by the Volkssturm during the previous fighting.[50]

At 2240 hours on 1 May the 79th Guards Rifle Division picked up the following radio message in Russian:

> Hello, hello. This is the LVIth German Panzer Corps. We ask you to cease fire. At 0050 hours Berlin time we are sending envoys to parley at the Bendlerstrasse Bridge.[51] The recognition sign is a white flag with a red light. We await your reply.

This message was repeated five times. The Soviets then replied:

> Your message received, message received. Request passed to superior officer.

The Germans then acknowledged with:

> Russian station I am receiving you. You are reporting to a superior officer.[52]

Colonel-General Chuikov then called for a cessation of fighting in the area where the envoys were due to appear. Colonel von Dufving, accompanied by two majors, one of whom was an interpreter, and a soldier carrying the white flag, set off down Bendlerstrasse to where the Soviets had established a small bridgehead behind an impromptu barricade at the northern end of the bridge. The bridge had been blown, but the surviving cables previously strung underneath it had been bound together as an improvised footbridge.

Unfortunately, the German troops had not been informed in advance of the mission, and the Soviets had mistakenly recorded Potsdamer instead of Bendlerstrasse for the name of the bridge for the rendezvous. Consequently when Colonel von Dufving shouted out for the German troops to hold their fire, abuse and even grenades were hurled at them, and their unexpected arrival at the Soviet barricade nearly resulted in von Dufving's being clubbed down. Through his interpreter, Colonel von Dufving managed to explain to the Soviet major in charge that they were authorized parliamentarians seeking to establish contact with the Soviet High Command. Von Dufving then had to return to the Bendlerblock to get the orders issued for a local ceasefire before he could proceed. He and his party were then led across the bridge to where a vehicle was now waiting for them, and taken on via a regimental command post to that of the 47th Guards Rifle Division, where von Dufving was received by Guards-Colonel Semchenko, the acting divisional commander. Once General Weidling's suggested terms had been agreed, Semchenko asked how long the Germans would require to prepare themselves. Colonel von Dufving replied three to four hours, but that the task would have to be accomplished in darkness as Goebbels had issued instructions that anyone attempting to surrender should be shot in the back and there were plenty of fanatical Nazis who might not comply with Weidling's instructions to surrender. (Weidling and von Dufving already knew that Goebbels was dead.) The message then came from Chuikov that Colonel von Dufving was to return to General Weidling immediately and inform him that his offer to surrender was accepted. General Weidling would be expected to surrender himself at 0600 hours, the troops at 0700 hours. Honourable terms were guaranteed: officers would be allowed to keep their side-arms, each could take as much hand baggage as he could carry and the Soviet High Command would ensure the protection of the civilian population and care for the wounded. The two German majors were obliged to remain behind as hostages. Colonel von Dufving returned unharmed to the Bendlerblock at about 0300 hours and reported the success of his mission to General Weidling.[53]

In the meantime Dr Hans Fritzsche, Permanent Under-Secretary at the Propaganda Ministry, had discovered that he was the senior government official left after the death of Goebbels and the evacuation of the Führer-bunker, and decided to act in the interests of the civilian population by asking the Soviets to take them under their protection. His delegation arrived at Chuikov's headquarters at 0350 hours bearing a letter from him and a request to allow him to broadcast to the people and the garrison. Although the Soviets were primarily interested in the military surrender, they agreed to Dr Fritzsche's request and sent an escort to take him to a radio station to make the broadcast. While they were still discussing this, a report came in from the 47th Guards Rifle Division that the German troops were forming up in columns. Colonel-General Chuikov then ordered an immediate ceasefire in his area of operations.[54]

At 0500 hours, two Soviet officers arrived at the Bendlerblock asking for General Weidling. Working on Moscow time, they were an hour earlier than anticipated. Weidling accompanied them, crossing the Landwehr Canal by the same improvised bridge that von Dufving had previously used. With him too went the retired Lieutenant-Generals Woytasch and Schmidt-Dankward, who had volunteered to assist with the defence. When Weidling reached General Chuikov's headquarters, he told the latter that he had decided not to consult Goebbels about the surrender of the garrison. Colonel-General Sokolovsky then appeared from Marshal Zhukov's headquarters and, after answering a few questions, General Weidling sat down to compose his formal order of surrender to the garrison, which read as follows:

> On the 30th April the Führer, to whom we had all sworn an oath of allegiance, forsook us by committing suicide. Faithful to the Führer, you German soldiers were prepared to continue the battle for Berlin even though your ammunition was running out and the general situation made further resistance senseless.
>
> I now order all resistance to cease immediately. Every hour you go on fighting adds to the terrible suffering of the Berlin population and our wounded. In agreement with the High Command of the Soviet Forces, I call on you to stop fighting forthwith.
>
> > Weidling
> > General of Artillery
> > Former Commander
> > Berlin Defence Area

This format was accepted by the Soviets, and his staff, including Generals Woytasch and Schmidt-Dankward, were called in to produce and arrange the distribution of copies of this order. Weidling was then driven to a Political Department office in Johannisthal, where he recorded his order to surrender for broadcasting by Soviet propaganda vehicles around the remaining areas of resistance.[55]

All hostilities were due to cease by 1300 hours but it was nearer 1700 hours before the fighting finally came to an end in the city. Endless columns of prisoners began the long trek eastward, the 1st Byelorussian Front's prisoners being collected for sorting in the open chalk mines at Rüdersdorf, just beyond the autobahn ring. The Soviets claim to have taken 134,000 prisoners in Berlin that day, but this actually amounted to a big round-up of all able-bodied men, and even women, for the labour camps back in the Soviet Union.[56]

On the night of 1/2 May the remains of the 20th Panzergrenadier Division and other elements of the Army Detachment 'Spree', to which Lieutenant-Colonel Weiss's party had attached themselves, attempted to break out of the Wannsee 'island' position. Their plan was to force their way through the Soviet lines at Wannsee Railway Station and then turn south through the dense woods to meet up with the 12th Army. However, when they charged across the bridge taking the Potsdamer Chaussee across the water to pass under the railway bridge next to the station, they found the underpass blocked by an anti-tank barrier and the Soviets met them with a hail of fire. The Germans managed to establish a small bridgehead before the Soviets counterattacked.[57] Weiss was captured but the other two of his party managed to escape by hiding in a fir thicket. In the morning they discarded their uniforms and donned old civilian clothes before crawling though the lines of Soviets still scouring the woods for survivors. They eventually escaped to the west in the guise of returning foreign labourers.[58]

The heavy shelling that this escape attempt had attracted all over Wannsee 'island' also affected Major Johannmeier's courier party. During the fighting a three-engined Dornier flying boat landed on the Havel close to Pfaueninsel and contact was established with the couriers but the shelling forced the pilot to take off again without them. Although they all eventually reached safety, none of these couriers accomplished their missions and the documents were all subsequently recovered by the Western Allies during the investigation into Hitler's death.[59]

According to Marshal Koniev, General Lelyushenko had an unpleasant surprise that day when a large groups of Germans, estimated at 2,000 strong, attacked his headquarters in the village of Schenkenhorst. These were in fact the survivors of the breakout from Wannsee making their way to Beelitz, where they hoped to find Wenck's Army. Although Koniev says that it took two hours of hard fighting by the headquarters staff and guards, eventually reinforced by the 7th Guards Motorcycle Regiment and other units nearby, before the Germans were defeated,[60] the German group continued on to cross the autobahn ring, as Friedhelm Schöneck relates:

> Our advance is suddenly interrupted as we unexpectedly emerge from a little wood on to a Russian airfield. We can see the aircraft all lined up on it. We have no time to think. We can neither go back nor turn away. We charge on to the airfield like a crowd of demons and, before the Russian guards can grasp what is happening, grenades and Panzerfausts are going off and machine-guns making sieves out of the silver birds with their 'Red Star'. The chaos is complete, with screams, curses and explosions mingling. The dazed pilots try to get to their machines, and only on the far left do some succeed. With a thundering roar they race over the runway and gain height, but they don't fly away, they turn in a big loop and are then above us. Their cannon rake the airfield shooting up the machines and the mob of German and Russian soldiers running around firing indiscriminately.

The screams of the wounded mix with the sounds of cannon fire. We seek cover in the furrows of a ploughed field beyond the airfield. Lying on our backs, we aim with our weapons at the low flying IL-2s attacking us. They fly so low we can pick out the pilots' faces in their cockpits. The wounded scream and call out for medical orderlies. Some try and run for it but are shot down immediately … . It seems an eternity before the planes pull away, leaving behind a field full of stunned and screaming people, full of collapsed, torn bodies.

But this infernal finale is not over yet. Something growls in the shadow of the trees of the little wood and tank tracks screech. Shells burst in the field with hellish din among our lost band. Machine-guns rattle, completing the deadly work. Russian infantry storm in from left and right. We no longer have a chance. Our fate is sealed …

From the two or three thousand that broke out from 'Festung Wannsee' only 187 are still alive, some lightly wounded … Among us are Wehrmacht administrators, RAD men, Hitlerjugend, female auxiliaries, civilians and RAD girls. The sorting out begins. The women disappear from our view, pushed into a barn. Their cries and screams, the joking and laughing of the Russian guards, drives home to us with loathing and disgust the fact that we have been conquered.[61]

That same day, Marshal Koniev started withdrawing his forces from the Berlin area in preparation for another big operation in conjunction with the 2nd and 4th Ukrainian Fronts, which was due to start on 6 May against Army Group 'Mitte' in Czechoslovakia.[62]

The 1st Polish Infantry Division also pulled out of Berlin at noon on the 2nd May to rejoin their parent formation at Nauen, but not before the Polish soldiers had had the opportunity of hoisting their white and red national flags on the Siegessäule (Victory Column) and the Brandenburg Gate.[63]

The same day the 2nd Byelorussian Front reached the line Wittenberge/Parchim/Bad Doberan, pushing back the remains of the 3rd Panzer and 21st Armies. Meanwhile, the British 21st Army Group had taken Lübeck and Wismar, and the American 9th Army had taken Ludwigslust and Schwerin, so that the German forces now found themselves crushed into a pocket barely 15–20 miles wide. That night Generals von Manteuffel and von Tippelskirch surrendered their armies to the Americans.

The 1st Byelorussian Front still had to finish clearing up to the Elbe to complete their part of 'Operation Berlin', and so during 1 May the flanking armies were moved forward so that on the morning of the 2nd progress could be maintained westward. The 33rd Army started off from Kropstädt, the 69th

Army from Niemegk, the 3rd Army from Brandenburg, the 47th Army from Rathenow, the 1st Polish Army south and the 61st Army north of Havelberg. By 6 May they had closed up to the river everywhere except in Wenck's army's sector, where the XX Corps held them at bay for yet another day to enable the evacuation to be completed.

So 'Operation Berlin' ended, and it was time to count the cost. The tally given by the Soviets for the three fronts claim 480,000 prisoners (of which over 70,000 were taken in Berlin), 1,500 tanks and self-propelled guns, 8,600 guns and mortars, and 4,500 aircraft taken. Their own casualties they give as 304,887 killed, wounded and missing between 16 April and 8 May 1945, together with the loss of 2,156 tanks and self-propelled guns, 1,220 guns and mortars, and 527 aircraft. The Red Air Force claim to have destroyed 1,132 German aircraft in combat, plus another 100 on the ground, and to have knocked out some 400 tanks and self-propelled guns.[64]

In their brief appearance within the city, the 1st Polish Infantry Division and the accompanying 1st Polish Field Artillery Regiment lost 88 killed and 441 wounded.[65]

The Soviet medal for the capture of Berlin was awarded to 1,082,000 persons, which gives some indication of the numbers involved, including rear area personnel, in the actual taking of the city. Over 600 officers and men were awarded the gold star of 'Hero of the Soviet Union', and a further 13 received their second gold star. The Soviet military cemeteries in the city at Treptow, Pankow and in the Tiergarten hold the bodies of approximately 20,000 of their dead.[66]

It is not possible to give any accurate figures on German casualties within Berlin's perimeters, for the city administration collapsed during the critical period. From his immediate postwar research Colonel Pierre Rocolle gave a figure of 22,349 civilian deaths directly attributable to the battle and suggested that the military losses would have been about the same. More recently the Berlin Branch of the German War Graves Commission (Landesverband Berlin, Volksbund Deutsche Kriegsgräberfürsorge e.V.) records 18,320 Wehrmacht, 33,420 Berlin-registered civilians and 2,010 refugees buried in the Western Sectors of the city alone, but these figures relate to the whole of the war and include members of the Volkssturm as civilians. Throughout the Soviet Zone and Sector of Berlin, except in rare instances, the 'Fascist Wehrmacht' dead were accorded no honourable burial, being merely tumbled uncounted into mass graves or buried in the trenches they had defended.

APPENDIX 1

SOVIET ORDER-OF-BATTLE FOR 'OPERATION BERLIN'

Drawn from F.D. Vorbeyev, I.V. Propotkin and A.N. Shimanky's *The Last Storm*, with additional information on units identified in the encirclement of the city. The armies are listed in order of deployment from north to south as at 16 April 1945.

2ND BYELORUSSIAN FRONT
(*Marshal K.K. Rokossovsky*)

2nd Shock Army (*Col.-Gen. I.I. Fedyurinsky*)
108th, 116th Rifle Corps

65th Army (*Col.-Gen. P.I. Batov*)
18th, 46th, 105th Rifle Corps

70th Army (*Col.-Gen. V.S. Popov*)
47th, 96th, 114th Rifle Corps

49th Army (*Col.-Gen. I.T. Grishin*)
70th, 121st Rifle Corps
191st, 200th, 330th Rifle Divs

19th Army
40th Gds, 132nd, 134th Rifle Corps

5th Gds Tk Army
29th Tk Corps
1st Tk and 47th Mech Bdes

Appendix 1

Air Forces

4th Air Army (*Col.-Gen. K.A. Vershinin*)
4th Air Aslt, 5th Air Bomber and 8th Air Fighter Corps

1ST BYELORUSSIAN FRONT
(*Marshal G.K. Zhukov*)

61st Army (*Col.-Gen. P.A. Belov*)
9th Gds Rifle Corps (*Lt-Gen. G.A. Halyuzin/Lt-Gen. A.D. Shtemenko*)
    12th, 75th Gds and 415th Rifle Divs
80th Rifle Corps (*Maj.-Gen. V.A. Vyerzhbitsky*)
    212th, 234th, 356th Rifle Divs
89th Rifle Corps (*Maj.-Gen. M.A. Siyzov*)
    23rd, 311th, 397th Rifle Divs, 312th Gds, 1811th, 1899th SP Aslt Arty
    Regts

1st Polish Army (*Lt-Gen. S.G. Poplowski*)
1st Pol Inf Div 'Tadiuscz Kosciuszko' (*Maj.-Gen. W. Bewziuk*)
2nd, 3rd, 4th, 6th Pol Inf Divs
1st Pol Cav Bde
4th Pol Hy Tk Regt
13th Pol SP Aslt Arty Regt
7th Pol SP Aslt Arty Bn

47th Army (*Lt-Gen. F.I. Perkhorovitch*)
77th Rifle Corps (*Maj.-Gen./Lt-Gen. Y.S. Vorobyev*)
    185th, 260th, 328th Rifle Divs
125th Rifle Corps (*Maj.-Gen./Lt-Gen. A.M. Andreyev*)
    60th, 76th, 175th Rifle Divs
129th Rifle Corps (*Maj.-Gen. M.B. Anashkin*)
    82nd, 132nd, 143rd Rifle Divs
70th Gds Ind Tk Regt
334th, 1204th, 1416th, 1825th, 1892nd SP Aslt Arty Regts

3rd Shock Army (*Col.-Gen. V.I. Kutznetsov*)
7th Rifle Corps (*Maj.-Gen. V.A. Christov/Col.-Gen. Y.T. Chyervichenko*)
    146th, 265th, 364th Rifle Divs
12th Gds Rifle Corps (*Lt-Gen. A.F. Kazanin/Maj.-Gen. A.A. Filatov*)
    23rd Gds Rifle Div
        63rd Gds Rifle Regt
    52nd Gds and 33rd Rifle Divs

<u>79th Rifle Corps</u> (*Maj.-Gen. S.I. Perevertkin*)
    150th Rifle Div (*Maj.-Gen. V.M. Shatilov*)
        469th, 674th, 756th Rifle Regts
    171st Rifle Div (*Col. A.P. Negoda*)
        380th, 525th, 713rd Rifle Regts
    207th Rifle Div (*Col. V.M. Asafov*)
        594th, 597th, 598th Rifle Regts
<u>9th Tank Corps</u> (*Lt-Gen. I.F. Kirichenko*)
    23rd, 95th, 108th Tk Bdes
    8th Mot Rifle Regt
    1455th, 1508th SP Aslt Arty Regts

5th Shock Army (*Gen./Col.-Gen. N.E. Berzarin*)
<u>9th Rifle Corps</u> (*Maj.-Gen./Lt-Gen. I.P. Rossly*)
    230th Rifle Div (*Col. D.K. Shiskov*)
        988th Rifle Regt
        990th Rifle Regt
    248th Rifle Div (*Maj.-Gen. N.Z. Galai*)
        902nd Rifle Regt
    301st Rifle Div (*Col. V.S. Antonov*)
        1050th Rifle Regt
        1052nd Rifle Regt
        1054th Rifle Regt (*Col. Peshkov*)
<u>26th Gds Corps</u> (*Maj.-Gen. P.A. Firsov*)
    89th Gds Rifle Div (*Maj.-Gen. M.P. Seryugin*)
    94th Gds Rifle Div (*Maj.-Gen. I.G. Gospoyan*)
        283rd Gds Rifle Regt (*Lt-Col. A.A. Ignatiev*)
        286th Gds Rifle Regt (*Lt-Col. A.N. Kravchenko*)
        288th Gds Rifle Regt (*Lt-Col. V.V. Kondratenko*)
        199th Gds Arty Regt (*Lt-Col. J.F. Zherebtsov*)
    266th Rifle Div (*Col./Maj.-Gen. Fomichenko*)
        1006th Rifle Regt (*Lt-Col. I.I. Terjochin*)
        1008th Rifle Regt (*Col. Borisov*)
        1010th Rifle Regt (*Col. Zagoredski*)
<u>32nd Rifle Corps</u> (*Lt-Gen. D.S. Zherebin*)
    60th Gds Rifle Div (*Maj.-Gen. V.P. Sokolov*)
    295th Rifle Div (*Maj.-Gen. A.P. Dorofeyev*)
        1040th Rifle Regt
    416th Rifle Div (*Maj.-Gen. D.M. Syzranov*)
        1368th Rifle Regt (*Lt-Col. Kurkatischvili*)

1373rd Rifle Regt (*Lt-Col. S.M. Saidbatulov/Maj.-Gen. V.P. Siuvanov*)
1374th Rifle Regiment
1054th Arty Regt
11th, 67th Gds, and 220th Tk Bdes
92nd Ind Tk Regt (*Lt-Col. Miasnikov*)
396th Gds and 1504th SP Aslt Arty Regts

8th Gds Army (*Col.-Gen. V.I. Chuikov*)
<u>4th Gds Rifle Corps</u> (*Lt-Gen. V.A. Glazonov*)
   35th Gds Rifle Div (*Col. Grigoryev*)
      102nd Gds Rifle Regt
   47th Gds Rifle Div (*Lt-Gen. V.M. Shugeyev*)
      137th, 140th, 142nd Gds Rifle Regts
   57th Gds Rifle Div (*Maj.-Gen. P.I. Zalizyuk*)
      170th, 172nd, 174th Gds Rifle Regts
<u>28th Gds Rifle Corps</u> (*Lt-Gen. A.I. Ryzhov*)
   39th Gds Rifle Div (*Col. E.T. Marchenko*)
      117th, 120th Gds Rifle Regts
   79th Gds Rifle Div (*Col. S.I. Gerasimenko*)
      216th, 220th, 227th Gds Rifle Regts
   88th Gds Rifle Div (*Maj.-Gen. G.I. Pankov*)
      266th, 269th, 271st Gds Rifle Regts
<u>29th Gds Rifle Corps</u> (*Lt-Gen. A.D. Shemenkov/Maj.-Gen. G.I. Hetariov*)
   27th Gds Rifle Div (*Maj.-Gen. V.S. Glebov*)
      74th, 76th, 83rd Gds Rifle Regts
   74th Gds Rifle Div (*Maj.-Gen. D.E. Bakanov*)
      226th, 236th, 240th Gds Rifle Rgts
   82nd Gds Rifle Div (*Maj.-Gen. M. Duka*)
      242nd Gds Rifle Regt (*Col. I.F. Sukhorukov*)
      271st Gds Rifle Regt
7th Gds Tk Bde
84th Gds, 65th, 259th Ind Tk Regts
371st, 374th Gds, 694th, 1026th, 1061st, 1087th and 1200th SP
  Aslt Arty Regts

69th Army (*Col.-Gen. V.Y. Kolpakchi*)
<u>25th Rifle Corps</u> (*Maj.-Gen. N.I. Trufanov*)
   77th Gds and 4th Rifle Divs
<u>61st Rifle Corps</u> (*Lt-Gen. I.F. Grigoryevsky*)
   134th, 246th, 247th Rifle Divs

<u>91st Rifle Corps</u> (*Lt-Gen. F.A. Volkov*)
  41st, 312th, 370th Rifle Divs
117th, 283rd Rifle Divs
68th Tk Bde
12th SP Aslt Arty Bde
344th Gds, 1205th, 1206th, 1221st SP Aslt Arty Regts

33rd Army (*Col.-Gen. V.D. Svotaev*)
<u>16th Rifle Corps</u> (*Maj.-Gen. / Lt-Gen. E.V. Dobrovolsky*)
  323rd, 339th, 383rd Rifle Divs
<u>38th Rifle Corps</u> (*Maj.-Gen. / Lt-Gen. A.D. Tyershkov*)
  64th, 89th, 169th Rifle Divs
<u>62nd Rifle Corps</u> (*Lt-Gen. V.S. Vorobyev*)
  49th, 222nd, 362nd Rifle Divs
<u>2nd Gds Cav Corps</u> (*Lt-Gen. V.V. Krukov*)
  3rd, 4th, 17th Gds Cav Divs
  1459th SP Aslt Arty Regt
95th Rifle Div
257th Ind Tk Regt
360th, 361st SP Aslt Arty Regts

Air Forces

16th Air Army (*Col.-Gen. S.I. Rudenko*)
<u>3rd Air Bomber Corps</u> (*Maj.-Gen. A.Z. Karavacki*)
  241st, 301st Air Bomber Divs
<u>6th Air Bomber Corps</u> (*Maj.-Gen. I.P. Skok*)
  326th, 339th Air Bomber Divs
<u>6th Air Aslt Corps</u> (*Maj.-Gen. B.K. Tokarev*)
  197th, 198th Air Aslt Divs
<u>9th Air Aslt Corps</u> (*Maj.-Gen. I.V. Krupski*)
  3rd Gds and 300th Air Aslt Divs
<u>1st Gds Air Fighter Corps</u> (*Lt-Gen. E.M. Belecki*)
  3rd, 4th Gds Air Fighter Divs
<u>3rd Air Fighter Corps</u> (*Lt-Gen. E.Y. Savicki*)
  265th, 278th Air Fighter Divs
<u>6th Air Fighter Corps</u> (*Maj.-Gen. I.M. Dzusov*)
  234th, 273rd Air Fighter Divs
<u>13th Air Fighter Corps</u> (*Maj.-Gen. B.A. Sidnev*)
  193rd, 283rd Air Fighter Divs

1st Gds, 240th, 282nd, 286th Air Fighter Divs
2nd, 11th Gds Air Aslt Divs
113th, 183rd, 188th, 221st Air Bomber Divs
9th Gds and 242nd Air Night Bomber Divs
16th, 72nd Air Recce Regts
93rd, 98th Air Observation Regts
176th Gds Air Fighter Regt
226th Air Tpt Regt

18th Air Army (*AVM A. Y. Golovanov*)
<u>1st Gds Air Bomber Corps</u>
   11th, 16th Gds, 36th, 48th Air Bomber Divs
<u>2nd Gds Air Bomber Corps</u>
   2nd, 7th, 13th, 18th Gds Air Bomber Divs
<u>3rd Gds Air Bomber Corps</u>
   22nd Gds, 1st, 12th, 50th Air Bomber Divs
<u>4th Gds Air Bomber Corps</u>
   14th, 15th Gds, 53rd, 54th Air Bomber Divs
45th Air Bomber
56th Air Fighter Div
742nd Air Recce Regt

Mobile Forces

1st Gds Tk Army (*Col.-Gen. M. Y. Katukov*)
<u>8th Gds Mech Corps</u> (*Maj.-Gen. I.F. Drygemov*)
   19th, 20th, 21st Gds Mech Bdes
   1st Gds Tk Bde
   48th Gds Tk Regt
   353rd, 400th Gds SP Aslt Arty Regts
   8th Gds M/C Bn
<u>11th Gds Tk Corps</u> (*Col. A.H. Babadshanian*)
   40th, 44th, 45th Gds Tk Bdes
   27th Gds Mech Bde
   362nd, 399th Gds and 1454th SP Aslt Arty Regts
   9th Gds M/C Bn
<u>11th Tk Corps</u> (*Maj.-Gen. I.I. Jushuk*)
   20th, 36th, 65th Tk Bdes
   12th Mot Rifle Bde
   50th Gds Tk Regt

1461st, 1493rd SP Aslt Arty Regts
64th Gds Tk Bde
19th SP Aslt Arty Bde
11th Gds Ind Tk Regt
12th Gds M/C Bn

2nd Gds Tk Army (*Col.-Gen. S.I. Bogdanov*)
<u>1st Mech Corps</u> (*Lt-Gen. S.M. Krivosheina*)
19th, 35th, 37th Mech Bdes
219th Tk Bde
347th Gds, 75th, 1822nd SP Aslt Arty Regts
57th M/C Bn
<u>9th Gds Tk Corps</u> (*Maj.-Gen. A.F. Popov*)
47th, 50th, 65th Gds Tk Bdes
33rd Gds Mech Bde
341st, 369th, 386th Gds SP Aslt Arty Regts
17th Gds M/C Bn
<u>12th Gds Tk Corps</u> (*Maj.-Gen. M.K. Teltakov/Col. A.T. Shevchenko*)
48th, 49th, 66th Gds Tk Bdes
34th Gds Mech Bde
79th Gds Tk Regt
387th, 393rd Gds SP Aslt Arty Regts
6th Gds Ind Tk Regt
5th Gds M/C Regt
16th Gds M/C Bn

Front Reserves

3rd Army (*Col.-Gen. A.V. Gorbatov*)
<u>35th Rifle Corps</u> (*Maj.-Gen. N.A. Nikitin*)
250th, 290th, 348th Rifle Divs
<u>40th Rifle Corps</u> (*Lt-Gen. V.S. Kuzynetsov*)
5th, 129th Rifle Divs
<u>41st Rifle Corps</u> (*Lt-Gen. V.K. Ubranovich*)
120th, 269th Rifle Divs
1812th, 1888th, 1901st Sp Aslt Arty Regts
<u>2nd Gds Cav Corps</u> (*Lt-Gen. V.V. Kruhkov*)
3rd, 4th, 17th Gds Cav Divs
1459th SP Aslt Arty Regt
10th Gds RL Regt

3rd Gds Cav Corps (*Lt-Gen. N.S. Oslikovsky*)
    5th, 6th, 32nd Gds Cav Divs
    1814th SP Aslt Arty Regt
    3rd Gds RL Regt
7th Gds Cavalry Corps (*Maj.-Gen. M.P. Konstantinov*)
    14th, 15th, 16th Gds Cav Divs
    1816th SP Aslt Arty Regt
    7th Gds RL Regt
3rd Gds Tk Corps (*Lt-Gen. A.P. Panfilov*)
    3rd, 18th, 19th Gds Tk Bdes
    2nd Gds Mot Rifle Bde
    375th Gds, 1436th, 1496th SP Aslt Arty Regts
    10th Gds M/C Bn
8th Gds Tk Corps (*Maj.-Gen. A.F. Popov*)
    58th, 59th, 60th Gds Tk Bdes
    28th Gds Mot Rifle Bde
    62nd Gds Ind Tk Regt
    301st Gds and 1817th SP Aslt Arty Regts
    6th Gds M/C Bn
244th Ind Tk Regt
31st, 39th, 51st, 55th Ind Armd Train Bns

Naval Forces

Dnieper Flotilla (*Rear Adm V.V. Grigoryev*)
1st, 2nd, 3rd River Boat Bdes
[*8 Monitors, 34 Gunboats and 20 Antiaircraft Gunboats*]

1st UKRAINIAN FRONT
(*Marshal I.S. Koniev*)

3rd Gds Army (*Col.-Gen. V.N. Gordov*)
21st Rifle Corps (*Maj.-Gen. A.A. Yamanov*)
    58th, 253rd, 329th Rifle Divs
76th Rifle Corps (*Lt-Gen. M.I. Gluhov*)
    106th, 287th Rifle Divs
120th Rifle Corps (*Maj.-Gen. S.I. Donskov*)
    127th, 149th, 197th Rifle Divs

<u>25th Tk Corps</u> (*Maj.-Gen. E.I. Fominich*)
   111th, 162nd, 175th Tk Bdes
   20th Mot Rifle Bde
   262nd Gds and 1451st SP Aslt Arty Regts
389th Rifle Div
87th Gds Ind Tk Regt
938th SP Aslt Arty Regt ·

13th Army (*Col.-Gen. N.P. Phukov*)
<u>24th Rifle Corps</u> (*Maj.-Gen. D.P. Onoprienko*)
   121st Gds and 395th Rifle Divs
<u>27th Rifle Corps</u> (*Maj.-Gen. F.M. Chyerokmanov*)
   6th Gds, 280th, 350th Rifle Divs
[*350th Rifle Div later detached to 4th Gds Tk Army*]
<u>102nd Rifle Corps</u> (*Maj.-Gen./Lt-Gen. I.M. Puzikov*)
   117th Gds, 147th, 172nd Rifle Divs
88th Ind Tk Regt
327th, 372nd Gds, 768th, 1228th SP Aslt Arty Regts

5th Gds Army (*Col.-Gen. A.S. Zhadov*)
<u>32nd Gds Rifle Corps</u> (*Lt-Gen. A.I. Rodimtsev*)
   13th, 95th, 97th Gds Rifle Divs
<u>33rd Gds Rifle Corps</u> (*Maj.-Gen. N.F. Lyebedyenko*)
   9th Gds Airborne, 78th Gds and 118th Rifle Divs
<u>34th Gds Rifle Corps</u> (*Maj.-Gen. E.V. Boklanov*)
   14th, 15th, 58th Gds Rifle Divs
<u>4th Gds Tk Corps</u> (*Lt-Gen. P.P. Poluboyarov*)
   12th, 13th, 14th Gds Tk Bdes
   3rd Gds Mot Rifle Bde
   29th Gds Tk Regt
   293rd, 298th Gds SP Aslt Arty Regts
   76th M/C Bn

2nd Polish Army (*Lt-Gen. K.K. Swiersczewski*)
5th, 7th, 8th, 9th, 10th Pol Inf Divs
<u>1st Pol Tk Corps</u>
   2nd, 3rd, 4th Pol Tk Bdes
   1st Pol Mot Rifle Bde
   24th, 25th, 26th Pol SP Aslt Arty Regts
   2nd Pol M/C Bn

16th Pol Tk Bde
5th Pol Ind Tk Regt
28th Pol SP Aslt Arty Regt

52nd Army (*Col.-Gen. K.A. Koroteyev*)
<u>48th Rifle Corps</u> (*Maj.-Gen. Z.Z. Roganzy / Lt-Gen. A.A. Gryechkin*)
  116th, 294th Rifle Divs
<u>73rd Rifle Corps</u> (*Maj.-Gen. S.S. Martirosyan*)
  50th, 111th, 254th Rifle Divs
<u>78th Rifle Corps</u> (*Lt-Gen. A.I. Akimov*)
  31st, 214th, 373rd Rifle Divs
<u>7th Gds Mech Corps</u> (*Lt-Gen. I.P. Korchagin*)
  24th, 25th, 26th Gds Mech Bdes
  57th Gds Tk Bde
  291st, 355th Gds, and 1820th SP Aslt Arty Regts
  5th Gds M/C Bn
213th Rifle Div
8th SP Aslt Arty Bde
124th Ind Tk Regt
1198th SP Aslt Arty Regt

Air Forces

2nd Air Army (*Col.-Gen. S.A. Krasovsky*)
<u>1st Gds Air Aslt Corps</u>
  8th, 9th Gds Air Aslt Divs
  12th Gds Air Fighter Div
<u>2nd Gds Air Aslt Corps</u>
  5th, 6th Gds Air Aslt Divs
  11th Gds Air Fighter Div
<u>3rd Air Aslt Corps</u>
  307th, 308th Air Aslt Divs
  181st Air Fighter Div
<u>4th Air Bomber Corps</u>
  202nd, 219th Air Bomber Divs
<u>6th Gds Air Bomber Corps</u>
  1st, 8th Gds Air Bomber Divs
<u>2nd Air Fighter Corps</u>
  7th Gds, 322nd Air Fighter Divs

<u>5th Air Fighter Corps</u>
    8th Gds, 256th Air Fighter Divs
<u>6th Air Fighter Corps</u>
    9th, 22nd, 23rd Gds Air Fighter Divs
208th Air Night Bomber Div
98th, 193rd Gds Air Recce Regts
222nd Air Tpt Regt

Mobile Forces

3rd Gds Tk Army (*Col.-Gen. P.S. Rybalko*)
<u>6th Gds Tk Corps</u> (*Maj.-Gen. V.A. Mitrofanov*)
    51st, 52nd, 53rd Gds Tk Bdes
    22nd Gds Mot Rifle Bde
    385th Gds, 1893rd, 1894th SP Aslt Arty Regts
    3rd Gds M/C Bn
<u>7th Gds Tk Corps</u> (*Maj.-Gen. V.V. Novikov*)
    54th Gds Tk Bde
    55th Gds Tk Bde (*Col. D. Dragunsky*)
    56th Gds Tk Bde (*Col. Z. Slyusarenko*)
    23rd Gds Mot Rifle Bde
    384th Gds, 702nd, 1977th SP Aslt Arty Regts
    4th Gds M/C Bn
<u>9th Mech Corps</u> (*Lt-Gen. I.P. Suchov*)
    69th, 70th, 71st Mech Bdes
    91st Tk Bde
    383rd Gds, 1507th, 1978th SP Aslt Arty Regts
    100th M/C Bn
16th SP Aslt Arty Bde
57th Gds, 90th Ind Tk Regts
50th M/C Regt

4th Gds Tk Army (*Col.-Gen. D.D. Lelyushenko*)
<u>5th Gds Mech Corps</u> (*Maj.-Gen. I.P. Yermankov*)
    10th, 11th, 12th Gds Mech Bdes
    24th Gds Tk Bde
    104th, 379th Gds and 1447th SP Aslt Arty Regts
    2nd Gds M/C Bn
<u>6th Gds Mech Corps</u> (*Col. V.I. Koryetsky/Col. S.F. Puthkaryev*)
    16th, 17th, 35th Gds Mech Bdes

28th, 117th, 118th Gds Tk Regts
423rd, 424th Gds SP Aslt Arty Regts
19th Gds M/C Bn
10th Gds Tk Corps (*Lt-Gen. Y. Y. Belov*)
    61st, 62nd, 63rd Gds Tk Bdes
    29th Gds Mot Rifle Bde
    72nd Gds Tk Regt
    416th, 425th Gds SP Aslt Arty Regts
    7th Gds M/C Bn
68th Gds Tk Bde
70th Gds SP Aslt Arty Bde
13th, 119th Gds Ind Tk Regts
7th Gds M/C Regt

Reserves

28th Army (*Lt-Gen. A.A. Luchinsky*) *[w.e.f. 20 Apr 45]*
38th Gds Rifle Corps (*Maj.-Gen. P.A. Alexandrov*)
    50th, 54th, 96th Gds Rifle Divs
20th Rifle Corps (*Maj.-Gen. N.A. Shvarev*)
    48th, 55th Gds and 20th Rifle Divs
128th Rifle Corps (*Maj.-Gen. P.F. Batirsky*)
    61st, 130th, 152nd Rifle Divs

31st Army
1st Gds Cav Corps (*Lt-Gen. V.K. Baranov*)
    1st, 2nd, 7th Gds Cav Divs
    143rd Gds A/Tk Arty Regt
    1224th SP Aslt Arty Regt
152nd Tk Bde
98th Ind Tk Regt
368th Gds, 416th, 1976th SP Aslt Arty Regts
21st, 45th, 49th, 58th Ind Armd Train Bns

APPENDIX 2

ORDER-OF-BATTLE OF THE MAIN GERMAN FORCES ENGAGED IN 'OPERATION BERLIN'

ODER–NEISSE FRONT

Army Group 'Vistula'
(*Col.-Gen. Gotthard Heinrici*)

3rd Pz Army (*Gen. Hasso von Manteuffel*)
'Swinemünde' Corps (*Lt-Gen. Ansat*)
   402nd Inf Div (*Maj.-Gen. Wittkopf*)
   3rd Naval Div (*Col. von Witzleben*)
XXXII Corps (*Lt-Gen. Schack*)
   'Voigt' Inf Div (*Maj.-Gen. Voigt*)
   549th VGr Div (*Maj.-Gen. Jank*)
   Stettin Garrison (*Maj.-Gen. Brühl*)
   281st Inf Div (*Lt-Gen. Ortner/Col. Schmidt*)
'Oder' Corps (*SS Lt-Gen. von dem Bach-Zelewski/Gen. Hörnlein*)
   610th Inf Div (*Col. Summer/Col. Fullriede*)
   'Klossek' Inf Div (*Maj.-Gen. Klossek*)
XXXXVI Panzer Corps (*Gen. Martin Gareis*)
   547th VGr Div (*Maj.-Gen. Fronhöfer*)
   1st Naval Div (*Maj.-Gen. Bleckwenn*)

9th Army (*Gen. Theodor Busse*)
CI Corps (*Gen. Wilhelm Berlin/Lt-Gen. Friedrich Sixt*)
   5th Lt Inf Div (*Lt-Gen. Friedrich Sixt/Lt-Gen. Edmund Blaurock*)
     56th Lt Inf Regt [3 Bns] (*Col. Haidlen*)

75th Lt Inf Regt [3 Bns] (*Col. Sparrer*)
5th Arty Regt [4 Bns]
606th Inf Div (*Maj.-Gen. Maximilian Rosskopf*)
   3rd Pz Depot Bn
   'Potsdam' Emergency Bn
   'Brandenburg' Emergency Bn
   'Spandau' Emergency Bn
   Bremen Police Bn
309th 'Berlin' Inf Div (*Maj.-Gen. Heinrich Voigtsberger*)
   'Grossdeutschland' Gd Regt [2 Bns]
   365th Gren Regt [2 Bns]
   652nd Gren Regt [2 Bns]
   4th Luftwaffe Trg Regt
   5th Luftwaffe Trg Regt
   309th Arty Regt [1 Bn]

Corps Reserve

25th PzGr Div (*Lt-Gen. Arnold Burmeister*)
   35th PzGr Regt [3 Bns]
   119th PzGr Regt [3 Bns]
   5th Pz Bn
   25th Arty Regt
111th SPG Trg Bde (*Capt Schmidt*)
'1001 Nights' Combat Gp (*Maj. Blancblois*)
<u>LVI Pz Corps</u> (*Gen. Helmuth Weidling*)
   9th Para Div (*Gen. Bruno Bräuer / Col. Harry Herrmann*)
      25th Para Regt [3 Bns]
      26th Para Regt [3 Bns]
      27th Para Regt [4 Bns]
      9th Para Arty Regt [3 Bns]
   20th PzGr Div (*Col. / Maj.-Gen. Georg Scholze*)
      76th PzGr Regt [3 Bns] (*Col. Rheinhold Stammerjohann*)
      90th PzGr Regt [3 Bns] (*Col. von Loisecke*)
      8th Pz Bn
      20th Arty Regt [3 Bns]

Corps Reserve

'Müncheberg' Pz Div (*Maj.-Gen. Werner Mummert*)
   1st 'Müncheberg' PzGr Regt [2 Bns] (*Col. Goder*)
   2nd 'Müncheberg' PzGr Regt [3 Bns] (*Lt-Col. Werner Rodust*)

'Müncheberg' Pz Regt (*Lt-Col. Kuno von Meyer*)
   1st Bn 'Müncheberg' Pz Regt (*Maj. Marquard*)
   2nd Bn 'Müncheberg' Pz Regt (*Capt/Maj. Horst Zobel*)
'Müncheberg' Armd Arty Regt [2 Bns] (*Lt-Col. Martin Buhr*)
920th SPG Trg Bde (*Maj. Wolfgang Kapp*)
<u>XI SS Pz Corps</u> (*SS Gen. Mathias Kleinheisterkamp*)
   303rd 'Döberitz' Inf Div (*Col. Scheunemann/Col. Albin*)
      300th Gren Regt [2 Bns] (*Lt-Col. Helmut Weber*)
      301st Gren Regt [2 Bns]
      302nd Gren Regt [2 Bns]
      303rd Arty Regt
   169th Inf Div (*Lt-Gen. Georg Radziej*)
      378th Gren Regt [3 Bns]
      379th Gren Regt [2 Bns]
      392nd Gren Regt [3 Bns]
      230th Arty Regt [4 Bns]
   712th Inf Div (*Maj.-Gen. Joachim von Siegroth*)
      732nd Gren Regt [2 Bns]
      745th Gren Regt [2 Bns]
      764th Gren Regt [2 Bns]
      1712th Arty Regt

Corps Reserve

'Kurmark' PzGr Div (*Col./Maj.-Gen. Willy Langkeit*)
   'Kurmark' PzFus Regt [2 Bns]
   1234th PzGr Regt [2 Bns]
   'Kurmark' Pz Regt [2 Bns]
502nd SS Hy Tk Bn (*SS Maj. Hartrampf*)
<u>Frankfurt an der Oder Garrison</u> (*Col./Maj.-Gen. Ernst Biehler*)
<u>V SS Mtn Corps</u> (*SS Gen. Friedrich Jackeln*)
   286th Inf Div (*Maj.-Gen. Emmo von Rohde*)
      926th Gren Regt [2 Bns]
      927th Gren Regt [2 Bns]
      931st Gren Regt [2 Bns]
      286th Arty Regt [3 Bns]
   32nd SS '30. Januar' VolGr Div (*SS Col. Kempin*)
      86th SS Gren Regt [2 Bns] (*SS Lt-Col. Eccer*)
      87th SS Gren Regt [2 Bns] (*SS Lt-Col. Voss*)
      88th SS Gren Regt [2 Bns] (*SS Lt-Col. Becker*)

Appendix 2

32nd SS Arty Regt [3 Bns] (*SS Lt-Col. Lorenz*)
391st Sy Div (*Lt-Gen. Rudolf Sickenius*)
   95th Gren Regt
   1233rd Offr Cadet Regt
   391st Arty Regt

Corps Reserve

561st SS Tk-Hunting Bn (*SS Capt Jakob Lobmeyer*)

Army Troops

156th Inf Div (*Gen. Siegfried von Rekowksy*)
   1313th Gren Regt [3 Bns]
   1314th Gren Regt [3 Bns]
   1315th Gren Regt [3 Bns]
541st VGr Div
   'Dorn' JagdPz Bde
   'Pirat' JagdPz Bde
   'F' and 'R' JagdPz Bdes
404th Volks Arty Corps (*Col. Bartels*)
406th Volks Arty Corps (*Lt-Col. Adams*)
408th Volks Arty Corps (*Col. Vogt*)

Army Group Reserve

<u>III SS 'Germanic' Pz Corps</u> (*SS Lt-Gen. Felix Steiner*)

   [a. Divisions later allocated to the 9th Army]
11th SS 'Nordland' PzGr Div (*SS Maj.-Gen. Jürgen Ziegler/ SS Maj-Gen. Dr Gustav Krukenberg*)
   23rd SS 'Norge' PzGr Regt (1st Norwegian)
   24th SS 'Danmark' PzGr Regt (1st Danish) (*SS Lt-Col. Klotz/ SS Maj. Sörensen*)
   11th SS 'Hermann von Salza' Pz Bn [4 Coys] (*SS Lt-Col. Paul Kausch*)
   503rd SS Hy Tk Bn (*SS Maj. Friedrich Herzig*)
   11th SS 'Nordland' Armd Recce Bn [4 Coys] (*SS Maj. Saalbach*)
23rd SS 'Nederland' PzGr Div (*SS Maj.-Gen. Wagner*)
   48th SS 'Gen. Seyffarth' PzGr Regt (1st Dutch) (*SS Lt-Col. Scheibe*)
   49th SS 'de Ruiter' PzGr Regt (2nd Dutch) (*SS Lt-Col. Lohmanns*)

[b. Divisions later allocated to the 3rd Pz Army]
27th SS 'Langemarck' Gren Div (*SS Col. Müller*)
28th SS 'Wallonien' Gren Div

OKW RESERVE
[Later allocated to the LVI Pz Corps, 9th Army]

18th PzGr Div (*Maj.-Gen. Josef Rauch*)
    30th PzGr Regt [2 Bns]
    51st PzGr Regt [2 Bns]
    118th Pz Regt [part only]
    18th Arty Regt [3 Bns]

Army Group 'Mitte'
(*FM Ferdinand Schörner*)

4th Pz Army (*Gen. Fritz-Herbert Gräser*)
<u>V Corps</u> *[Later transferred to the 9th Army]* (*Lt-Gen. Wagner*)
    35th SS Police Gren Div (*SS Col. Rüdiger Pipkorn*)
        89th SS Police Gren Regt [2 Bns]
        90th SS Police Gren Regt [2 Bns]
        91st SS Police Gren Regt [2 Bns]
    36th SS Gren Div (*SS Maj.-Gen. Dirlewanger*)
        72nd SS Gren Regt [2 Bns]
        73rd SS Gren Regt [2 Bns]
    275th Inf Div
        983rd Gren Regt [2 Bns]
        984th Gren Regt [2 Bns]
        985th Gren Regt [2 Bns]
        275th Fus Bn
        275th Arty Regt
    342nd Inf Div
        554th Gren Regt [2 Bns]
        697th Gren Regt [2 Bns]
        699th Gren Regt [2 Bns]

Corps Reserve
21st Pz Div (*Maj.-Gen. Marcks*)
    125th PzGr Regt [2 Bns] (*Col. Hans von Luck*)

192nd Pz Gr Regt [2 Bns]
22nd Pz Regt
155th Pz Arty Regt [3 Bns]
305th Army Flak Bn

ELBE FRONT

12th Army (*Gen. Walter Wenck*)
<u>XX Corps</u> (*Gen. Carl-Erik Koehler*)
'Theodor Körner' RAD Div (3rd RAD) (*Lt-Gen. Bruno Frankewitz*)
    1st 'TK' RAD Gren Regt [2 Bns] (*Maj. Bieg*)
    2nd 'TK' RAD Gren Regt [2 Bns] (*Maj. Becker*)
    3rd 'TK' RAD Gren Regt [2 Bns] (*Maj. Menzel*)
'Ulrich von Hutten' Inf Div (*Lt-Gen. Gerhard Engel*)
    1st 'UvH' Gren Regt [2 Bns] (*Maj. Wesemann*)
    2nd 'vH'Gren Regt [2 Bns] (*Maj. Anton Siebert*)
    3rd 'UvH' Gren Regt [2 Bns] (*Maj. Hobra*)
    2nd 'Potsdam' Gren Regt [2 Bns] [w.e.f. 20 Apr 45]
'Ferdinand von Schill' Inf Div (*Lt-Col. Alfred Müller*)
    1st 'FvS' Gren Regt [2 Bns] (*Maj. Carstens*)
    2nd 'FvS' Gren Regt [2 Bns] (*Maj. Kley*)
    3rd 'FvS' Gren Regt [2 Bns] (*Maj. Müller*)
'Scharnhorst' Inf Div (*Lt-Gen. Heinrich Götz*)
    1st 'S' Gren Regt [2 Bns] (*Maj. Mathias Langmaier*)
    2nd 'S' Gren Regt [2 Bns] (*Maj. Mahlow*)
    3rd 'S' Gren Regt [2 Bns] (*Lt-Col. Gerhard Pick*)
<u>XXXIX Pz Corps</u> (*Lt-Gen. Karl Arndt*)

[a. 12-21 Apr 45 under command OKW with following structure]
'Clausewitz' Pz Div (*Lt-Gen. Unrein*)
'Schlageter' RAD Div (1st RAD) (*Lt-Gen. Hein*)
    1st, 2nd, 3rd 'Schlageter' Gren Regts [each 2 Bns]
84th Inf Div

[b. 21-26 Apr 45 under command 12th Army with the following structure]
'Clausewitz' Pz Div [3 Bns only] (*Lt-Gen. Unrein*)
84th Inf Div [3 Bns only]
'Hamburg' Res Inf Div [2 Regts]
'Meyer' Inf Div [2 Regts]
<u>XXXXI Pz Corps</u> (*Lt-Gen. Holste*)
    'von Hake' Inf Div (*Col. Friedrich von Hake*)

  1st 'vH' Gren Regt (*Lt-Col. Joachim Bahr*)
  2nd 'vH' Gren Regt (*Lt-Col. von dem Bottlemberg*)
199th Inf Div [1 Regt only]
'V-Weapons' Inf Div
1st HJ Tk-Destroyer Bde
'Hermann Göring' JagdPz Bde
<u>XXXXVIII Pz Corps</u> (*Gen. Maximillian Reichsherr von Edelsheim*)
  14th Flak Div
  'Leipzig' Battle Gp [8 Bns] (*Lt-Gen. Rathke*)
  'Halle' Battle Gp [8 Bns] (*Col. von Poncet*)

Ungrouped Formations

'Friedrich Ludwig Jahn' RAD Div (2nd RAD) (*Col. Gerhard Klein/Col. Franz Weller*)
  1st 'FLJ' RAD Gren Regt [2 Bns] (RAD *Lt-Col. Gerhard Konopka*)
  2nd 'FLJ' RAD Gren Regt [2 Bns] (*Maj. Bernhard Schulze-Hagen*)
  3rd 'FLJ' RAD Gren Regt [2 Bns] (*Maj. Dahms*)
'Potsdam' Inf Div (*Col. Erich Lorenz*)
  1st, 2nd, 3rd 'Potsdam' Gren Regts [each 2 Bns]

APPENDIX 3

ZHUKOV'S ORDERS FOR ARTILLERY SUPPORT IN THE BERLIN STREET-FIGHTING PHASE

1. The artillery support for street-fighting in Berlin will be organised on the following principles:

a. Each Army will retain only one Long Range Artillery Group (drawn from the Army's Field Artillery Brigade and Artillery Division's Gun Artillery Brigade resources; if these resources are inadequate, the Artillery Division's Howitzer Brigade's resources may be included).

b. All remaining artillery resources will be distributed between the Rifle Corps and Divisions. Rifle Corps will establish powerful, destructive groups, which will include:

Heavy Artillery Brigades
Heavy Howitzer Brigades
Heavy Mortar Brigades
Howitzer/Mortar Brigades
Super Heavy Artillerty Battalions

The Rifle Divisions will establish Divisional Artillery Groups from the Artillery Division's Howitzer Brigade, Mortar Brigade and M-13 [Rocket-Launcher] Battalion resources. The Light Artillery Brigade, Antitank Artillery Brigade and the Army's Regimental batteries will be incorporated into the assault detachments (companies and battalions).

2. Assault detachment operations will be preceded by a short, powerful artillery preparation using Army, Corps and Divisional Artillery Group

resources. While firing is still in progress, a penetration of one kilometre in depth will be made in the sector of the Army's main thrust.

3. Simultaneously, the Long Range Artillery Group will suppress all known enemy artillery batteries and all likely battery locations in the tactical depth.

4. Corps and Divisional Artillery Group fire will overlap in the following instances:

a. *In city blocks being tackled by the advancing infantry* to a depth of 400 metres along the entire breakthrough frontage with the task of softening up the entire built-up area and the streets and street junctions between.

b. *While key buildings and open spaces are being tackled* further on to a depth of one kilometre.

M-31 Brigades, and in isolated cases M-31 Regiments, will be allocated their own sectors without any overlap between them and tube artillery sectors.

5. As soon as the artillery preparation commences, the assault detachment ordnance will roll out to previously surveyed firing positions and open fire on targets presenting an immediate threat to the infantry.

6. As the infantry advances to a depth of 600 metres, the artillery executing the opening bombardment and the Divisional Artillery Group will soften up the next kilometre in accordance with the principle for the initial artillery bombardment. This method of support will continue until the enemy resistance has been completely suppressed.

7. Assault detachments (companies) will have 8–12 × 75–203mm guns and 4–6 × 88–122mm mortars. Detachments of battalion size will have 16–24 guns and 8–12 mortars.

8. To implement this directive, the Front Artillery Commander will issue explicit instructions to the Armies with a detailed plan for the use of artillery in street-fighting.

G. ZHUKOV
Comd
1st Byelorussian Front

Lt-Gen. TELEGIN
Member War Council
1st Byelorussian Front

APPENDIX 4

FÜHRER ORDER

I order as follows: 21 January 1945

1. Commanders-in-Chief, Commanding Generals and Divisional Commanders are personally responsible to me for reporting in good time:

   a. Every decision to carry out an operational movement.
   b. Every attack carried out in divisional strength and upwards that does not conform with the general directives laid down by the High Command.
   c. Every offensive action in quiet sectors of the front over and above normal shocktroop activities that is calculated to draw the enemy's attention to that sector.
   d. Every plan for disengaging or withdrawing forces.
   e. Every plan for surrendering a position, a local strongpoint or a fortress.

They must ensure that I have time to intervene in the decision if I think fit, and that my counterorders can reach the front line in time.

2. Commanders-in-Chief, Commanding Generals and Divisional Commanders, the Chiefs of the General Staffs, and each individual officer of the General Staff, or officers employed with the General Staffs, are responsible to me that every report made to me either directly, or through the normal channels, should contain nothing but the unvarnished truth. In future I shall impose draconian punishment on any attempt at concealment, whether deliberate or arising from carelessness or oversight.

3. I must point out that maintenance of signals communications, particularly in heavy fighting or critical situations, is a prerequisite for the conduct of the

battle. All officers commanding troops are responsible to me for ensuring that these communications both to higher formations and to subordinate commanders are not broken, and for seeing that, by exhausting every means and engaging themselves personally, permanent communications are ensured with commanders above and below, whatever the situation.

Adolf Hitler

NOTES

GENERAL

Square brackets have been used throughout to denote the sources of the reference, or to indicate which of several books attributable to an author is applicable.

I have drawn heavily on Gosztony's excellent 1970 collection of pertinent extracts of source material, which otherwise would have been difficult to come by in original form. No Soviet source material was published before 1952, and what appeared during Stalin's reign was designed to show that he alone was responsible for the victory over Fascist Germany. Zhukov was progressively humiliated during the remainder of Stalin's lifetime and reappeared to public view only after Khruschev's denunciation of the dictator. Then he was quickly promoted to Deputy Minister and then Minister of Defence, only to be deposed again for a further seven years of rustication. While he worked on his memoirs, his political enemies eliminated him from the histories being published. Subsequent rewriting of Soviet history to meet changes in the political climate has not altered the original bland presentation of all having gone to plan, whoever was in charge. Little has emerged to indicate what really went on behind the scenes or to give colour to the principal players. However, Chuikov's book, having been published as an attack on Zhukov, inevitably pointed to some cracks in the façade, and some of the articles published on the activities of individual formations have proved useful in revealing certain important aspects of the overall operation not properly covered in the major works. Bokov's book on the 5th Shock Army also provides a useful source. Then the Order-of-Battle in Appendix 1 reveals a surprising amount of upheaval among the commanders of formations during the course of this 'Operation Berlin', well beyond what could be attributable to battle casualties.

The German source material has proved more generous in scope, especially since the publication of the German-language version of the first edition of this book and the collapse of the Communist regimes in Europe, all of which has given me a great advantage over the earlier writers on this subject, such as Kuby, Ryan, Toland, Tully and Ziemke, who were obliged to work within much narrower parameters in describing the military aspects of the battle.

Details of all the books I have cited will be found in the Bibliography. Where I have quoted from more than one title by the same author I have used initials to identify the title in question.

Throughout, I have placed much emphasis on the detailed examination and appreciation of maps in the study of the operation. Water courses provided the most significant geographical factor, both as obstacles and in channelling the lines of attack, especially as all bridges could be expected to be destroyed. One aspect that became particularly significant once fighting began within the devastated city was the establishment of formation

219

boundaries readily identifiable to the troops on the ground, and here water courses and railway lines had far greater value than named but rubble-choked streets. At this stage, too, the changes of scale in the maps having to be used, and the narrowing of formation and unit frontages as they gradually converged on the city centre, all added to the difficulties of command.

1: THE GOAL

1. Shtemenko [*SGSW*], p. 320; Koniev, p. 83; Erickson, pp. 532–3.
2. Professor Michael Parrish to the author.
3. *The Great Patriotic War of the Soviet Union, 1941–5* (hereafter referred to as *GPW*), p. 381; Zhukov, p. 607; Erickson, pp. 558–9.
4. Novikov, p. 90.
5. Koniev, pp. 105–6; Spahr, p. 175. Chuikov's account of Zhukov's incredulous reaction to the discovery of some of Koniev's troops on what he presumed to be his own preserve on the morning of the 24th supports this contention and will be discussed later. Zhukov later admitted that he lied to his Chief-of-Staff when he told the latter that Stalin had informed him about this move.
6. Koniev, pp. 107–8.
7. *Neue Zürcher Zeitung* of 18 April 1945 [Gosztony, pp. 217–20]; Ryan, p. 27.
8. Busse, p. 165; Tieke, pp. 169, 278.
9. Busse, pp. 165–6; Tieke, p. 160.
10. Tieke, p. 135.
11. Ibid., pp. 168–9.
12. Von Oven, p. 307 [Gosztony, p. 201].

2: BERLIN

Much of the basic material for this chapter comes from *Götterdämmerung – La Prise de Berlin* by Colonel Pierre Rocolle, who conducted his own investigations when stationed in Berlin shortly after the war, and Willemer's report on *The German Defense of Berlin* for HQ USAREUR.

The defence plans for Berlin will be found incorporated on the applicable maps. However, the implementation of these plans and the manning of these positions does not necessarily follow.

1. Ziemke, p. 75; Ryan, pp. 13–16; O'Donnell, p. 18; Tully, p. 111 – since September 1944 the British had dropped 42,825 tons of bombs on Berlin and the Americans 28,268 tons.
2. Rocolle, pp. 5, 10–11; Ryan, pp. 26–7.
3. Arnold and Körner, personal correspondence.
4. Rocolle, pp. 7–9; Ryan, pp. 137–8; Willemer, p. 33; plus assistance from Wolfgang-Dietrich Neumann, who was in Turmflakabteilung 123, 1st Flak Division. See Borkowski for descriptions of conditions in the big flak-towers, and Altner, pp. 170–4. The Berlin-based Stiftung Preussischer Kulturbesitz published a report by Irene Kühne-Kunze on the subject of art treasures stored in these towers in a special supplement to its 1984 annual review. The Humboldhain tower is the only one to have

partially survived demolition, being concealed on three sides by an artificial hill with a rubble core. The demolished Friedrichshain tower is almost completely concealed in this manner and that at the Zoo has been removed.

5. Willemer, p. 15; Clark, pp. 388–9. Detailed information on the basic German Army organization in the city comes from Zippel.
6. Willemer, p. 8; Tieke, pp. 58–9.
7. Von Dufving, personal correspondence.
8. Refior Berlin Diary, (BMA Freiburg, RH 53-3/24), pp. 1, 14, 15; Tieke, p. 50.
9. This 35-page document is headed 'Verteidigungsbereich Berlin, Abt Ia/Op., Nr. 400/45 geh., Berlin–Grunewald den 9.3.1945', so must have been prepared before-hand.
10. Oberst von Dufving's archives; Refior Berlin Diary (BMA Freiburg, RH 53-3/24).
11. Refior Berlin Diary (BMA Freiburg, RH 53-3/24); Rocolle, p. 6; Willemer, pp. 26–7.
12. Willemer, p. 28.
13. Ibid., p. 27.
14. Ibid., pp. 28–31.
15. Ibid., pp. 31–3.
16. Jacob Kronika's *Der Untergang Berlins* (Flensburg/Hamburg, 1946), p. 114 [Burkert, p. 41], Refior Berlin Diary (BMA Freiburg, RH 53-3/24); Willemer, pp. 33–4.
17. Refior Berlin Diary (BMA Freiburg, RH 53-3/24); Willemer, p. 22.
18. Refior Berlin Diary (BMA Freiburg, RH 53-3/24); Rocolle, p. 16.
19. Willemer, p. 38; Trevor-Roper [*LDH*], p. 96.
20. Although various dates in March have been given for this visit, the date of the 3rd is confirmed by Goebbels' *Tagebuche 1945: Die letzte Aufzeichnungen* (Hamburg, 1977), pp. 100, 108, 206, and Schenk's *Patient Hitler: Eine medizinische Biographie* (Düsseldorf, 1989), p. 159 [Dr Raiber MD to the author], and Tiecke, p. 22. Erich Kempa's *Ich habe Adolf Hitler verbrannt* (Munich, undated), p. 76, and Hans Schwarz's *Brennpunkt FHQ – Menschen und Maßstäbe im Führerhauptquartier* (Buenos Aires, 1950), p. 25 [Gosztony, pp. 91–3] give no date; Kohlase, p. 33, says the 9th, and Ziemke, p. 65, gives the 11th.
21. Von Loringhoven in *Der Todeskampf der Reichshauptstadt*, p. 139; O'Donnell, pp. 40–3, says that the Führerbunker balloon was shot down twice during the fighting.
22. Rocolle, p. 14.
23. Toland, pp. 1118–19. These bunkers were later used by the Soviet Army High Command in East Germany.
24. Trevor-Roper [*LDH*], pp. 65–6.
25. Kitchen, pp. 16–17: Kuby, pp. 87–8; Refior Berlin Diary (BMA Freiburg, RH 53-3/24), p. 6.
26. Willemer, pp. 40–2.
27. From Milton Schulmann's *Defeat in the West* (London: Secker & Warburg, 1947) [Flower and Reeve, p. 1004].
28. Dr Johannes Stumm's statement comes from his denazification process questionnaire.
29. Pourroy MS. Colonel Refior in his Berlin Diary (BMA Freiburg, RH 53-3/24), p. 12, mentions a VS Bn commanded by a retired Admiral von Fischel that acquitted itself particularly well, but does not give any details.
30. Trevor-Roper [*LDH*], p. 161.
31. Rocolle, p. 16. See also Koch and an extract from Axmann's article in Stern magazine, 'Mit Hitler im Führerbunker' of 25 April 1965 [Gosztony, pp. 202–20]. A similar hanging is described in Altner, pp. 123–4.
32. Loewe. The Deutschen Jungvolk was the junior branch of the Hitlerjugend.

33. Wöhlermann MS, p. 8.
34. Rogmann correspondence with the author re Mohnke's units and BDM girls at the Rotes Rathaus. Tieke, p. 192, says that BDM girls served as 'Kampfhelferinnen' with the HJ Regiment 'Frankfurt/Oder', which formed part of the Frankfurt garrison and later took part in the 9th Army's breakout to the west.
35. Rogmann, pp. 18–19; Tieke, pp. 233–4. Mohnke's forces are also described in Tully, further information coming from Mohnke in O'Donnell, Tully again being the source *re* the Allgemeine-SS, the police, fire brigade, etc. Mohnke was accused by the British of ordering the murder of some British POWs near Dunkirk in 1940, but was never brought to trial for this alleged crime.
36. Willemer, pp. 42–3.
37. Trevor-Roper [*LDH*], pp. 207–8; Tully, p. 83.
38. Trevor-Roper [*LDH*], pp. 119–22.
39. Trevor-Roper [*HWD*], pp. 207–8; Trevor-Roper [*LDH*], pp. 123–4; O'Donnell, pp. 51–75.
40. Speer, pp. 575–7; O'Donnell, pp. 56–62; Trevor-Roper [*LDH*], pp. 124–6. I remain sceptical about Speer's alleged plot to kill Hitler with poison gas, even though it was raised at his trial at Nuremberg.
41. Thorwald, pp. 67–8; Reymann in Tieke, pp. 57–8.
42. Speer, pp. 624–5; Speer says that only 84 out of 950 were blown, but it is difficult to define exactly what constituted a bridge in this context, or what was the actual cause of damage to those found wrecked after the battle. Colonel Refior in his Berlin Diary (BMA Freiburg, RH 53-3/24), p. 10, says that no orders for blowing bridges were issued by his headquarters.
43. Toland, p. 10.
44. Trevor-Roper [*HWD*], pp. 209–12.
45. Trevor-Roper [*LDH*], pp. 135–8.

3: THE RUSSIANS ARE COMING!

1. See Tony Le Tissier, *Zhukov at the Oder*.
2. The change of plan involving the 2nd Guards Tank Army is drawn from Pykathov and from Skorodumov's article, whose accompanying map shows exactly how the formations were split and functioned in the advance on the city after the breakthrough at the Seelow Heights. The chronology of this phase emphasizes the exhaustion of the combatants, the infantry in particular, for there was virtually no enemy resistance to overcome, despite Zhukov's allegations. See Edward Kmiecik, *Berliner Victoria* (Warsaw: Verlag 'Ruch', 1972), p. 31.
3. Wagener, p. 348.
4. Skorodumov, p. 90.
5. Ibid., p. 93.
6. Chuikov, p. 164; Koniev, pp. 701–2.
7. Koniev, p. 111.
8. Tieke, pp. 144, 171; Steiner, p. 228 [Gosztony, p. 207].
9. Tieke, p. 295; Seaton [*RGW*], p. 575; Willemer, pp. 14, 18.
10. Gosztony, pp. 228–9, including quotation from *Der grundlegende Befehl des Führers vom 21 April 1945* (National Archives, Washington DC).
11. Kuby, p. 105 (quoting Colonel Refior); Tieke, p. 214.
12. *Neue Zürcher Zeitung*, 20 April 1945 [Gosztony, pp. 196–8]; Thorwald, pp. 152–3.

13. Novikov, p. 93 – 'We did not know that the enemy had so few troops to defend this boundary and expected strong opposition.'
14. Zhukov, p. 609 – but not mentioned in Koniev!
15. Koniev, p. 115.
16. In discussion some 40 years later at Spandau Allied Prison with Soviet Army officers, who regarded this incident as common knowledge.
17. Gerhard Boldt's *Die letzten Tage der Reichskanzlei* (Hamburg: Rohwolt Verlag, 1947), p. 49 [Gosztony, pp. 193–5]; Tieke, p. 147, says originally 12 tanks had set off from the Kummersdorf Training Area nearby.
18. Kuby, p. 97; Koniev, p. 115.
19. Refior Berlin Diary (BMA Freiburg, RH 53-3-24, p. 20) Koniev, p. 122; Tieke, p. 183; Gellermann, p. 35.
20. Chuikov, pp. 153–4.
21. Tieke, pp. 159–71.
22. Skorodumov, pp. 90–3.
23. Komornicki, p. 116 and map on p. 112; but Erickson, p. 577 – Bernau taken by the 125th Rifle Corps of the 47th Army.
24. Zhukov, pp. 609, 612.
25. Ryan, pp. 414–15; Tieke, p. 282; Klaus Scheel's *Die Befreiung Berlins* (East Berlin: VEB Deutscher Verlag der Wissenschaft, 1975), pp. 73ff. [Burkert, pp. 58–60]. What exactly this 'Müller Brigade' was is not quite clear. Döberitz had already provided the 303rd 'Döberitz' and 309th 'Gross-Berlin' Infantry Divisions for the Oder Front, and then yielded up further trainees to found the 'Potsdam' and 'Theodor Körner' Infantry Divisions on 30 March and 9 April respectively, so it is extremely doubtful whether any further manpower remained there. When threatened with being overrun by the Americans from the west, a Major Alfred Müller had organized some 8,000–10,000 trainees from the Assault Artillery School at Burg into the semblance of an infantry division and placed them on the east bank of the Elbe. On 20 April this group was officially named the 'Ferdinand von Schill' Infantry Division and assigned to the 12th Army, its commander being promoted Lieutenant-Colonel. It was only partly motorized and it is unlikely that it could have reached the Havel in time to support Steiner, even if it had been so ordered [Gellermann, p. 39].
26. Seaton [*RGW*], p. 578; Novikov, p. 94.
27. Axmann, p. 66 [Gosztony, pp. 202–3]. Attendance of diplomats recorded in the Visitors' Book later taken to Moscow [Chronos-Film].
28. Rogmann, pp. 5–6.
29. Gorlitz, pp. 196–7.
30. Ibid., p. 199.
31. Trevor-Roper [*LDH*], p. 151; Thorwald, pp. 91–2.
32. Trevor-Roper [*LDH*], p. 148.
33. Tieke, p. 159.
34. Trevor-Roper [*LDH*], pp. 151–2; Thorwald, p. 93.
35. Dönitz, p. 435; Trevor-Roper [*LDH*], pp. 153–5.
36. Trevor-Roper [*LDH*], pp. 130, 155–6; Borkowski, pp. 126–7.
37. Dönitz, pp. 436–7; Speer, p. 634; Trevor-Roper [*LDH*], pp. 153–5.
38. O'Donnell, p. 101; Ryan, p. 403.
39. Koller, pp. 38–42; Trevor-Roper [*LDH*], p. 153.
40. Altner was with the 156th Infantry Division at Lietzen – pp. 38–44.
41. Tieke, pp. 129–80.
42. Novikov, pp. 93–4; Wagener, p. 357.

4: ENCIRCLEMENT

1. Ryan, p. 324. The location of the Luftwaffe Academy given in Ryan as Potsdam has been corrected to Gatow (later a Royal Air Force establishment and now the General-Steinhoff-Kaserne of the Bundeswehr's Luftwaffe) by Colonel Herrmann. It seems that the location of the Gatow establishment was meant to be secret (the Berliners of course soon knew about it, but it was not marked on contemporary maps), and was more commonly referred to as Potsdam, that being the nearest communications centre.
2. Bokov, pp. 196–7; Pourroy, p. 27; Skorodumov, p. 93.
3. Rocolle, p. 44.
4. Bokov, p. 198; Skorodumov, p. 93.
5. Lothar Loewe to the author; Ryan, pp. 27, 484–94; O'Donnell, p. 143 – Governing Mayor Ernst Reuter once quoted the figure of 90,000 Berlin rape victims.
6. Chuikov, pp. 156–7.
7. Diem, pp. 47–52.
8. Colonel von Dufving told the author that he may inadvertently have been responsible for some of these rumours through having ordered all the corps's non-combatant troops to Döbberitz on 18 April.
9. Willemer, p. 19; Tieke, pp. 240–3 – *'Fall Ziegler und Hintergrund'*. (General Weidling's own account only covers the period 23 April–5 May 1945.) Ziegler's motives were no doubt honourable in this matter, but from a disciplinary and command point of view his conduct was clearly unacceptable. In his interview with Ryan, Refior said that he had heard rumours that Himmler had given secret orders for all SS commanders to get their units out of Berlin and take them to Schleswig-Holstein, or to keep them out of Berlin if they could [von Dufving].
10. Gorlitz, p. 201; Schumann, p. 720.
11. Kuby, p. 111; *GPW*, p. 382.
12. Koller, pp. 43–4.
13. Koller, pp. 44–5.
14. Seaton [*GPW*], p. 576; Gorlitz, p. 199 – Keitel says Schörner was promoted that day, but Ziemke, p. 78, gives his date of promotion as 5 April 1945 (Hitler's birthday on 20 April was a common date for promotions); Koniev, p. 119; Erickson, p. 591.
15. Seaton [*GPW*], p. 576; Gorlitz, pp. 199–200.
16. Ryan, p. 426.
17. Thorwald, pp. 144–5; K.G. Klietmann's *Die Waffen-SS. Ein Dokumentation* (Osnabrück, 1965), p. 56 [Gosztony, p. 206]; *GPW*, p. 382. Steiner, p. 328, says only 4,000–5,000 reinforcements reached Liebenwalde.
18. Steiner, p. 328; Tully, p. 138.
19. Ryan, pp. 375, 475; Thorwald, p. 87.
20. Koniev, pp. 120–1.
21. *GPW*, p. 381.
22. Novikov, p. 95; Wagener, pp. 355–6.
23. Thorwald, pp. 88–9.
24. Koller, p. 45; Speer, p. 571 – the division had been at Carinhall when he visited in February 1945. The Schönewalde mentioned here is most likely to have been the one between Oranienburg and Spandau, as opposed to the one due north of the city, for Steiner would have been concerned with the line of the Havel at this stage of the battle.
25. Koller, pp. 46–7.

26. Ibid., p. 47.
27. Ibid., pp. 48–9.
28. Ibid., p. 50.
29. Novikov, p. 93.
30. Diem, pp. 52–56.
31. Trevor-Roper [*LDH*], p. 157.
32. Busse, p. 166; Ryan, p. 325.
33. Busse, p. 166; Tieke, p. 193.
34. Busse, pp. 166–7.
35. Ibid., pp. 166–7.
36. Komornicki, p. 116.
37. Seaton [*RGW*], p. 578. Also a Polish map that was previously on display in the Soviet Army Museum, Karlshorst, Berlin.
38. Ziemke, pp. 92, 95.
39. Altner, pp. 123–4. 'Stalin-Organs', otherwise known as 'Katyushas,' were rocket-launchers mounted in batteries on standard truck beds.
40. Bokov, p. 205; Skorodumov, p. 93.
41. Pourroy, pp. 27–30, 38–9.
42. Chuikov, pp. 156, 160–1.
43. Willemer, pp. 29–30.
44. Kuby, p. 108; Tieke, pp. 216–17. However, in a letter to the author, Colonel Hermann, who was at that time commanding the 9th Parachute Division, says that he was not present at this meeting. Wagener, p. 63 – the explanation for the rumour of the retreat to Döberitz appears to spring from 'Seydlitz-Troops' spreading false orders for the LVI Panzer Corps to regroup at Güterfelde, east of Potsdam. Many of those who followed these false orders were caught by the Soviets in Marienfelde.
45. Koniev, pp. 126–8.
46. Rocolle, p. 30.
47. Ibid., p. 31. The Soviets tried to get all Allied POWs to head for Odessa for repatriation by ship, but not all made it, for Stalin had some 23,500 Americans and 31,000 British kept back as hostages that were eventually treated as common criminals in his NKVD camps (Saunders, Sauter and Kirkwood's *Soldiers of Misfortune*, p. 15).
48. Skorning report.
49. Koniev, pp. 131–2.
50. Ibid., pp. 128–9, 132.
51. Trevor-Roper [*LDH*], pp. 158–9; O'Donnell, pp. 93–5; Koller, p. 54; Thorwald, pp. 109–13.
52. Trevor-Roper [*LDH*], pp. 159–60; O'Donnell, pp. 94–7; Koller, p. 55.
53. O'Donnell, pp. 81, 97–9; Koller, p. 63; *Stern* magazine, no. 18 (28 April 1983) – abortive authentification of *The Hitler Diaries*.
54. Trevor-Roper [*LDH*], pp. 160–1; Gorlitz, p. 202; Thorwald, pp. 116–17.
55. Trevor-Roper [*LDH*], pp. 161–2; Gorlitz, pp. 202–3; Thorwald, pp. 118–19.
56. Von Loringhoven article in *Der Todeskampf der Reichshauptstadt* (Chronos-Film).
57. Trevor-Roper [*LDH*], pp. 163–5; O'Donnell, p. 126.
58. Kuby, p. 109; Willemer, pp. 16–17; Tieke, p. 215; Refior Berlin Diary (BMA Freiburg, RH 53-3/24), p. 25.
59. Kuby, p. 118; Tieke, pp. 184, 214, 223.
60. From a photocopy of a memo from Beate Rotermund-Uhse, quoting an extract from her pilot's logbook, together with a cutting of an article on her flight in *Neue Revue* magazine (date unknown). She later became famous for founding a chain of sex shops.

5: SIEGE PREPARATIONS

General Helmuth Weidling's account covering the period 23 April–5 May 1945 was written in Soviet captivity (where he later died), and was translated from Russian and introduced in German by Wilhelm Ahrens in the *Wehrwissentschaftliche Rundschau*, No. 1/1962, as 'Der Todeskampf der faschisten Clique in Berlin aus der Errinerung des Generals Weidling'. It was therefore subject to censorship but appears authentic in content, as confirmed to the author by Oberst von Dufving.

1. Gosztony, pp. 232–4; Tieke, p. 214.
2. Rocolle, pp. 34–5; Tieke, p. 141.
3. Trevor-Roper [*LDH*], p. 197; Rocolle, p. 35; Wenck, pp. 64–5; Thorwald, pp. 133–4; Kuby, p. 1113; Strawson, p. 132.
4. Schwarz, p. 108 [Gosztony, pp. 262–3]; Thorwald, p. 145.
5. Gellermann, p. 97.
6. Wenck, p. 64; Gorlitz, pp. 203–4; Tieke, pp. 196–7.
7. Wenck, p. 64; Gellermann, pp. 80–3; Ryan, p. 351.
8. Gellermann, p. 48; Ryan, p. 443.
9. Gorlitz, pp. 204–5.
10. Ibid., p. 205.
11. Ibid., pp. 206–8; Thorwald, p. 163.
12. Gorlitz, pp. 207–9.
13. Kuhlmann article in the *Ruhr-Nachrichten* (April 1985); article by Dr -Ing. Joachim Sierck, in which Kulhmann's staff are given as Lieutenants Wolf and Zuborg, and Sub-Lieutenant Böing [Chronos-Film].
14. Thorwald, p. 142.
15. Ibid., pp. 138–9.
16. Ibid., pp. 125–6.
17. Mayer, pp. 16ff.
18. Weidling p. 42; Gorlitz, p. 221; Tieke, pp. 216–18. Ryan's interview notes with Refior [von Dufving]. Wagner, p. 67 – the 9th Parachute Division's route into the city was via Friedrichshagen, Köpenick and Alt Glienicke to Hermannplatz in Neukölln. Hölz was promoted Major-General on 25 April.
19. Weidling, pp. 42–5; Willemer, p. 19; Tieke, p. 224.
20. Weidling, pp. 45–6. However, although Weidling may have intended the 9th Parachute Division to occupy Lichtenberg, it seems the Soviets arrived there first. Wagner (p. 67), makes no mention of Lichtenberg (see Note 18 above) but says that the 9th Parachute Division were ordered to Sector 'H'. Colonel Herrmann in a letter to the author denied having been to Lichtenberg, the division having passed through Neukölln, which he had known well as a policeman before joining the Luftwaffe.
21. Engelmann, p. 646 – The 'Müncheberg' lost 12 tanks and 30 APCs in this action at Rudow: Weidling, p. 46; Tieke, p. 227.
22. Weidling, pp. 46–7; Tieke, p. 224.
23. Weidling, pp. 47–8; Tieke, pp. 227–8.
24. Discussions with von Dufving; Refior Berlin Diary [BMA Freiburg RH 53-3/24]; Weidling, p. 48; Willemer, p. 17.
25. Willemer, p. 46; Kuby, pp. 83–4; Tieke, p. 226. *Der Spiegel* in an article dated 10 January 1966 quoted in Gosztony, p. 228, gives 44,630 soldiers, 42,531 Volkssturm and 3,532 Hitlerjugend, RAD and Organisation Todt members as constituting the Berlin Garrison on 23 April.

26. Tieke, p. 349 – Major-General Scholze's wife and children had been killed in the British air raid on Potsdam of 14 April 1945.
27. Tieke, p. 55.
28. Ibid., pp. 231–2 – quoting from Wöhlermann's MS *'Notizen über der letzten Einsatz ostwärts und in Berlin im April/Mai 1945'*.
29. Willemer, pp. 48–9.
30. Trevor-Roper [*LDH*], p. 204.
31. Ryan, p. 479.
32. Chuikov, p. 156. Co-location of the two armies' headquarters later in the battle confirmed to the author by Joachim Krüger.
33. Wagner, p. 356; Novikov, p. 95 – 'The smoke of countless fires and the dust hindered the pilots in seeking their objectives. It demanded exceptionally accurate bombing not to hit our own troops. In these tasks only the best of bomber pilots were sent, real virtuosos of the strike assault.'
34. Kuby, p. 60.
35. Thorwald, p. 176; Kuby, pp. 153–4.
36. Rocolle, p. 43.
37. A copy of the 'Berlin Street Index and Key to Numbered Buildings for use with the Town Plan of Berlin (GSGS 4480), 3rd Edition 1945' (GSGS [Misc] No. 201) in the author's possession appears to have code numbers to the buildings identical to those used by Chuikov in his sketch of the Government Quarter.

6. ENCIRCLEMENT COMPLETED

Inevitably, Koniev's and Zhukov's forces meet up. We can only presume that Stalin had briefed Novikov to keep Zhukov in the dark about the 3rd Guards Tank Army's advance into the southern suburbs beyond the boundary originally laid down by the Stavka at Easter, but that Zhukov would be aware of their rapid progress northwards from the news bulletins and that his suspicions would have been aroused. This appears to have been part of Stalin's plot to eventually humiliate Zhukov by throwing the latter's plans off balance by introducing Koniev into the race for the Reichstag.

The diarist of the 'Müncheberg' Panzer Division has been identified as Professor Dr h.c. Walter Kroemer, who has confirmed the content of his previously quoted extracts to the author.

1. Thorwald, pp. 166–7.
2. *GPW*, p. 381; Ziemke, p. 94.
3. Chuikov, p. 177.
4. Willemer, p. 30. The Wittler Bakery was at Pankstrasse 47 in Wedding.
5. Rocolle, p. 31.
6. Ibid., p. 45.
7. Bokov, pp. 206–11; Chuikov, p. 163 and map on p. 161; Zhukov, pp. 614–15. The Karlshorst Engineer Barrack complex was later to contain the Soviet Berlin Garrison, the KGB Headquarters and the Soviet Army Museum, where the German surrender was signed by Field Marshal Keitel on 8 May 1945.
8. Chernyayev, p. 105.
9. Chuikov, pp. 162–3.
10. *GPW*, p. 383.
11. Willemer, p. 29.

12. Skorning Report.
13. Koniev, p. 132.
14. Ibid., pp. 134–5. Koniev estimated that he was faced by 15,000 enemy (p. 132) at a density of 1,200 per kilometre, against which he placed 650 guns per kilometre along his attack front!
15. Ibid., p. 135.
16. Ibid., p. 135.
17. Ibid., p. 137.
18. Ibid., pp. 137–41; Komornicki, pp. 128–34.
19. Koniev, p. 124.
20. Trevor-Roper [*LDH*], pp. 168–9; Koller, pp. 64–73; Emmy Göring's *An der Seite meines Mannes: Begebenheiten und Bekenntnisse* (Göttingen, 1967), pp. 240ff., as quoted in Gosztony, pp. 294–6.
21. Trevor-Roper [*LDH*], pp. 176–9; O'Donnell, p. 110; Boldt, p. 72 [Gosztony, pp. 297–8].
22. Trevor-Roper [*LDH*], pp. 173–5; O'Donnell, pp. 102–5, 108–9; Speer, pp. 638, 643–5.
23. Trevor-Roper [*LDH*], pp. 175–6; O'Donnell, p. 104; Speer, pp. 639–40.
24. Trevor-Roper [*LDH*], p. 179; O'Donnell, pp. 115–16; Speer, pp. 647–8.
25. Willemer, pp. 57, 61; Tieke, p. 288; Komornicki, p. 117.
26. Rocolle, pp. 37–8.
27. Altner, pp. 94–9.
28. Willemer, p. 31.
29. Tieke, pp. 234–8 quoting SS Major-General Dr Gustav Krukenberg's MS 'Kampftage in Berlin – 24.4.–2.5.1945', p. 4.
30. Tully, p. 163. The Jungfernheide is the heath on which Tegel Airport now stands, and is where Professor Wernher von Braun conducted his early rocket experiments, which later led to the 'V' series of rocket weapons and ultimately took man into space.
31. Tully, p. 201. The barracks later became 'Quartier Napoléon', the main French military installation in Berlin, and is now the Bundeswehr's 'Julius-Lehr-Kaserne'.
32. Rocolle, p. 44.
33. Pykathov *et al.*
34. The late Wolfgang Karow's article '*Bei der Verteidigung von Berlin*' in *Alte Kameraden* No. 5/1965 (Karlsruhe), p. 14 [Gosztony, pp. 267–8].
35. Pykathov *et al.*
36. Pourroy, pp. 38–43.
37. Ryan, p. 45.
38. Bokov, pp. 221–31; Chernyayev, p. 105; Zhukov, p. 615. Treptow Park now contains the main Soviet cemetery in Berlin.
39. Tieke, p. 229.
40. Bokov, p. 229; Rocolle, p. 46.
41. Chuikov, p. 164; Kuby, pp. 52–3; Tieke (p. 201) gives the time of encounter as 0900 hours. Zhukov does not even mention it! According to Koniev this was 23 April, but it is quite clear from the accounts of both Zhukov and Chuikov that it must have occurred on the 24th.
42. Koniev, p. 131. The new interfront boundaries followed the main railway lines into Berlin, being clearly discernible to the troops on the ground however badly damaged the environment, then crossed the Landwehr Canal to the Anhalter Railway Station. Any extension of that line left the Reichstag clearly to the west and in Koniev's path. (Here I disagree with both Ryan, p. 354, and Erickson, p. 586, for the reasons stated.) North of the canal Zhukov could now only approach the Reichstag from the east,

north or west. Chuikov's group, originally intended to cover the whole southern arc of the city, could now, however, concentrate a disproportionately powerful punch on the eastern flank of that arc in competition with the 3rd Guards Tank Army. From then on one suspects that Zhukov must have pushed Chuikov deliberately to block Koniev's route to the Reichstag, thus causing the forthcoming changes in the interfront boundary with a *fait accompli*. Koniev, p. 90, writing of the opening battle of 16 April, says, 'The fighting at both fronts was coordinated by GHQ, and the fronts, as usual, exchanged information and reconnaissance summaries.'

43. Chuikov, p. 163.
44. Ibid., pp. 159–60.
45. Dragunsky, pp. 68–9.
46. Koniev, pp. 155–6.
47. Dr Averdieck to the author, personal communication, and discussions with survivors of the 20th Panzergrenadier Division; Engelmann, pp. 645–6; Tieke, p. 244.
48. Koniev, p. 178.
49. Ibid., pp. 158, 161; Wagener, p. 350; Erickson, p. 592.
50. Chernyayev, p. 105.
51. Koniev, pp. 161–2; Zhukov, p. 610.
52. Koniev, p. 120.
53. Weidling, p. 49.
54. Dr Kroemer to author.
55. Discussion with von Dufving; Refior Berlin Diary (BMA Freiburg RH 53-3/24), p. 25.
56. Koller, pp. 88–9; Tieke, p. 301.
57. Trevor-Roper [*LDH*], p. 183; Koller, pp. 81–2.
58. Gellermann, p. 101; Ziemke, p. 105.
59. Tieke, p. 245.
60. Zhukov, p. 616.

7. THE NOOSE TIGHTENS

Dragunsky's *A Soldier's Life* not only provides a most interesting account of his brigade's activities as Koniev's flank guard, but also neatly dovetails with Altner's account of his experiences based on Ruhleben at this time.

1. Friedrich Husemann's *Die guten Glaubens waren* (Osnabrück, 1973), p. 558 [Tieke, p. 297].
2. Thorwald, p. 165.
3. Ryan, pp. 374–5.
4. Tieke, pp. 204–13.
5. Von Luck, pp. 272–3
6. Koniev, p. 168; Lakowski and Stich, pp. 72–96; von Luck, pp. 272–6.
7. Glaser appeared as part of the Red Army delegation to the 50th anniversary commemoration of the breakout from Halbe organized by the *Förderkreis Gedenkstätte Halbe e.V.*, whose chairman was Horst Wilke, a former member of the 32nd Waffen-SS Volunteer '30. Januar' Grenadier Division. He had been born a German Baltic Jew in Lithuania 1926 and fled the persecution of the Jews sponsored by the German invasion of his country in 1941. Eventually he joined the Red Army and was awarded the Order of Glory (second to 'Hero of the Soviet Union') for valour.

8. *GPW*, p. 382; Koniev, p. 172; Toland, p. 451.
9. Weidling, pp. 48–9.
10. Ibid., p. 112.
11. Von Dufving to the author, re: the Liesegang Report, in the former's possession.
12. *GPW*, p. 382; Zhukov, p. 610.
13. Weidling, p. 49. Heissmeyer was Inspector of the Napola Schools, one of which was in Spandau and whose pupils formed part of his command. His wife, who was also with him, was the Reichsfrauführerin (Leader of the Reichs Womenfolk) Scholtz-Klink – Refior, Berlin Diary (BMA Freiburg, RH 53-3/24).
14. Novikov, p. 94; Wagener, pp. 357–8.
15. Komornicki, p. 146; Pourroy, pp. 54–6.
16. Tully, p. 203. This area has changed considerably since the battle. The 'T'-shaped canal has been extended at either end to connect the Westhafen with the Spree and the original canal filled in.
17. Bokov, p. 259; Rocolle, p. 53; Rogmann, pp. 25–7, 45.
18. Pourroy, pp. 44–8.
19. Bokov, pp. 231–7, 247. Although Bokov's chronology here, apart from Zhukov's order, is definitely askew.
20. Rogmann, pp. 22–32. These rockets are believed to have been the 150mm type intended for the largest calibre Nebelwerfer (smoke launcher) in service.
21. Rocolle, p. 53.
22. Chuikov, pp. 182–3, Plievier, p. 151; Tully, pp. 182, 189–90; Peter de Mendelssohon's *Zeitungsstadt Berlin* (Berlin: Ullstein Verlag, 1959), pp. 416–22 [Burkert, pp. 117–22]; Skorning Report.
23. Chuikov, pp. 182–3; Kroemer.
24. Rocolle, p. 53; Skorning Report.
25. Krukenberg, p. 14 [Tieke, pp. 246, 353]; Kuby, pp. 122, 125–7; Venghaus, p. 91. Krukenberg says that there were only 90 Frenchmen with him, but SS Captain Henri Fenet, the battalion commander, says that there were in fact 300.
26. Venghaus, pp. 56–58.
27. Krukenberg, p. 14 [Tieke, p. 246].
28. Rocolle, p. 47.
29. Later to become the US Sector Headquarters on the renamed Clayallee. Having been constructed about the time when Goering said that should enemy aircraft penetrate German airspace one could call him 'Meyer', this complex contained no air raid shelters and so the staff were obliged to take cover in trenches dug on the other side of the main road whenever there was an alert (Ralph Stiewe to author).
30. Koniev, pp. 167–8, 184.
31. Dragunsky, pp. 61–2, 93.
32. Novikov, p. 95; Koniev, p. 171. This change of interfront boundary still kept the Reichstag within Koniev's reach for the same reason as before, that is, the boundary projected beyond Potsdamer Railway Station would pass well to the east of the Reichstag building.
33. Koniev, p. 171. The later East German Government falsely attributed the damage and casualties from the Soviet artillery bombardment and attack on Potsdam to the air raid of 14 April 1945 by the Royal Air Force, which had in fact been directed at the main railway station east of the Havel and the old part of the historic city (Mihan).
34. Rocolle, p. 53.
35. This truly extraordinary woman, holder of the Iron Cross First and Second Class, was the first woman to hold an airline pilot's licence, the first to become a test pilot,

the first to fly a helicopter and the first to fly a jet. She continued flying until her death in 1979 at the age of 67, having established a new women's world long-distance gliding record of 805 km only four months previously.

36. Trevor-Roper [*LDH*], pp. 183–5; O'Donnell, p. 127; Koller, pp. 83–5, 94.
37. Tieke, p. 355; Kuby, pp. 136–7.
38. Tieke, p. 304.
39. Seaton [*RGW*], p. 574.
40. Tieke, pp. 301–2; Ziemke, pp. 99, 104.
41. Altner, pp, 128–35; Weidling, p. 51.
42. Wenck, pp. 65, 66; Gellermann, pp. 83–7; Tieke, p. 331. Patients from the main civilian and military hospitals in Berlin and Potsdam had been evacuated here to a lung clinic and adjacent barracks (Ramm, p. 228).
43. Novikov, p. 94.
44. Tully, pp. 203–4; Borkowski, p. 131. Beusselstrasse Station held out until 27 April 1945 (Rocolle, p. 51).
45. Weidling, p. 52. Research into Bärenfänger's background reveals that he had been a member of the SA since 1933 and promoted *Sturmbannführer* (major) on 23 March 1944, well after his equivalent promotion in the Army on 1 January 1943. He had gained rapid promotion to lieutenant-colonel by the age of 30 in his brief military career, winning many decorations for bravery, including the Knights' Cross of the Iron Cross with Oak Leaves and Swords, and was exactly the kind of soldier that appealed to Hitler (Berlin Document Centre).
46. Liesegang Report, p. 6 [von Dufving archives].
47. Rocolle, p. 53.
48. Kroemer.
49. Weidling, p. 111.
50. Bokov, pp. 245, 250.
51. Pourroy, pp. 48–50.
52. Rocolle, pp. 53–4. The fire in the Karstadt department store was due to the SS having blown up the food stocks contained there.
53. Rocolle, p. 42.
54. Chuikov, pp. 196–7.
55. Ibid., pp. 184–5.
56. Skorning Report.
57. Engelmann, pp. 647–9; Tieke, p. 350. From the number of tanks given it seems that part of the 503rd SS Heavy Tank Battalion, which is later reported operating in Wilmersdorf, was involved.
58. Dragunsky, pp. 93–104; Grunewald flak battery destroyed by 33 'Stormovik' ground-attack aircraft (Rocolle, p. 51).
59. Koniev, pp. 179–80.
60. Von Dufving; Refior Berlin Diary (BMA Freiburg RH 53-3/24), p. 26; Weidling, p. 52.
61. Von Dufving; von Loringhoven [Chronos-Film]; Refior Berlin Diary (BMA Freiburg RH 53-3/24), p. 26.
62. Boldt, p. 71 [Gosztony, p. 311], confirmed by von Loringhoven [Chronos-Film]. The telephone conversation with Goebbels is taken from Kuby, pp. 57–9.
63. Trevor-Roper [*LDH*], pp. 185–7; O'Donnell, pp. 127–8; Tully, p. 193; Koller, pp. 94, 103; Hanna Reitsch's *Fliegen, mein Leben* (Stuttgart, 1951), pp. 296–8 [Gosztony, pp. 298–300], describes the flight, while General Hans Baur's *Ich flog Mächtige der Erde* (Kempten, Allgäu, 1956), p. 269 [Gosztony, p. 299] describes how he was engaged

in having the East–West Axis landing strip widened to 120 yards by having the bordering trees chopped down when von Greim's aircraft landed.
64. Ziemke, p. 98.

8: NO RELIEF

1. Tieke, pp. 348–52.
2. Kroemer.
3. Tieke, p. 303.
4. Lakowski and Stich, pp. 97–108; Tieke, p. 346; Weidling, p. 112.
5. Rocolle, pp. 34–5; Tieke, p. 141.
6. Dragunsky, pp. 104–20.
7. Tully, pp. 203–4.
8. Karow, p. 15 [Gosztony, pp. 386–7].
9. Zhukov, p. 611. Chuikov [1978], p. 205, quotes his 8th Guards Army order of 27 April, viz: '1. During the night the offensive will be continued by assault detachments. The main forces will rest, and artillery, tanks and ammunition will be brought up.'
10. Zhukov, pp. 211–12.
11. Borkowski, pp. 132–7; Pourroy, pp. 51–2.
12. Chuikov, p. 188; Kuby, p. 139.
13. Chuikov, pp. 188–9. I have adhered to Chuikov's chronology in his accounts of the 8th Guards Army, which does not always tally with German accounts but seems the more reliable in this respect.
14. Tieke, p. 355.
15. Engelmann, p. 651.
16. Altner, pp. 155–62.
17. Later to house the British Sector Headquarters and British Military Government.
18. Kroemer. However, Karen Meyer's 1991/92 investigation into this subject, *Die Flutung des S-Bahn-Tunnels*, indicates that whatever flooding may have occurred at this stage could not have been of any significance and that it was not until 0755 hours on 2 May that a massive explosion under the Landwehr Canal caused the tunnel system to be inundated as far north as the Stettiner Railway Station. Such a demolition had required the expert positioning of an enormous amount of explosives and was presumably the work of a Waffen-SS team being detonated by the Soviets either deliberately or accidentally. After the war the canal had to be diverted to enable the tunnel to be pumped out and repaired. The city records for this period are incomplete, but it seems that only about 100 bodies were found, many of whom could have died from causes other than drowning. (See also Curth and Dittfurth's *Nord–Sud-Bahn – Vom Geistertunnel zur City-S-Bahn.*)
19. Kuby, pp. 141–2; O'Donnell, quoting Mohnke, p. 226.
20. Kuby, p. 141; Tieke, p. 352.
21. O'Donnell, pp. 151–60.
22. Baur, p. 272 [Gosztony, pp. 327–8]; Trevor-Roper [*LDH*], pp. 277–8. Von Loringhoven says Fegelein was shot at dawn on 29 April [Chronos-Film].
23. Rocolle, pp. 49–50.
24. Tieke, pp. 354–5; Thorwald, pp. 169–70; Gorlitz, pp. 216–17.
25. Thorwald, pp. 197–9; Gorlitz, pp. 217–19.
26. Wenck, p. 66.

27. Tieke, p. 238.
28. Busse, pp. 167–8; Tieke, pp. 195, 204.
29. Domank article and map; Koniev, p. 153 – the Berlin–Breslau autobahn was the main line of communication.
30. Tieke, pp. 204–13.
31. Tieke, pp. 332–3; Ziemke, p. 119; Komornicki, p. 143.
32. Komornicki, pp. 146–8.
33. Tully, pp. 200, 204–6; Tieke, pp. 361–2, 369.
34. Reichhardt and Schäche's *Von Berlin Nach Germania*; RNZAF aerial photograph of February 1945 and numerous postwar photographs show clearly the actual layout of the battlefield, but Soviet maps erroneously show the pre-war layout of Königsplatz with a straight anti-tank ditch drawn diagonally across and no pit. The two 88mm guns seen in post-battle photographs in front of the Reichstag, one with nine and the other with 16 'score' rings painted on their barrels, belonged to the 5th Battery of the 211th Heavy Flak Battalion from Zehlendorf. They had been towed there by fire-engines after having been engaged in the defence of the Teltow Canal on the 24th and then at Tempelhof Airport on the 26th. From this exposed position they had been used in the indirect-fire role – one for which they were ill-suited – firing north across the Spree, but had suffered heavy casualties among their mainly schoolboy crews and were knocked out before the attack on the Moltke Bridge by the heavy Soviet artillery fire directed on this area. (Author's interview with survivors Ernst Bittcher, Professor Oskar de la Chevallerie and Professor Reinhard Pohl.)
35. Rudenko.
36. Tully, and Tiecke as above, together with numerous Soviet sources; Rogmann, pp. 62–4; Wagener, p. 69.
37. Bokov, pp. 262–3; Borkowski, pp. 136–7; Venghaus, p. 110.
38. Bokov, pp. 253–4; Tieke, pp. 361–2, 369.
39. Liesegang Report, pp. 6–7 [von Dufving archive]; Tieke, p. 360.
40. Chuikov, p. 189.
41. Ibid., p. 193.
42. Ibid., p. 201.
43. Ibid., pp. 190–2.
44. Koniev, p. 184; Erickson, p. 600 – Koniev was still aiming for the Reichstag.
45. Dragunsky, p. 120.
46. Engelmann, p. 653; Koniev, p. 185; Lothar Loewe to author; Tully, p. 221.
47. Koniev, p. 187. Some texts quote Ruhleben instead of Witzleben Station, but this does not tally with either the final deployment of the 55th Guards Tank Brigade or the geographical factors.
48. Altner, pp. 163–79.
49. Kroemer. The route to Nollendorfplatz would have been via the Lützowplatz bridgehead across the Landwehr Canal.
50. Trevor-Roper [*LDH*], p. 202; O'Donnell, pp. 171–2; Axmann, 'Mit Hitler im Bunker' in *Stern* magazine (25 April 1965), p. 70 [Gosztony, p. 313].
51. Trevor-Roper [*LDH*], pp. 205–6; O'Donnell, pp. 128–9; Thorwald, pp. 208–9; Reitsch, p. 302 [Gosztony, p. 311].
52. Weidling, p. 115; Tieke, p. 357.
53. Kuby, p. 133; Ziemke, p. 105.
54. Thorwald, pp. 201–5; Gorlitz, p. 220; Percy Ernst Schramm's edition of the *Kriegestagebuch des Oberkommandos der Wehrmacht (Wehrmachtführungsstab)* (Frankfurt: Bernard & Graefe Verlag, 1961), Vol. 4, p. 1466 [Gosztony, p. 319].

55. Trevor-Roper [*LDH*], pp. 207–13; O'Donnell, pp. 132–5; Nerin E. Gun's *Eva Braun – Hitler, Leben und Schicksal* (Stuttgart, 1968), p. 199 [Gosztony, pp. 325–6].
56. Averdieck papers; Koniev, pp. 186, 188; Schöneck, pp. 118–21 – at this stage a member of the 5. *Versprengtenkompanie*.
57. Refior Berlin Diary (BMA Freiburg RH 53-3/24), p. 28.
58. Koniev, p. 188.

9: THE LAST ROUND

This chapter includes the story of the battle of the Reichstag, which has been completely revised since the first edition, blowing away some of the myths about this 'play within a play', which took place as a virtually separate event within the main battle on a stage only 700 yards square. As late as 1993 I was given the information about the flags through *After the Battle* magazine, and then in 1994 I encountered my first German witness of the battle of the Reichstag, Willi Rogmann.

1. Wenck, pp. 66–7; Strawson, p. 146. Neither von Dufving nor Refior mentions it.
2. Wenck, p. 68.
3. Busse, p. 168.
4. *GPW*, p. 383; Kuby, p. 211; Ziemke, p. 110 – the writer was Konstantin Simonov; Strawson, pp. 125–6.
5. Thorwald, p. 190.
6. Wenck, p. 66; Gellermann, pp. 93–4.
7. Gellermann, p. 176.
8. Thorwald, p. 205; Ziemke, pp. 119–20; Tieke, p. 306; Gorlitz, p. 22.
9. Thorwald, pp. 193–4.
10. Gorlitz, pp, 220–2.
11. Trevor-Roper [*LDH*], pp. 218–21; Tieke, p. 358.
12. Trevor-Roper [*LDH*], pp. 221–5; Boldt, p. 83, as quoted in Gosztony, p. 329; von Loringhoven [Chronos-Film].
13. Trevor-Roper [*LDH*], pp. 221–5.
14. Ibid. [*LDH*], pp. 221–5, 248–9.
15. Kmiercik, pp. 25–6; Komornicki, pp. 148–57; Kmiecik, p. 26, says that Zhukov had arranged with the 1st Polish Army at 1500 hours on the 24th for this division to be available in Reinickendorf on the 30th.
16. Rogmann, pp. 64–8.
17. Tully, pp. 206–7.
18. Bokov, p. 269–70; Tieke, p. 366; Zhukov, pp. 616–17.
19. Bokov, pp. 265–7.
20. Chuikov, pp. 197–9, who mistakenly calls the Viktoria Bridge (sometimes known as the Potsdamer) the Möckern Bridge, but the location is given on his map in the 1967 Panther edition. Like most Soviet military writers, Chuikov interlards his work with reminiscences about individuals and tales of heroism. Unfortunately the presentation and style are so blatantly dictated by political considerations that it is often difficult to give them full credence. However, this incident was immortalized by the symbolic statue now dominating the Soviet War Cemetery in Treptow Park.
21. Chuikov, p. 196; Koniev, p. 177.
22. Chuikov, p. 202.
23. Ibid., p. 200.

24. Bokov, pp. 265–7, map, p. 277; Chuikov, p. 238.
25. Dragunsky, pp. 124–33.
26. Engelmann, pp. 653–5: Tieke, pp. 359, 362; Tully, p. 222.
27. Boldt.
28. Weidling, pp. 117, 169.
29. Trevor-Roper [*LDH*], p. 229; Artur Axmann's article 'Das Ende im Führerbunker', *Stern* magazine (2 May 1965), p. 82 [Gosztony, p. 330].
30. Gellermann, p. 177.
31. Ibid., pp. 97–8; Gorlitz, p. 223.
32. These were probably just rumours, for the Soviets showed a marked reluctance to use the tunnels, and the Stadtmitte and Kaiserhof U-Bahn stations were still in German hands at midnight on 1 May.
33. Trevor-Roper [*LDH*], p. 229; O'Donnell, pp. 147–50.
34. Weidling, p. 170; von Dufving to author; Refior Berlin Diary (BMA Freiburg, RH53-3/24), p. 29.
35. Weidling, p. 169.
36. Rocolle, p. 59.
37. Tully, pp. 248–58; Report by Colonel V.B. Seoev and N.G. Bodrikhin, Delta Productions, Moscow, dated 30 April 1993 [*After the Battle*]; Subbotin, pp. 46–8. Captain Makov's group consisted of S/Sgts A.P. Bobrov, A.F. Lisimenko and G.K. Zagitov, and Sgt M.P. Minin. The survivors of the flak battery on Königsplatz sheltering in the cellars beneath the southwest corner of the Reichstag deny that the building was stormed as such. They maintain that all was quiet that afternoon and evening, for previously the building had been shaking with the effects of the bombardment directed at it, and were surprised to be told that the Soviets were already inside above them. However, they had not been called upon to defend the building and only on 1 May took part in an ineffective counterattack within the building, so have no direct evidence of what occurred on 30 April. (Author's interview with survivors Ernst Bittcher, Professor Oskar de la Chevallerie and Professor Reinhard Pohl.) The comparative quiet they experienced during the Soviet assault may have been due to the front's siege artillery having been called off the area, leaving it to the resources of the 79th Rifle Corps.
38. Bokov, pp. 264, 287–8. Evidence of the severity of the exchange of fire between Museum Island and the west bank can still be found in the buildings on either side of the Kupfergraben Canal.
39. Trevor-Roper [*LDH*], pp. 230–3; O'Donnell, pp. 179–93; Axmann [Ende], p. 82 [Gosztony, pp. 332–3]; Erich Kempa's *Ich habe Adolf Hitler verbrannt* (Munich, undated), p. 108 [Gosztony, pp. 333–4].
40. Gorlitz, p. 226; Dönitz, pp. 443–4.
41. Trevor-Roper [*LDH*], pp. 236–7; Dönitz, p. 441.
42. Weidling, pp. 169–71.
43. Trevor-Roper [*LDH*], p. 238.
44. Bokov, pp. 283–6. General Berzarin did not consult his superiors before giving these instructions, and so it is possible that Chuikov was truly unaware of Hitler's death when Krebs told him later that night.
45. Liesegang's report of 1985 [von Dufving archive]. Krukenberg (BMA MSG2/1283) says that Mohnke telephoned him at 0700 hours on the 1st May to tell him that Krebs, von Dufving and Seifert had set off during the night from the latter's sector to negotiate with the Soviets. They had failed to return or communicate through the telephone link that had been established, and Mohnke feared treachery. Krukenberg

was to take over Seifert's sector.
46. Dragunsky, p. 134.
47. Komornicki, pp. 166–75
48. Rogmann; Hildegard Springer's *Es sprach Hans Fritzsche, Nach Gesprächen, Briefen und Dokumenten* (Stuttgart, 1949), pp. 51–2 [Gosztony, pp. 365, 369].
49. Busse, p. 168; Tieke, pp. 309–45.
50. Busse (p. 168) describes the breakout as having taken place on the night of 26/27 April and the union with the 12th Army on the morning of 29 April, but this is in conflict with Wenck's chronology and that of other witnesses, and allowance should be made for the fact that Busse's article was apparently written in captivity some ten years after the event; Wenck, pp. 68–9; Koniev (pp. 180–2) denies the breakout was effective.

10: ULTIMATE VICTORY

The accuracy of O'Donnell as a source regarding certain points remains doubtful.

1. Chuikov, pp. 228–32.
2. Von Dufving; Steiner, p. 333; Weidling, p. 172. The choice of Colonel von Dufving to accompany General Krebs resulted from the latter having no senior staff officers of his own that he could call on! Neilands' change of uniform has proved misleading in subsequent accounts. The 'safe passage' through to the Soviet lines appears to have been Möckernstrasse, for when Neilands reported back to Chuikov about a Soviet major having been shot by German troops, he said the firing appeared to come from the Hotel Excelsior, which faced down this street from opposite the Anhalter Station. Although reference is made to a suspension bridge in some versions of Chuikov's book, this should not be confused with the Bendlerstrasse bridge used later by von Dufving and General Weidling.
3. Chuikov, pp. 205–37; Tully, pp. 261–70.
4. Von Dufving.
5. Kuby, pp. 61, 198–9.
6. Trevor-Roper [*LDH*], pp. 239–40; Dönitz, pp. 444–5.
7. Axmann [Ende], p. 86 [Gosztony, pp. 363–4]; Tieke, p. 378.
8. Trevor-Roper [*LDH*], pp. 241–2; Tieke, p. 378.
9. Kuby, pp. 61, 198–9.
10. Communications with Jo Brettschneider, who negotiated the surrender as a Second Lieutnant with Second Lieutnant Ebbinghaus, Werner Mihan, who saw some of the tanks, and the late Heinz Vogt, who worked in the laboratories. The buried remains of the poison gas samples were to prove a problem when discovered some 20 years later. See also Vladimir Gall's *Mine Weg Nach Halle*, pp. 88–103, and Colonel-General M.C. Kalashnick's *Im Feuer geprüft*, pp. 359–65, both published by the Militärvelag der DDR, East Berlin.
11. *GPW*, p. 384; Kuby, pp. 66–9; Strawson, pp. 153–5.
12. Bokov, p. 286.
13. Ibid., p. 301–4. The fighting had been particularly severe and tank losses high. SS Captain Henri Fenet of the SS Division 'Charlemagne', who received the last Knight's Cross to be awarded on 29 April, claims that his unit had destroyed 62 Soviet tanks during this battle. [Article by Jörg von Uthmann in the Tagesspiegel of 22 Jan. 98.]
14. Zhukov, pp. 622–3; Chuikov, pp. 238–9; Tully, p. 218.

15. O'Donnell, p. 247; Kuby, p. 186; photographic evidence.
16. Kmiecik, pp. 52–6, 63; Kormonicki, pp. 178–97.
17. Kmiecik, pp. 52–6, 63; Kormonicki, pp. 200–9.
18. Kmiecik, pp. 52–6, 63; Kormonicki, pp. 210–21.
19. Engelmann, p. 659; Koniev, p. 191.
20. Kroemer.
21. Weidling, pp. 173–4.
22. Gellermann, pp. 105–19.
23. Theophil Sawadda and Anton Schmied to the author re: transfer to Soviets.
24. Engelmann, p. 658. Wöhlermann, pp. 23–4. The Neuen-Siegesallee was lined with 70 statues of figures from German history erected in the original Siegesallee at the instigation of Kaiser Wilhelm II and transferred to this new site in 1934. The statues were later buried behind Schloss Bellevue on British instructions but have since been retrieved, restored and resited under cover at the Lapidarium on the Landwehr Canal.
25. Weidling, p. 173; Kuby, pp. 201–2.
26. Refior interview with Ryan [von Dufving]. Von Dufving was promoted to Colonel on the 22nd April, but General Weidling omitted to tell him until the night of 1/2 May.
27. Before the breakout attempts began it was estimated that there were some 29,000 civilians sheltering in the Zoo bunkers.
28. Wöhlermann MS, pp. 30–1.
29. Loewe.
30. Tieke, pp. 415, 419 – possibly more than 10,000 took part in this breakout to the west; Altner, pp. 210–45; Engelmann, pp. 660–5: Lothar Loewe, Werner Mihan and Oberst a.d. Horst Zobel to author: Zhukov, p. 605.
31. Loewe. Shortly before the agreed time of surrender, Major Baechle lead a small breakaway group, including Lothar Loewe, along a track towards Wachow, but they too were captured next morning. Altner, p. 242, found 'Leibstandarte SS Adolf Hitler' armbands discarded in a wood near Roskow, some six to seven miles from Brandenburg. Major Horst Zobel escaped on foot when his tank ran out of fuel and passed through both the Soviet and American lines without being captured.
32. Tully, pp. 276–80.
33. Tieke, p. 386; Zhukov, p. 623.
34. Helmut Später's *Die Geschichte des Panzerkorps Grossdeutschland* (Duisburg, 1958), Vol. 3, p. 748 [Gosztony, p. 383]; Borkowski, pp. 136–7.
35. Borkowski, pp. 136–9; Pourroy, p. 52; Horst Denkinger to author re: Bärenfänger.
36. O'Donnell, pp. 213–17. According to Armin Lehmann, who was present as Axmann's HJ runner at Mohnke's planning conference, it was rudely interrupted by a drunken Bormann, who demanded that Axmann provide him with an escort of Hitlerjugend drawn from the Reichs Chancellery and Propaganda Ministry units to get him through the Soviet lines under the command of Major Weltzin, Axmann's Wehrmhacht aide. Axmann refused as this would have required the permission of General Weidling, which he knew he would not get. (Armin Lehmann in a letter to the author.)
37. Rogmann, pp. 93–7; Tieke, p. 390 – Krukenberg says that in order to avoid confusion, he had not intended issuing his own orders for the breakout before 2200 hours.
38. Trevor-Roper [*LDH*], p. 243; O'Donnell, pp. 217–18.
39. Trevor-Roper [*LDH*], p. 243; O'Donnell, pp. 221–7. A picture of the bulkhead (*Wehrtor*) in *Nord–Sud–Bahn – Vom Geistertunnel zur City-Bahn*, published by the Interessengemeinschaft Eisenbahn und Nahverkehr Berlin in 1992, shows that it operates vertically, dropping on to the track from above. A later group apparently got through by borrowing through the track ballast! (Venghaus, p. 60).

40. Trevor-Roper [*LDH*], pp. 243–4; O'Donnell, pp. 227–9.
41. Armin Lehmann, who was a Hitlerjugend runner at Axmann's command post, in a letter to the author.
42. Rogmann, pp. 99, 104–7; Trevor-Roper [*LDH*], p. 244; O'Donnell, p. 222; Venghaus, pp. 26, 30–1, 69. Venghaus's analysis of the chaotic circumstances of the breakout over the Weidendammer Bridge taken from survivors' reports establishes five separate attempts:

    The first, shortly after midnight, was supported by an armoured four-barrelled 20mm flak tracked vehicle ('Wirbelwind'), but collapsed within 250 metres of the bridge.

    The second, about 15 minutes later, was led by a 'Tiger' tank and two other armoured vehicles, and collapsed about 300 metres from the bridge when the 'Tiger' blew up. (See Note 43 below.)

    The third, at about 0100 hours, was supported by APCs of the 11th SS 'Nordland' Armoured Recce Bn, and stalled when the leading APC burst into flames, blocking the route.

    The fourth, at about 0200 hours, was supported by an SPG, which destroyed a Soviet machine-gun commanding the street from a corner building, but caused the building to collapse into the street, again blocking the route.

    The fifth, at about 0400 hours, turned left on the Schiffbauerdamm and then north towards the Charité Hospital area, where it petered out.

    Tennede eventually got away on foot and hid in the Charité Hospital area for four days before making a sucessful escape to the west. Krukenberg got through to Schönhauser Allee by 1000 hours and headed north through Pankow, only to be captured three hours later.
43. O'Donnell, pp. 229–32.
44. Trevor-Roper [*LDH*], p. 245; O'Donnell, pp. 239–50; Axmann, as quoted in Venghaus, pp. 39–41. Other Venghaus witnesses confirm that this group had first crossed the Weidendamm Bridge under cover of a 'Tiger' tank, which then exploded, the explosion apparently throwing them unconscious to the ground, where several surviving witnesses took them to be dead, giving rise to the myth that Bormann had been killed on the bridge.
45. O'Donnell, pp. 249–50. The remains of Bormann and Stumpfegger were found nearby in a shallow grave in 1972 and positively identified by forensic tests, finally putting paid to the Bormann survival myths.
46. Trevor-Roper [*LDH*], p. 245; O'Donnell, pp. 232–5. O'Donnell alleges that at the Humboldthain flak-tower Monhke's group found flags flying and companies of troops parading for orders as if on peacetime manoeuvres, with Major-General Bärenfänger, the senior officer there, sitting on one of ten 'Tiger' tanks surrounding the tower, together with several artillery pieces and armoured personnel carriers. This I assume to be poetic licence, for Bärenfänger and his wife and brother-in-law committed suicide in the Schönhauser Allee break-out, which had already taken place earlier that morning (Horst Denkinger to author, personal communication). Some sources erroneously name the surrender location as the Schultheiss Brewery.
47. Trevor-Roper [*LDH*], p. 246; O'Donnell, pp. 235–7, 256–61.
48. Tieke, p. 237; Steiner, pp. 332–3.
49. Tieke, p. 232. Another version of this story is that the French had omitted to post sentries and were captured sound asleep.
50. Bokov, pp. 308–16, quoting Zhukov, p. 357; Rogmann letter to author.
51. This was erroneously given as the Potsdamer Bridge in the recorded text, for the bridge intended and used was in fact the Grossadmiral von Maltzendorff Bridge,

otherwise known as the Bendler Bridge, and its present name.
52. Chuikov, p. 240; von Dufving.
53. Chuikov, pp. 248–9; a classified Soviet report on this incident translated for Ryan [von Dufving]; von Dufving report [Chronos-Film].
54. Trevor-Roper [*LDH*], p. 244; Zhukov, pp. 392–3; Chuikov, pp. 241–4; Thorwald, p. 243; Kuby, p. 203.
55. Weidling, p. 174; Chuikov, pp. 244–67; Kuby, p. 206.
56. Willemer, p. 46.
57. Koniev, p. 189: Wannsee breakout given as 30 April 1945; author's discussions and correspondence with survivors of the 20th Panzergrenadier Division and from an unpublished manuscript '*Die Zange – Tagebuch und Erlebnisberichte aus dem Jahr 1945*' by Friedhelm Schöneck, pp. 125–9.
58. Trevor-Roper [*LDH*], p. 249.
59. Ibid., pp. 247–8.
60. Koniev, pp. 190–1.
61. Schöneck, pp. 132–4.
62. Koniev, p. 192.
63. Komornicki, pp. 232–48; Ryan, p. 520.
64. *GPW*, p. 385; Novikov, p. 95.
65. Komornicki, p. 251.
66. Abyzow; *GPW*, p. 385. Col.-Gen. G.F. Krivosheev's *Stamped 'Removed from Secrecy' – Losses of the Armed Forces in Wars, Battles and Military Conflicts* (Moscow: MOD Military Publishing House), pp. 219–20, gives the following casualty figures for the period 16 April–8 May 1945:

	Killed	*Wounded*	*Missing*
2nd Bye. Front	13,070	46,040	2,570
1st Bye. Front	37,610	141,880	7,804
1st Ukr. Front	27,580	86,245	4,949
1st/2nd Pol. Armies	2,825	6,067	387

However, with the 33,000 killed admitted at Seelow and another 20,000 buried in Berlin, apart from those in between these two points, these figures appear dubious.

BIBLIOGRAPHY

The editions listed below are those to which I have referred in my research. Alternative editions are given in parentheses.

Abyzov, Vladimir. *The Final Assault*. Moscow: Novosti Press Agency Publishing House, 1985.

Altner, Helmut. *Totentanz Berlin: Tagebuchblätter eines Achtzehnzahriger*. Offenbach-am-Main: Bollwerk Verlag, 1947.

Babadshanian, Colonel A.H. *Hauptstosskraft*. East Berlin: Militärverlag der DDR, 1981.

Bauer, Dr Frank, Karen Pfund and Tony Le Tissier. *Der Todeskampf der Reichshauptstadt*. Berlin: Chronos-Film, 1994.

Bezymenski, Lev. *The Death of Adolf Hitler*. New York: Harcourt, Brace & World, 1968.

Bieller, Seweryn. *Stalin and his Generals*. New York: Pegasus, 1969.

Blond, Georges. *Death of Hitler's Germany*. New York: Macmillan, 1954.

Boehm, Oberst a.D. Prof. Erwin. *Geschichte der 25. Division*. Stuttgart, undated.

Bokov, Lt-Gen. F.I. *Frühjahr des Sieges und der Befreiung*. Berlin: Militärverlag der DDR, 1979.

Boldt, Gerhard. *Die letzten Tage der Reichskanzlei*. Hamburg: Rohwolt Verlag, 1947.

Borkowski, Dieter. *Wer weiss, ob wir uns wiedersehen – Erinnerungen an eine Berliner Jugend*. Frankfurt-am-Main: Fischer Taschenbuch Verlag, 1980.

Buchner, Alex. *Das Handbuch der deutschen Infanterie 1939–1945*. Friedberg: Podzun-Pallas Verlag, 1989.

Bullock, Alan. *Hitler: A Study in Tyranny*. London: Penguin Books, revised edn 1962. (Originally published by Oldhams, London, 1952.)

Burkert, Hans–Norbert, Matussek, Klaus and Obschernitzki, Doris. *Zerstört Besiegt Befreit – Der Kampf um Berlin bis zur Kapitulation 1945*. Stätten der Geschichte Berlins, Bd. 7, Berlin: Edition Hentrich im Verlag Fröhlich & Kaufmann, 1985.

Burn, Jeffrey. *The Waffen-SS*. London: Osprey, 1982.

Carter, Field Marshal Sir John. *The War Lords*. London: Weidenfeld & Nicolson,1976.

Chaney, Otto P. Jr. *Zhukov*. Norman: University of Oklahoma Press, 1971.

Chuikov, Vasilii I. *The End of the Third Reich*. Moscow: Progress Publishers, revised 1978, and Panther edition 1969.

Clark, Alan. *Barbarossa – The Russo-German Conflict 1941–45*. London: Hutchinson, 1965.

Curth, Gerhard and Udo Dittfurth. *Nord–Sud-Bahn – Vom Geistertunnel zur City-S-Bahn*. Berlin: Interessengemainschaft Eisenbahn und Nahverkehr Berlin e.V., 1992.

David, Paul. *Am Königsplatz: die letzten Tage der Schweizerischen Gemeindschaft in Berlin*. Zurich: Thomas Verlag, 1948.

Diem, Liselotte. *Fliehen oder bleiben?* Freiburg im Breisgau: Verlag Herder, 1982.

Doernberg, Dr Stefan. *Befreiung 1945*. East Berlin: Dietz Verlag, 1985.

Dönitz, Karl. *Memoirs – Ten Years and Twenty Days*. London: Weidenfeld & Nicolson, 1959.

Dragunsky, David. *A Soldier's Life*. Moscow: Progress Publishers, 1977.

Eichholz, Diedrich. *Brandenburg in der NS-Zeit*. Berlin: Verlag Volk und Welt, 1993.

Eisenhower, Dwight D. *Crusade in Europe*. London: Heinemann, 1949.

Engelmann, Joachim. 'Lohn der Tapferkeit', unpublished MS, Oldenburg, undated.

—— 'Geschichte der 18. Panzergrenadier-Division', Part IV, unpublished MS, Oldenburg, undated.

Erickson, John. *The Road to Berlin*. London: Weidenfeld & Nicolson, 1983.

Fest, Joachim C. *Hitler*. New York: Harcourt Brace Jovanovich, 1973 (Weidenfeld & Nicolson, London, 1974).

Fey, Will. *Panzer im Brennpunkt der Fronten*. Munich: J.F. Lehmanns Verlag, undated.

Flower, Desmond and Reeve, James. *The Taste of Courage*. New York: Harper, 1960.

Gall, Vladimir. *Mein Weg nach Halle*. East Berlin: Militärverlag der DDR, undated.

Gellermann, Günter W. *Die Armee Wenck – Hitlers letzte Hoffnung*. Koblenz: Bernard & Graefe, 1983.

Gorlitz, Walter. *The Memoirs of Field Marshal Keitel*. London: William Kimber, 1965.

Gosztony, Peter. *Der Kampf um Berlin in Augenzeugenberichten*. Düsseldorf: Deutscher Taschenbuch Verlag, 1970.

The Great Patriotic War of the Soviet Union, 1941–5 (GPW). Moscow: Progress Publishers, 1974.

Groehler, Olaf. *Das Ende der Reichskanzlei*. East Berlin: Deutscher Verlag der Wissenschaften, 1976.

Guderian, Col.-Gen. Heinz. *Panzer Leader*. New York: Ballantine Books, 1965.

Hansen, Hans. '… allzeit meine Pflicht zu tun', unpublished MS, Kropp, rev. 1993.

Höcker, Karla. *Die letzten und die ersten Tage: Berliner Aufzeichnungen 1945*. Berlin: Verlag Bruno Hessling, 1966.

Höhne, Heinz. *The Order of the Death's Head*. New York: Ballantine Books, 1971.

Houston, Donald E. *Hell on Wheels – the 2nd Armored Division*. Novato, CA: Presido Press, 1977.

Irving, David. *Hitler's War*. London: Hodder & Stoughton, 1977.

Kalschnik, Col.-Gen. M.C. *Im Feuer geprüft*. East Berlin: Militärverlag der DDR, undated.

Keegan, John. *Waffen SS: The Asphalt Soldiers*. London: Pan/Ballantine, 1972. London: Purnell, 1971.

Keilig, Wolff. *Das deutsche Heer 1939–1945 – Gliedung, Einsatz, Stellenbesetzung, Abschnitt 211: Die Generalität des Heeres im 2. Weltkrieg 1939–1945* (Truppenoffiziere). Bad Nauheim, 1956–70.

Kitchen, Martin. *Nazi Germany at War*. Harlow: Longman, 1995.

Klimov, Gregory. *The Terror Machine*. London: Faber & Faber, 1953.

Kmiecik, Edward. *Berliner Victoria*. Warsaw: Verlag 'Ruch', 1972.

Knappe, Siegfried. 'Tagebuch-Aufzeichnungen', unpublished MS, 1985.

Knappe, Siegfried and Ted Brusaw. *Soldat – Reflections of a German Soldier*. Shrewsbury, England: Airlife Publishing, 1993.

Knüppel, Fritz. *Kreis Lebus – Ein leidgeprüftes Land*. Lebus: Eigenverlag des Heimatkreises, 1990.

Koch, H.W. *The Hitler Youth*. New York: Stein & Day, 1976.

Kohlase, Fritz. *Mit dem Füsilier-Bataillon 303 in Küstrin*. Berlin: Brandenburgisches Verlagshaus, 1993.

Koller, Karl. *Der letzte Monat*. Munich: Bechtle, 1985.

Komornicki, Stanislaw. *Polnische Soldaten stürmten Berlin*. Warsaw: Polish Military History Institute, Ministry of Defence, undated.

Koniev, Marshal I.S. *Year of Victory*. Moscow: Progress Publishers, 1969.

Kuby, Erich. *The Russians and Berlin 1945*. New York: Hill & Wang, 1964.

Lakowski, Richard and Karl Stich. *Der Kessel von Halbe 1945*. Berlin: Brandenburgisches Verlaghaus, 1997.

Lindner, Gen.-Maj. a.D. Rudi. 'Der Tod war unser Begleiter', unpublished MS, 1993.

von Luck, Hans. *Gefangener meiner Seit – Ein Stück Weges mit Rommel*. Herford and Bonn: Verlag E.S. Mittler & Sohn, 1991.

Luethen, Hanns and Wilke, Horst. *Am Rande der Strassen*, Arbeitsgemeinschaft Suchdienst – Archiv – Dokumentation, March 1991.

Mabire, Jean. *Berlin in Todeskampf (Mourir à Berlin)*. Preussisch Oldendorf: Verlag K.W. Schütz KG, 1977.

—— *La Division Nordland*. Paris: Librairie Arthème Fayard, 1982.

Mackintosh, Malcolm. *Juggernaut*. London: Secker & Warburg, 1967.

Melzheimer, Werner. *Die Festung und Garnison Küstrin*. Berlin: Landmannschaft Berlin-Mark Brandenburg, 1989.

Menvell, Roger and Fraenkel, Heinrich. *Heinrich Himmler*. London: Heinemann, 1965.

Meyer, Karen, *Die Flutung des Berliner S-Bahn-Tunnels in den letzten Kriegstagen – Rekonstruktion und Legenden*. Berlin: Kunstamt Kreuzberg, 1992.

Michaelis, Rolf. *Kampf und Untergang der 32. SS-Freiwillige-Grenadier-Division '30. Januar'*. Erlangen: 1993.

Mihan, Hans-Werner. *Die Nacht von Potsdam*. Potsdam: Kurt Vowinckel Verlag, 1997.

Montgomery-Hyde, H. *Stalin – the History of a Dictator*. London: Rupert Hart-Davis, 1971.

Nicolaevsky, Boris L. *Power and the Soviet Elite*. New York: Praeger Publications, 1964.

O'Donnell, James P. *The Berlin Bunker*. London: J.M. Dent, 1979.

Plievier, Theodor. *Berlin*. London: Panther, 1976. (London: Hammond & Co., 1956.)

Pourroy, Dr G.A. Unpublished MS on the fate of the Siemens Volkssturm units, undated.

Pykathov, B.V.K., Belov, K.S. and Frolov, S.S. *History of 3rd Shock Army*. Moscow: Ministry of Defence, 1976.

Quarrie, B. *Hitler's Samurai*. Cambridge: Patrick Stephens, 1984.

Ramm, Gerald. *Gott mit uns – Kriegserlebnisse aus Brandenburg und Berlin*. Woltersdorf Schleuse: Verlag Gerald Ramm, 1994.

Reichhardt, Hans J. and Schäche, Wolfgang. *Von Berlin nach Germania*. Berlin: Transit Buchverlag, 1990.

Reimann, Viktor. *Goebbels*. New York: Doubleday, 1976.

Reinicke, Adolf. *Die 5. Jäger-division*. Freidberg: Podzun-Pallas-Verlag, undated.

Rocolle, Colonel Pierre. *Götterdämmerung – La Prise de Berlin*. Indo-China: French Military Press, 1954.

Rogmann, Willi. 'Dabei im Endkampf um Berlin 1945 – An der Seite von europäischen Freiwilligen', unpublished MS.

Rshewskaja, Jelena. *Hitlers Ende ohne Mythos*. East Berlin: Deutscher Militärverlag, 1967.

Ryan, Cornelius. *The Last Battle*. New York: Simon & Schuster, 1966 (London: Collins, 1973).

Salisbury, Harrison E. *Marshal Zhukov's Greatest Battles*. London: Macdonald, 1969.

Saunders, James D., Mark A. Sauter and R. Cort Kirkwood. *Soldiers of Misfortune*. Washington, DC: National Press Books, 1992.

Scheel, Klaus. *Hauptstossrichtung Berlin*. East Berlin: VEB Deutscher Verlag der Wissenschaften, 1983.

Schöneck, Friedhelm. 'Die Zange: Tagebuch und Erlebnisberichte aus dem Jahr 1945', unpublished MS.

Schramm, Percy Ernst. *Kriegestagesbuch des OKW 1940–1945*. Frankfurt-am-Main: Vol. IV, Bernard & Graefe, Verlag für Wehrwissen, 1961.

Schrode, Wilhelm. *Die Geschichte der 25. Division – Die Wiederaufstellung der 25.Panzergrenadier-Division, Herbst 1944 bis Kriegsende*. Ludwigsburg: 1980.

Schumann, Wolfgang and Olaf Groehler. *Deutschland im zweiten Weltkrieg*. Berlin: Akademie Verlag, 1988.

Seaton, Albert. *The Russo-German War 1941–45*. New York: Praeger Publications, 1971. (London: Arthur Barker, 1971.)

—— *Stalin as a Warlord*. London: Batsford, 1976.

Sethi, Colonel (Retd) A.L. *Marshal Zhukov – The Master Strategist*. Dehra Dun: Natraj Publishers, 1988.

Shtemenko, S.M. *The Soviet General Staff at War*. Moscow: Progress Publishers, 1970.

—— *The Last Six Months*. New York: Doubleday, 1977.

Simon, Hauptmann Manfred. *Die Bildung und Erweiterung des Küstriner Brückenkopfes*. Dresden: 'Friedrich Engels' Military Academy, 1987.

Skorning, Lt-Col. *Wolfgang*. Unpublished report.

Spahr, William J. *Zhukov – The Rise and Fall of a Great Captain*. Novato, CA: Presidio Press, 1993.

Speer, Albert. *Inside the Third Reich*. London: Sphere Books, 1975 (London: Weidenfeld & Nicolson, 1970).

Steiner, Felix. *Die Freiwilligen*. Rosenheim: Deutsche Velagsgesellschaft, 1992.

Stich, Karl. 'Der Durchbruch der Verteidigung der faschistischen deutschen Truppen an der Oder durch die sowjetischen Streitkräfte in der Berliner Operation im Frühjahr 1945'. Dissertation. Dresden: 'Friedrich Engels' Military Academy, 1989.

Strawson, John. *The Battle for Berlin*. London: Batsford, 1974.

Strik-Strikfeld, Wilfried. *Against Stalin and Hitler*. London: Macmillan, 1970.

Subakov, W. *Der letzte Sturm*. Moscow: APN Verlag, 1975.

Subbotin, Vassili J. *Wir stürmten den Reichstag*. East Berlin: Militär Verlag der DDR, 1969.

Suvarov, Viktor. *Inside the Soviet Army*. London: Hamish Hamilton, 1982.

Tessin, Georg. *Verbände und Truppen der deutschen Wehrmacht und Waffen-SS im zweiten Weltkrieg 1939–1945*. Osnabrück: Biblio Verband, 1977.

Thorwald, Jürgen. *Das Ende an der Elbe*. Stuttgart: Steingrüben Verlag, 1950.

Thrams, Hermann. *Küstrin 1945 – Tagebuch einer Festung*. Berlin: Landesmannschaft Berlin–Mark Brandenburg, 1992.

Tieke, Wilhelm. *Das Ende zwischen Oder und Elbe – Der Kampf um Berlin 1945*. Stuttgart: Motorbuch Verlag, 1981.

Tiemann, Rolf. *Die Leibstandarte*, Part IV/2. Osnabrück: Munn Verlag GmbH, undated.

Tillery, Gerhard. 'Hinter uns lag Berlin – Mein Fronteinsatz bei der 309. I.D. 'Gross Berlin', unpublished MS.

Toland, John. *The Last Hundred Days*. London: Arthur Barker, 1965.

—— *Adolf Hitler*. New York: Doubleday, 1976 (London: Futura, 1978).

Tolstoy, Nikolai. *Stalin's Secret War*. London: Jonathan Cape, 1981.

Trevor-Roper, H.R. *Hitler's War Directives 1931–45* (HWD). London: Sidgwick & Jackson, 1964.

—— *The Last Days of Hitler* (*LDH*). London: Macmillan, rev. 1972.

Tully, Andrew. *Berlin: Story of a Battle*. New York: Simon & Schuster, 1963.

Venghaus, Wolfgang. *Berlin 1945: 24 April bis 2. Mai: Eine Dokumentation in Berichten, Bildern, Bermerkungen*. Undated, private distribution.

Vorbeyev, F.D., Propotkin, I.V. and Shimansky, A.N. *The Last Storm*, 2nd edn. Moscow: Ministry of Defence, 1975.

Wagner, Gerd. *Der 9. Fallschirmjägerdivision im Kampf um Pommern, Mark Brandenburg und Berlin*. Cologne: Author (private circulation), 1985.

Wagener, Ray. *The Soviet Air Forces in World War II*. New York: Doubleday, 1973.

Waldmüller, Wolfdieter. 'Von Böbligen bis Magdeburg – die letzte 130 Tage'. Geislingen/Steige: unpublished MS, 1982.

Weber, Helmut. *Greif-Rundbrief,* Nos 93–8. Oberaudorf: 1990–92.
Werth, Alexander. *Russia at War 1941–1945.* New York: E.P. Dutton, 1964.
Wilke, Horst. 'Wilke Archiv', unpublished MS.
Willemer, William. *The German Defense of Berlin.* HQ USAREUR, 1953. (Now part of the US Army's Foreign Military Studies series.)
Wöhlermann, Col. Hans-Oskar. 'Notizen über den letzten Einsatz ostwärts und in Berlin in April/Mai 1945', unpublished MS.
Wolkogonow, Dimitri. *Stalin: Triumph und Tragödie. Ein politisches Porträt.* Düsseldorf: Claasen Verlag, 1989.
Zhukov, Georgii Konstantinovitch. *The Memoirs of Marshal Zhukov.* London: Jonathan Cape, 1971.
Ziemke, Earl F. *Battle for Berlin – End of the Third Reich.* London: Purnell, 1968.
Zippel, Martin. *Untersuchungen zur Militärgeschichte der Reichshauptstadt Berlin von 1871–1945.* Berlin: 1982.

Sundry articles from Soviet, East and West German journals and magazines, in particular:

Busse, Theodor. 'Die letzte Schlacht der 9. Armee', *Wehrwissenschaftliche Rundschau*, 1954.
Chernyayev, V. 'Some Features of Military Art in the Berlin Operation', *Soviet Military History Journal*, April 1955.
Domank, A. '1st Guards Artillery Division beats off Counterattacks of the Enemy attempting to break out of Encirclement during the Berlin Operation', *Soviet Military History Journal*, March 1978.
von Hopffgarten, Gen.-Lt a.D. Hans-Joachim. 'Der Kampf um die Oder-brückenköpfe Lebus und Göritz', *Wehrkunde*, 11 (1955).
Interviews in Chronos-Film GmbH films. Arthur Axmann in *Der Geschichte der Hitlerjugend*.
Kuhlmann, Franz. 'Endkampf in den 'Führerbunker', *Ruhr-Nachrichten*, 1985.
Loewe, Lothar. 'In der Feuerpause erklangen vom Panzerturm Lieder von Marika Rökk', *Welt am Sonntag*, 23 April 1995.
Novikov, A.A. 'The Air Forces in the Berlin Operation', *Soviet Military History Journal*, May 1975.
Rudenko, Air Marshal S.I. 'On the Employment of Aviation in the Berlin Operation', *Soviet Military History Journal*, March 1985.
Sergeyev, S. 'Battle of the 150th Rifle Division for a Fortified Stronghold', *Soviet Military History Journal*, June 1977.
Skorodumov, N. 'Manoeuvres of 12th Guards Tank Corps in the Berlin Operation', *Soviet Military History Journal*, March 1978.

Weidling, Helmuth. 'Der Todeskampf der faschistischen Clique in Berlin aus der Erinnerung des Generals Weidling', *Wehrwissenschaftliche Rundschau*, 1962.

Wenck, Walter, 'Berlin war nicht mehr zu retten', *Stern*, April 1965.

Zelensky, Colonel V.D. 'Logistic Support of the 2nd Guards Tank Army in the Berlin Operation', *Soviet Military History Journal*, April 1985.

Zinchenko, Colonel F. 'Capture of the Reichstag Described', *Soviet Military History Journal*, April 1980.

INDEX

Index

251

Index

Index

255

Index

Index

ARMED FORCES INDEX